RULERS
OF
BRITAIN

RULERS

OF BRITAIN

Text by Plantagenet Somerset Fry F.R.S.A.

Illustrated by Clyde Pearson

HAMLYN

London · New York · Sydney · Toronto

First published 1967
Third Impression 1973

Published by
THE HAMLYN PUBLISHING GROUP LIMITED

London · New York · Sydney · Toronto
Astronaut House, Feltham, Middlesex, England
© Copyright The Hamlyn Publishing Group Limited 1967
ISBN 0 601 085108
Printed in Czechoslovakia by VST, Košice
51044/3

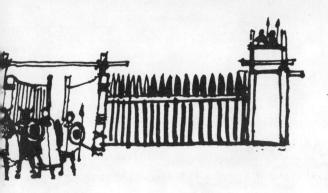

CONTENTS

The greater part of this book is devoted to the rulers of England. This is for two reasons. First, there were no more independent rulers of Ireland after Henry II's conquest of 1171 (until Ireland became a republic), nor of Wales after Edward I's conquest of 1282, nor of Scotland after the accession of King James VI to the throne of England as James I in 1603. Secondly, we know very much more about the earlier history of England than we do of Ireland, Wales or Scotland—indeed, it is said that the five hundred or so years of English history before the Norman Conquest of 1066 are more fully documented than those years of the same period in any country of Western Europe.

Rulers of ENGLAND

Several centuries before the birth of Our Lord, the Celtic peoples of central Europe began to move towards France and the Low Countries, in search of new living space. A branch of these, the Goidels, or Gaels, braved the uninviting channel across to the British Isles and there they overcame the savage inhabitants. These islanders, who knew nothing of farming and had not discovered the use of iron, dwelt in crude huts and caves and lived by hunting and fishing, for which they used weapons of flint and bone.

The Gaels brought with them the knowledge of how to work the land, and they taught the islanders to till the fertile valleys and plains. They also introduced them to trading with Europe.

Generations later, another and more developed branch of Celts, the Brythons, or Britons, came to the islands and drove their Gaelic kinsmen into the depths of South Wales, the Cumberland district, parts of Scotland and across the sea to Ireland. These Britons did not mix very much with the Gaels, but settled mainly in England and North Wales. They thought themselves superior, and it was this division between the peoples of the British Isles that was to prove, time and again, disastrous for them all, for it made invasion and conquest by new foreigners, such as the Romans and the Saxons, that much easier. Ireland, however, was not overrun by either of these peoples.

The Celts still kept some traces of barbarism. They worshipped strange gods with complicated rituals, which included the sacrifice of human lives. They continually warred amongst themselves. They painted their bodies with a bright blue dye called woad, a habit that continued among the Highland Scottish Celts for much longer than anywhere else.

At the same time, they were expert iron founders; they knew how to work bronze; and they could make jewellery from gold and tin. They were skilled in building and driving chariots, war vehicles which the Romans were later to find very frightening in their early battles with the Celts. They had laws, which were set down and administered by their religious chiefs, the Druids, the principal officers of government, such as it was.

In 55 B.C., the Roman general, Gaius Julius Caesar, regarded widely in history as the greatest man of the ancient world, invaded Britain to punish the people for giving assistance to the Gauls in his recent campaign of conquest in what is now France. He defeated a British army on the Kentish coast, but returned to Gaul within a few weeks. A year later, he came again, and this time advanced as far as Hertfordshire, where he forced a powerful British chief, Cassivelaunus, to surrender. He ordered the British to send money payments and took hostages with him back to Gaul.

Almost a century passed before the Romans turned their attention again to the British Isles.

The emperor Claudius, great-nephew of Caesar's nephew Augustus, sent a large army to Britain in A.D. 43, under the command of Aulus Plautius, who, in a short campaign, defeated the British and established a province bounded by a line running roughly from King's Lynn to Southampton.

Thereafter, a succession of Roman governors continued the conquest of Britain. This was not done without difficulty. In A.D. 60, when the governor Suetonius Paulinus was overcoming the people of North Wales and Anglesey, a dangerous rebellion broke out in East Anglia, led by a chieftainess, Boadicea. She roused the tribes there and managed to sack a number

Outside a typical Roman town

of important Roman settlements, including Colchester and St Albans. Then she was defeated by Suetonius, who had hurried back along Watling Street from Wales.

By about A.D. 84 the Romans were masters of all England, most of Wales and the Lowlands of Scotland. Thenceforth, the subject tribes were, in the main, quiet. They began to enjoy the benefits of Roman civilisation, its language of Latin, its laws which applied equally to all subjects, and its advanced ideas of business and trading.

The principal enemies of Roman Britain were the Picts from the Scottish Highlands (you can read of their activities in the introduction to the rulers of Scotland) and the Saxons, a warlike tribe from West Germany. To deal with the Saxons, the Romans appointed a special Count of the Saxon Shore, that is, most of the east coast of England where the raids took place. For many years, the Saxons were beaten off, but when the very heart of the Roman empire itself was threatened with invasion by barbarians at the end of the

fourth century, Roman troops in Britain were called home. This left the island at the mercy of the invaders.

At the beginning of the fifth century, the last Roman forces were withdrawn, and the requests for help sent by the Britons to Rome were met with refusal. At first they fought gallantly on their own against the Saxons, and also against raiding parties of Gaels from Ireland and Picts from the Highlands of Scotland. But they soon fell into disorder, and Britain broke up into small kingdoms, each fending for itself. The next hundred and fifty years are the story of how various invaders from north-western Europe came to Britain, conquered most of the little kingdoms and made settlements for themselves and their families.

In 449, the king of Kent, Vortigern, appealed to two Jutish chiefs, Hengist and Horsa, to help him beat off attacks from the Picts. They came over and drove the marauders out, but when Vortigern asked them to go home again, they refused. War followed, and Vortigern was defeated at the battle of Aylesford, at which Horsa was slain. Hengist then took over the kingdom of Kent.

A Saxon chief, Aella, landed near Pevensey in Sussex in 477, and he proceeded to overrun the district (called Sussex after his people, the South Saxons). He settled his followers on the chalky downs and battered the Britons in a number of bloodthirsty sieges.

Nearly twenty years later, another Saxon chief, Cerdic, brought a host to Southampton, and within a short while he had made himself master of Hampshire, Dorset and Wiltshire. He became king of Wessex (named after the West Saxons) and he was probably a direct ancestor of Ecgbert, the first real king of all England. At about the same time, another band of Saxons invaded Essex (the country of the East Saxons) and set up a kingdom there.

In 520, the Angles, a German tribe related to the Saxons, landed in Suffolk and set up a kingdom in what came to be called East Anglia. Further north, more Angles invaded Yorkshire, overran the district and went up as far as the Lowlands of Scotland. This new kingdom was called Northumbria, and it was divided into two, Bernicia (from the Forth to the Tees) and Deira (from the Tees to the Humber). Angles also created the kingdom of Mercia, which included parts of Lincolnshire and most of the midland counties of today.

The invaders had now entrenched themselves in the more easterly part of England and southern Scotland. There, for the most part, the land was flat or gently rising and it provided excellent ground for agriculture, at which the Angles and Saxons were expert. To the west of them the Britons remained, seeking their living in the more mountainous or hilly regions of Devon, Somerset, Wales, the Pennines and south-west Scotland. They were still divided and fought continually amongst themselves, instead of combining to drive out the invaders.

It was not long before the settlers

Aella lands near Pevensey in 477

decided to expand their kingdoms. Ceawlin, the grandson of Cerdic, won a great battle against the Britons at Dyrham, south of Gloucester, in 577, and by it added most of the West Country to his kingdom. In 613, Aethelfrith of Northumbria crushed the Britons at Chester, and then cut off the people of north-western England from their kinsmen in Wales.

Gradually, all England was won, and it then became divided into seven kingdoms, Wessex, Mercia, Northumbria, Essex, East Anglia, Sussex and Kent. From then on, there was a struggle between the kingdoms for supremacy, and also warfare with the Britons who were confined to the area that is now Wales, and to Strathclyde, which is the south-western portion of Scotland.

Northumbria was the first of the kingdoms to wield any power over its neighbours, but it was not complete, nor did it last. When its king, Ecgfrith, was killed in 685 in an attempt to conquer the Picts (see the introduction to the rulers of Scotland) his successors were so weak that they fell a prey to the growing might of Mercia.

The rulers of this central kingdom were tough men and for some time managed to make themselves feared by the rest of England. The last and greatest Mercian king was Offa, and he ruled from 757 to 796.

Offa extended the boundaries of Mercia right up to north Wales, and he defeated the king of Wessex at a great battle. Because his kingdom was raided so often by parties of Britons from Wales he decided once and for all to keep them out by building a huge dyke, stretching from the river Dee near Chester down to the river Severn near Chepstow. Along the dyke he placed garrisons at regular intervals, whose troops were in readiness to deal with the raiding Britons.

We do not know much about Offa, but his fame spread across Europe. He became a friend of Charlemagne, king of the Franks and the most powerful monarch of Western Europe of the time. Unfortunately, when he died, his successors were weak and let the supremacy of Mercia slip from their grasp. Meanwhile, Wessex was growing in strength, and in the person of its king, Ecgbert, we see for the first time a man able to assert a position as supreme king of England, and also to ensure that his successors would continue as overlords. Thereafter the kings of Wessex were kings of England, and it is with Ecgbert's life story that our chapters begin.

Offa's Dyke

ECGBERT [*King of Wessex, 802-839, and King of England, 828-839*]

Ecgbert was the ancestor of all the kings and reigning queens of England, with the exception of Canute, Harthacanute, Harold I, Harold II and William I.

Born in about 775, he suffered a stormy childhood, during which he was driven out of the country. He fled to the court of Charlemagne, and when he reached manhood he enlisted in that great emperor's army. His experiences in Europe taught him the arts of war and showed him how to lead men, two things which he was to find vitally important when he came back to his country in 802 to succeed to the throne of Wessex.

At his succession, England was still divided into several kingdoms, and no one king was able to assert his dominion over the others for any length of time. Ecgbert began by strengthening his own kingdom so that he could the more easily achieve his one great ambition, the unification of England under his rule.

With little difficulty he conquered Kent and Sussex, and he compelled the princes in Wales to pay him homage. By 825, he had united most of southern England, expanded its agriculture and trade, and given it wise and just government. He now felt strong enough to make the next move.

At Ellandun, in Wiltshire, he met the Mercian king, Beornwulf, in battle, and utterly defeated him. Beornwulf retired to the Midlands, having lost a great number of men. Immediately, the king of East Anglia acknowledged Ecgbert as overlord, and put himself under his protection.

Three years later, Beornwulf was killed, and Mercia submitted to Ecgbert. Northumbria soon followed suit, and by the end of 828, Ecgbert was overlord of all England.

His fighting days, however, were not over. England had, for the past forty years, been suffering pirate raids from the Vikings of Denmark and Norway. These warlike seafarers would land at a coastal town, sack it, and then put to sea again before the local army could be raised to fight them. Year by year the raids grew more frequent, and by 828, the Vikings had become bold enough to carry their attacks right into the heart of the country.

The king of East Anglia does homage to Ecgbert

In the southern half of England, Ecgbert successfully beat off these attacks, and at Hingston Down, near Plymouth, he inflicted such a crushing defeat on the Vikings that they avoided Wessex altogether for the rest of his reign.

In Mercia and Northumbria, however, it was a different story. Ecgbert could not always win, nor could he afford the time or the men to make endless counter-attacks on the invaders. The Northerners were often left to fend for themselves.

Ecgbert died in 839, sorely missed by his people to whom he had been a tower of strength. His own kingdom was free from Viking invasion, and it had begun to enjoy peace and prosperity. This happy situation was soon to change.

AETHELWULF [839-856]

Aethelwulf was Ecgbert's son. While he was a deeply religious and easy-going man,

he had none of his father's military or political ability, and so he was unable to preserve the peace in Wessex which he inherited. Indeed, during the first years of his reign, he sustained a number of defeats by the Vikings.

From time to time, answering calls for help from Mercia, he led armies into the Midlands, but as soon as his back was turned, other Vikings would ravage the coasts of Wessex, plunder the rich monasteries and destroy the villages.

The condition of England grew worse. Trade came to a standstill, harvests were not gathered in, and poverty spread throughout the land. Each year the Viking raiding parties appeared to be larger, and before long it seemed as if all England would break up.

There was one English success in this tale of disaster. In 852, at Ockley in Surrey, Aethelwulf defeated a large Viking army in battle. The Anglo-Saxon Chronicle

Battle of Ockley, 852

says that he ". . . there made the greatest slaughter of a heathen host that we have ever heard tell of." But it was only a respite.

The raids continued, and soon the invaders began to settle in England instead of sailing off to their own shores. Building strongholds in places like Thanet, Sheppey and Portsmouth, they defied Aethelwulf to drive them out.

In despair, the king made a pilgrimage to Rome to obtain the Pope's blessing for his efforts, but it availed him nothing. On his return journey, he begged the help of the French king, Charles the Bald, but he, too, was harassed by Viking raids and could spare no men.

At the French court, Aethelwulf met, and soon afterwards married, as his second wife, Judith, Charles's daughter. When the couple returned to England, Aethelwulf was met by an angry council who demanded his abdication. They offered the throne to his eldest son, Aethelbald.

Three years later, Aethelwulf, who had been allowed to maintain a royal court and household, died. He left four sons by his first wife, and all of them in turn became kings of England. The youngest of these was Alfred the Great.

AETHELBALD [856-860]

Little is known about the life of Aethelbald, Aethelwulf's eldest son. During his father's reign he commanded English armies in a number of battles against the Vikings, and he is said to have distinguished himself by his bravery. He assisted his father at the victory of Ockley, and it is likely that it was Aethelbald's leadership that won the day, for Aethelwulf was not a good general.

Aethelbald was one of the members of the council, called the Witanagemot, or the Witan for short, which deposed Aethelwulf, and it may have been due to him that his father was allowed to keep a royal household until his death. When his father died, Aethelbald married his stepmother, Judith, but they had no children, and when he died in 860, he was succeeded by his next brother, Aethelbert.

AETHELBERT [860-866]

The six-year reign of Aethelbert was as beset by Viking raids as those of his brother and father. In 864, an army of Vikings landed on the south coast between Portsmouth and Southampton. Aethelbert summoned the levies of Hampshire and Berkshire to meet the enemy, but while the army was being prepared, the Vikings reached Winchester, the capital city of Wessex, took it by storm and set it on fire.

Stirred by the knowledge that their capital was being burned by heathens, the levies called up by the king hurried towards the city, and a few miles north of it defeated the invaders and put them to flight.

Aethelbert lived for two more years, during which the Vikings did not again attack the south of England.

AETHELRED I [866-871]

Aethelred was the third son of Aethelwulf, and when the Witan elected him king, they did so because he had proved his ability as a leader serving with his brother Aethelbert. His reign saw a new development in the Viking raids. For the first time they were organised on a grand scale. The Vikings joined together and formed one vast league, called the Great Army.

The first arrival of this new and much better disciplined force was in the northeast, near Scarborough. Marching inland in great numbers, the Vikings reached a position near the city of York, and there annihilated the levies of Northumbria. Then they stormed York itself, a centre of religion and learning, and put the inhabitants to the sword.

Further invasions followed, and the Vikings overran nearly all England north of the river Trent. The victors, who were in many cases accompanied by their families, settled in this territory and made new homes for themselves. Some of them moved south-eastwards to East Anglia and in a pitched battle defeated the Anglian

A meeting of the Witan, the Council of England

under-king, Edmund, known as the Martyr, a brave and saintly man whom they captured. He was brought before the Viking chiefs and ordered to do homage to them, and to pray to their heathen gods. Being a devout Christian, Edmund refused. The Vikings shot him to death with arrows, and threw his body into a ditch. His followers buried him, marked the position with a cross, and in later years an abbey was built there, which is called Bury St Edmunds.

Aethelred, meanwhile, had been building up the army of Wessex, for he knew that as soon as the Vikings had finished in northern England, they would turn their attention to the south. In 871, the Great Army, led now by two chiefs, Guthrum and Bagsaeg, sailed up the Thames and began to ravage Surrey and Berkshire.

Aethelred's forces were now ready, and, with his younger brother, the twenty-year-old Alfred, who was commander of one of the detachments, he set out for the Thames valley. In more than one battle the English were forced to retire westwards, but each time they managed to inflict serious casualties among the Viking troops. At Ashdown, in Wiltshire, they gave the enemy a thorough beating and compelled them to withdraw towards Reading. In this engagement, the chief Bagsaeg was killed, along with many of his lieutenants.

Aethelred re-grouped his army and came to Merton, near Reading. There, in a skirmish with Viking patrols he was mortally wounded. The command of the English army was at once placed in the hands of young Alfred, and within days the Witan elected Alfred as successor to the dead king. Thenceforth began a reign that was to prove one of the most successful in the history of England.

In May, 878, the remnants of a defeated Viking army, under its leader Guthrum, lay inside a stockade at Chippenham, in Wiltshire, rapidly running out of food. Surrounding it was the army of Alfred of England, fresh from a great victory a few miles away at Ethandune. Then, one morning, a gate in the wall opened, and out walked Guthrum, accompanied by a number of officers. They walked over to Alfred's headquarters and asked for a meeting. They were, they said, ready to surrender.

Alfred invited them to sit down at a table. Then he spoke:

"These are our terms. To begin with, you must evacuate all Wessex at once. You must also move out of Mercia south of a line running from just north of London to Chester—roughly the Roman Watling street. Here," he said, as he stretched out a map, "this is the division."

He went on: "There are to be no more raids, no more violence. You must acknowledge us as your overlords. And one more thing, though we do not insist on this. We would like you to give up your heathen beliefs and become Christians. If you, Guthrum, will agree to be baptised, I am sure your people will follow."

Guthrum, tired of fighting and grateful for the generous peace terms, readily consented, and he was baptised, taking the new name of Aethelstan. Then he and his people retired to their territory.

Alfred had brought the war with the Vikings to a victorious conclusion. Now he could get on with the great schemes he was planning for the country.

Few leaders in the history of the world have been surnamed The Great, and Alfred deserved the title as much as any of them. This splendid Englishman, youngest son of Aethelwulf and grandson of Ecgbert, was almost unique in the variety of his talents and achievements, standing in this respect beside such figures as Alexander the Great and Julius Caesar, and, in our own time, Winston Churchill.

Alfred was born at Wantage in about

Alfred's Jewel. Discovered in the marshes at Athelney

849. At the age of five he was sent to Rome to be blessed by the Pope, who predicted a great future for him. His childhood must have been hard while his father and brothers, one by one, spent their reigns marching around England leading armies against the Vikings. Often, when they were defeated, they would have to move their courts elsewhere, and so Alfred's home was never in one place for long.

He inherited all the qualities of his grandfather, courage, leadership and patriotism. He was also learned, he loved books, he studied law closely, and he had an inventively scientific mind.

When king Aethelred died at Merton in 871, the men of Wessex retired to Wiltshire, pursued by the Vikings. More battles were fought and the English were defeated again and again. Eventually, young Alfred bought peace with a large sum of money. The Vikings then turned their attention to Mercia, crushed the levies sent against them, and settled in the districts around five towns, Nottingham, Leicester, Derby, Stamford and Lincoln, districts which came to be known as the Five Boroughs.

Alfred was determined to rebuild the strength of Wessex, and soon he created a body of tough, efficient fighting men, ready to follow wherever he led them.

In 877, the Viking chief, Guthrum, who

Alfred waits for Guthrum outside Chippenham

had sailed up the Thames in 871, again brought a host to the south. He captured London and Winchester, and drove the English farther and farther westwards. Alfred was driven off one battlefield and had to hide in the marshes at Athelney, Somerset, but this was to be his last defeat.

Gathering up his forces once more for a final effort, he marched to Ethandune and inflicted the heaviest defeat on the Vikings since the time of Ecgbert. Guthrum was forced to make peace terms, and these were confirmed at the Treaty of Wedmore.

The territory given to the Vikings was called the Danelagh, and there they settled down, mixing with the English, adopting their language and customs, united as they were by a common religion. England thus gained from the arrangement, for the Vikings were a hardy race, industrious and quick to learn.

The country, however, was in a desperate condition. Most of the towns were in ruins, monasteries were deserted and the fields had been left unploughed and unharvested. Worse, the steady growth of learning had been checked. It was a formidable task of repair that faced king Alfred, but he was more than equal to it.

He began by strengthening the royal power. Local lords, or thegns, were compelled to swear an oath of allegiance to him, and they had to serve him both in peace and in war. The village levies, called fyrds, were divided into two. One half would remain at home to plough the fields, the other half would accompany the king on

military expeditions, or if there was no fighting to do, would spend their time in military exercises and weapon training. The two halves would exchange duties every six months.

He then turned to the kingdom's laws which were in confusion. He examined the mass of conflicting rights and penalties, and after sorting them out, he embodied them in an orderly code. For generations afterwards people used to talk about "The Laws of Alfred" when they meant the statutes of the realm.

It was in the field of education that Alfred's greatest interest lay. Fifty years of incessant invasion had brought learning almost to an end, and so he founded new schools and invited scholars from England, Wales and Europe to teach there. He was particularly enthusiastic about literature and history, and to both he made important personal contributions. He made a collection of ancient British poetry, and he translated several famous Latin works into English, notably *The Ecclesiastical History of the English Nation* by Bede, and a history of the world by the Spanish monk, Orosius. He began the celebrated history of England called *The Anglo-Saxon Chronicle*, which started with the invasion of Britain by Julius Caesar in 55 B.C. This chronicle was continued for nearly three hundred years after his death.

Among many other activities was his creation of the English navy. Faced with more Viking raids in later years, he determined to beat them at sea as well as on land. He organised the building of new ships, which were larger than anything hitherto seen in Western Europe. Thus he was able to hold the Vikings at bay, and in this he was supported by Aethelstan (Guthrum) and his people, for they did not wish their kinsmen from Scandinavia to interrupt their new way of life in the Danelagh.

In spite of this full programme, Alfred found time to arrange the repair of monasteries and churches, and the building of new ones. Two foundations were at Winchester and Athelney. He would often

appear on the site to discuss progress with the master masons, suggesting this or that feature of design. He busied himself with scientific matters, inventing, among other things, a candle clock. This was a tallow candle divided into twelve equal parts by lines, each part of which burned for an hour. He adapted candles to another use— lanterns. These were boxes made of ox-horn ground so thin that a lighted candle inside would shine through.

Alfred was devoted to charitable work, and is even said to have sent money to India, to a small Christian community living there.

This extraordinary man died in October, 900, and was buried at Winchester. He left his kingdom in peace and order. The royal power was firmly established, the navy efficient, and the people once more filled with a sense of national pride. It was to the benefit of England that his descendants proved to be in many respects as able and as hardworking as himself.

EDWARD [*The Elder :900–924*]

Alfred the Great was followed by his son and three grandsons in succession, and all of them proved worthy heirs. Edward, known as The Elder to distinguish him from the later Edward of the royal Anglo-Saxon house, had assisted his father in many of his projects. When he was elected by the Witan in 900, he determined to continue his father's policies and reforms.

When Alfred died, the Danelagh people, no longer ruled by the peaceful and sensible Guthrum who had died, declared war in favour of a king of their own choosing. Immediately, Edward marshalled the royal forces, drove the pretender out, defeated Guthrum's son, Euric, and forced the rebels to accept his supremacy.

A few years later, they rebelled again. This time the king decided that if he should beat them, he would make them direct subjects of the crown rather than vassals. He enlisted the aid of his sister, Aethelflaed, the widow of Aethelred, Earl of Mercia, whom he found to be a staunch supporter of the royal family, and together they planned a series of campaigns.

Edward set out from London and worked his way into East Anglia, while Aethelflaed summoned the hosts of Mercia. Progressively, they built lines of fortified strongholds, called burghs, across the countryside. When the rebels attempted to take these by storm they were invariably driven off with great loss. One by one, their armies were beaten into submission, and by 920, Edward and his sister had conquered England as far north as the river Humber.

Their successes frightened the remaining Vikings in Northumbria and even the chiefs in southern Scotland, so that at a meeting which the king held near Sheffield in 924, they all acknowledged him as overlord of Britain from the south coast to the river Forth in Scotland.

Edward died that year, firmly established as ruler of a greater part of Britain than had been held by any of his predecessors.

ATHELSTAN [924-940]

Edward's son, Athelstan, who was elected to succeed him, was a tall, fair-haired, powerfully built man, whose bravery was matched by his military leadership. As a boy he was adored by his grandfather Alfred, who gave him a purple cloak, a jewelled belt and a little sword, and who encouraged him to learn the arts of war.

The territorial gains of his father had to be maintained, for while subject rulers would acknowledge the supremacy of one man, it did not follow that they would automatically transfer their allegiance to his son. This was the case with Athelstan, but in a reign that was filled with campaigning he set the seal on his father's conquests.

The Vikings who had been driven out of England by Edward now wanted to return, and they begged the help of Anlaf, the Viking ruler in Ireland. They planned an invasion of northern England, which was to coincide with another to be led by Constantine, King of Scotland. This great league was a serious threat.

Athelstan marched to Northumbria, gathering levies on the way, and led his forces to a favourable position at Brunanburgh, perhaps in Lancashire. The combined invasion forces were advancing swiftly down the country to meet him.

The battle began in the morning and it lasted throughout the day. Though outnumbered, Athelstan's men fought with superb gallantry and in the afternoon they were beginning to drive the enemy off the field. *The Anglo-Saxon Chronicle*, which describes in stirring terms the great slaughter inflicted on the enemy by the king, says that "the field grew dark with the blood of men." By eventide, Athelstan had won. Anlaf had fled to his ships and set sail for Ireland. Constantine was running back to Scotland, having left his son mangled with wounds on the battlefield.

Athelstan's victory resounded throughout Europe. Neighbouring kings eagerly sought alliance with him, and offered themselves as husbands for his sisters.

Otto the Great, king of Germany, married one of them, and Charles, king of France married another. Athelstan was regarded as the most powerful monarch in Western Europe.

He died in 940, leaving no children, and the Witan offered the throne to his next brother, Edmund.

EDMUND I [940-946]

When the Witan chose Edmund to succeed Athelstan, they chose well, for he continued his brother's consolidation of royal power. He had been commander of one of the wings at the battle of Brunanburgh, and had displayed the courage and leadership peculiar to his family.

Northumbria rebelled at the beginning of his reign, but Edmund dealt with the rebels severely. Then he decided to invade the lowlands of Scotland. He crossed the Solway river with a considerable force, harried the countryside from east to west and defeated the kingdom of Strathclyde which had been occupied for some time by the Celts, kinsmen of the Celts in Wales. Instead of bringing this kingdom into the English nation, he gave it to Malcolm I, King of Scotland, "on condition that he (Malcolm) should be his faithful fellow-worker by land and sea." This meant, among other things, that Edmund expected Malcolm to provide levies to fight off any Viking raids in the north.

Edmund came to a violent end, after a short reign of six years. In 946, he was dining at Pucklechurch, in Gloucestershire, when, to his anger, he noticed at one of the tables a notorious outlaw called Leofa. He rose from his chair and ordered the man to leave at once. When Leofa refused, Edmund strode over to the table, grabbed him by the hair and threw him to the ground, instructing the guards to take him out of the room. At that moment, Leofa pulled a dagger from his belt and plunged it into the king's chest, whereupon the guards killed him on the spot.

Edmund died a few minutes later, to the sorrow of all the nobles who were with him.

EADRED [946-955]

When Edmund died, his two sons were but children, and the Witan elected his brother Eadred as king.

Eadred had suffered from ill-health all his life, which meant that during his bouts of sickness he had to leave the management of the kingdom in the hands of the Witan. All the same, he continued to assert the power of the monarchy throughout England, and he put down a number of risings in the north.

He was, however, much fonder of the church than of the battlefield, and his greatest achievement was recognising the talents of an abbot called Dunstan, and giving him a hand in the control of the kingdom's affairs.

Dunstan was the wisest and most learned man of his day. He had strong ideas about the reform of the English church. He considered that there was too much feasting and neglect of duties among the clergy, and he wanted to make them return to the old rules of poverty, chastity and obedience.

Edmund seizes Leofa by the hair

In this he had the full support of Eadred, who gave him a free hand to "clean up" the monasteries and parishes.

In 955 Eadred had another attack of illness, and he did not recover. When he died, he was succeeded by his nephew, Eadwig, elder son of his brother Edmund I.

EADWIG [955-959]

Eadwig was fifteen when the Witan elected him successor to Eadred, but it was only a matter of weeks before they regretted choosing so headstrong and irresponsible a young man to rule. He was the first to break the uninterrupted line of strong, wise and popular rulers descending from Alfred.

Even at his coronation, by Odo, Archbishop of Canterbury, he behaved badly, and at the feast following the ceremony, he suddenly got up from the table, and walked out of the room without so much as saying where he was going. After a while, the thegns and bishops felt they could bear the insult no longer and they went to look for him. Odo and Dunstan found him upstairs enjoying a private drinking party.

When the two prelates told him that he

had offended the company by his behaviour, he laughed and said he would not come back to the feast. Then Dunstan reminded him that his position as king was the result of election by the Witan, and that under the laws of England that election could very easily be set aside. Sulkily, Eadwig left the room and returned to the feast.

He never forgave Dunstan, and at the first opportunity he banished him. This had an immediate result. To a man, the bishops and clergy, supported by many of the thegns, withdrew their allegiance and offered the throne to Eadwig's younger brother, Eadgar, and Archbishop Odo duly crowned the latter King of England.

Civil war followed, in which Eadwig, backed by only a few of the Wessex thegns, was defeated. He was compelled to allow Eadgar to rule all England north of the Thames.

Eadwig soon died, in 959, lamented only by his widow and a few friends, and the Witan elected Eadgar as his successor.

EADGAR [959-975]

The new king was very different from his brother, and soon began to show that he had the ability to rule. He brought Dunstan home from exile and appointed him as chief adviser, and between them they managed the kingdom with great success.

Dunstan was allowed to continue with his church reforms, and he enforced new standards of conduct among the clergy that set an example to the rest of Europe.

Eadgar, meanwhile, inheriting the fearlessness and all the military skill of his ancestors, dealt the Welsh chiefs in North Wales so severe a blow in a series of battles that they all acknowledged him as their overlord. In England Eadgar tried a policy of peaceful co-operation with the Viking settlers who once again had risen in revolt. He admitted some of their leaders to the Witan and even gave important positions in the church to their clergy. In this way England was really united as there was little cause left for revolt.

In 973, to demonstrate the extent of his power, Eadgar journeyed to Chester and there summoned a number of neighbouring rulers to pay him homage as their overlord. These included Kenneth the King of the Scots, the Viking chief of the Hebrides, and all the Welsh princes who had already acknowledged him. Then he instructed them all to get into a boat on the river Dee, and row him across, as a sign to the crowds gathered along both banks that he was "King of the English and all the nations round about."

Eadgar was a great lawgiver. He introduced a number of statutes which were added to Alfred's code, and brought existing laws up to date. He conceived the idea of a local police force organisation. He divided the shires of England into smaller areas called hundreds, districts large enough to hold a hundred families. The inhabitants of each hundred were made responsible for law and order there, although the supreme judicial authority rested in the hands of the king and the Witan.

This admirable descendant of Alfred died, at the early age of thirty-one, leaving two sons, Edward and Aethelred, both of whom were only children.

When Eadgar died, there were no adult members of the royal family and the Witan therefore elected Edward, his son by his first wife, who was only twelve years old. The thegns formed a council of regency, and Dunstan, who had become Archbishop of Canterbury when Odo died in 961, was appointed its head.

Dunstan had wielded great influence in the Witan for so long, however, that many thegns grew jealous, and they now tried to get the young king to dismiss him.

A meeting of the Witan was arranged in a large room on the first floor of a house at Calne, in Wiltshire. Suddenly, during the proceedings, the main beam of the floor cracked and the boards gave way, hurtling the occupants down to the stone floor below. *The Anglo-Saxon Chronicle* says that "some were severely injured there, and some did not escape with their lives." The piece of flooring on which Dunstan was standing did not give way, and he was unharmed. This was taken to be a sign from God that he should remain in office.

Edward died tragically, as the result of treachery, in 978. One day in March of that year he was hunting in Dorset, when he decided to visit his step-mother, Elfrida, at Corfe Castle. He arrived on horseback and was met at the door by Elfrida. He asked for a cup of wine, and she brought it to him. While he was drinking it, one of her attendants, at a signal, stabbed him in the back. He fell forwards, and the horse leapt into a gallop. Edward clutched at the reins for a while, but then fainted from loss of blood, and slipping from the saddle, was dragged along the ground. When Elfrida and her followers reached him, he was dead. They threw the body into a ditch, and sent messages to Dunstan and the other members of the Witan that the king died as the result of an accident.

No one believed this story, for it was well known that Elfrida wanted her son, Aethelred, Edward's half-brother, to be king. Dunstan prophesied that England would pay dearly for Elfrida's crime.

AETHELRED II [*The Unready: 978-1016*]

As there were no other members of the royal family to succeed, Aethelred was chosen as king, although he was only ten years old. For the first years, Dunstan and his colleagues governed the country, but before long Elfrida had managed to gather enough support to drive Dunstan out of office and take over the government.

When he was old enough, Aethelred began to rule in his own right. He proved to be one of the most incompetent monarchs of English history, and his long reign, filled with one disaster after another, finally brought England under the heel of a foreign conqueror. The strength and the prosperity of the country, so carefully built up by Alfred and his family for a hundred years, were all but swept away.

No historian seems to have a good word to say about Aethelred. He was selfish, lazy, cruel, extravagant, unjust, and, above all, weak-minded. He earned his nickname, the Unready, or Redeless, which means ill-advised, because whenever he did make up his mind he invariably chose the worst advice he could get.

Almost immediately Vikings from Denmark and Norway began to raid the coasts of England, as their ancestors had done a century before. Finding that England was no longer united, for the supporters of the dismissed Dunstan were bitterly opposed to Elfrida's party, they grew bolder in their invasions. It should have been easy to defeat them, because England had a strong fleet of ships, an organised system of military service, and a way of life that people would fight to the death to preserve.

To its detriment, however, the country had this weak king who had none of the fine martial qualities of his family. At first, he led armies against the invaders, and he was even successful on occasion, but he never managed to inflict the kind of total defeat on them that would put them off altogether. Then, in 991, he introduced for the first time a new and cowardly policy, that of bribing the Vikings to keep away. Not unnaturally, the invaders took the money and then came back for more.

For years these payments were made, and the money was raised by a special tax called the Danegeld. Aethelred paid

£10,000 in 991, but each time he entered into this unworthy bargain it cost him more —£16,000 in 994, £24,000 in 1002 and £30,000 in 1007. His imposition of the Danegeld caused much misery to the country.

In 1002, he perpetrated an appalling crime. He ordered all the Danish settlers in England to be massacred, without considering for a moment that many of them had been living in the country peacefully for a long time. On St Brice's Day, November 12th, thousands were put to the sword. Among them were relatives of Sweyn Forkbeard, the powerful king of Denmark.

Sweyn was infuriated and he began a series of raids which were backed by the whole might of the Danish army. Gradually, he occupied large tracts of England in the North and the Midlands, ravaging the countryside far and wide. Aethelred did little to check Sweyn or to help the victims, for he had fallen under the influence of a wicked and treacherous favourite, Eadric Streona.

Eadric, who cared nothing for England and thought only of increasing his own wealth and power, squeezed all he could out of the king, and then betrayed him. When, in 1013, Sweyn invaded again, Eadric brought most of the nation over to the Vikings, having persuaded the Witan that surrender to Sweyn would be better than living under the incompetence of Aethelred.

Aethelred, deserted by most of his thegns and people, fled overseas, and Sweyn became King of England.

He died very soon afterwards, and the Viking followers accepted his son, Canute, as successor. The English Witan, however, realising their mistake, would not have him, and sent for Aethelred to return. War broke out, and for some time it was not clear who was the effective ruler. The English levies were commanded by Aethelred's son by his first wife, Edmund Ironside, who was a worthy match for Canute.

Aethelred died in London, on April 23rd, 1016, after a reign of thirty-eight years. He left the kingdom in a condition totally different from that in which he had found it. The new system of law was being disregarded, trade and agriculture were severely hampered, the country's treasury was nearly empty, and the nation itself was torn by civil strife. No one could then imagine the outcome.

EDMUND II [*Ironside : April to November 1016*]

Edmund succeeded his father, and though his reign lasted only for seven months, in that brief spell he showed himself to be one of the greatest warrior kings ever to occupy the throne.

Edmund was born in about 980, and he grew up in the period when the fortunes of England were very low. When he reached manhood, he realised that his father's policy of buying off the Vikings could only lead to national disaster. He also saw that this weakness would continue so long as the treacherous Eadric Streona, who became Earl of Mercia, remained as his father's chief adviser.

While still a prince, Edmund encouraged the English to stand up to the Vikings, and sometimes they did. In 1015, when he was beating off an invasion in the north, he heard that Canute was ravaging Dorset and Wiltshire. He gathered an army and marched southwards, having arranged to meet Eadric, with another force, on the way. At the last moment, however, the false earl deserted him and joined Canute, and the two drove Edmund back into the Midlands. It has never been known why Edmund trusted Eadric in the first place.

A few months later, Aethelred lay dying in London, and Edmund was summoned to his bedside. He arrived just in time, for the king died the following day. The members of the Witan who were in London immediately elected Edmund as king. At the same time, however, Canute was chosen by his supporters and by other members of the English Witan in the south. He immediately assembled a great force and headed for London hoping to assert his claim.

Edmund left the city with his levies and marched towards the west country where, at Sherston in Wiltshire, he encamped, ready to give battle to Canute who was pursuing him.

At dawn the next day, Edmund's front line began the attack with a charge of foot-soldiers who fought at close quarters. Throughout the day the armies battled, until in the evening they both withdrew, exhausted.

On the following morning, the struggle continued. Edmund was beginning to get the upper hand when Eadric, commanding a wing of Canute's army, killed an Englishman, cut off his head and held it high on a stick, shouting: "Run away, you English. Edmund has been killed!"

Edmund's troops were panic-stricken, and would have fled in disorder. But the king rushed to a small hill, took off his helmet and showed them he was still alive and still fit to lead them on. Thereupon, they fought more gallantly than ever, and drove Canute's soldiers off the field. It was a great victory for Edmund, who had earned the nickname Ironside because of his valour.

Edmund and Canute, who were much alike in character, brave, just and resolute, fought several more battles, most of which Edmund won. But at Ashington, in Essex, Canute utterly defeated his rival, largely due to the treachery of Eadric who, inexplicably, had been forgiven by Edmund and employed again. Once more he had changed sides and led his wing over to the enemy.

After Ashington, the rivals agreed to divide the kingdom between them and live at peace.

A few weeks later, Edmund, worn out by his hard campaigning, died in London, on November 30th. For the time being the family of Alfred ceased to have any connection with the fortunes of England. The kingdom passed to Canute who ruled wisely and won the affection of the whole nation.

The tall, blond-haired and good-looking young Viking who succeeded Edmund Ironside was elected King Canute by the Witan. While they remembered the savage nature of his father, Sweyn Forkbeard, they had seen that Canute was a strong leader, fearless, and imbued with a sense of justice that they would not have expected from a Scandinavian heathen. They were ready to give him a chance to do what he promised, that is, to govern well. They were not to be disappointed.

The transformation of a heathen pirate who had followed his father around on numerous raids, and, later on, had organised them himself, into a civilised Christian ruler, adored by his subjects, is one of the most amazing stories in the history of the English monarchy. He was said to have become more English than most Englishmen, and though he was also ruler of Denmark, he was much happier governing in this country in which he spent most of his time.

Canute well understood the importance of being a strong king, and from the beginning he set out to curb the power of the thegns who had taken advantage of the war to increase their wealth. He removed many of them from their lands, and he put the treacherous Eadric Streona to death, an act that can have offended no one. He divided the country into great earldoms and gave them to trustworthy thegns.

He dismissed his Danish army and sent it back to Denmark, retaining only a small but tough bodyguard whose activities he watched closely. He employed Englishmen at court and in offices of state, chose English bishops where possible, and then allied himself to the house of Alfred by marrying Emma, the widow of Aethelred the Unready. He was baptised as a Christian, and thenceforth became a devout supporter of the church. He reviewed the country's laws and modernised them where necessary. He appointed a number of

Edmund Ironside removes his helmet at the battle of Sherston

sheriffs to see that they were observed. Indeed, his strict regard for justice prompted him, when on a visit to Rome in 1026, to write a "Letter to my people" in which he said: "I command all sheriffs, or governors, throughout my whole kingdom, not to commit injustice towards any man, rich or poor, but to allow all, noble and humble alike, to enjoy impartial law, from which they are never to deviate."

Perhaps the best evidence of his wise rule was the swift improvement in the country's prosperity and learning. In this respect he followed so closely in Alfred's footsteps that soon the thirty-eight years of misery under Aethelred were forgotten.

The Welsh and the Scots accepted him as their overlord. To Malcolm II of Scotland he gave the English-speaking territory of Lothian, and it was by this act that the English language and customs began to spread as far north as the Grampian mountains.

Canute was treated by his subjects with a veneration bordering on worship. Some said that he could even still the waves at his command. This kind of flattery did not impress him, and when he allowed himself to be put in a chair on the shore at Southampton, to order the incoming waves to recede, he said to those around him when his feet were drenched by a disobedient tide, "You see how weak an earthly king is

in comparison with Him Whom all things obey. Him, therefore, you should honour."

Canute died in 1035, only forty years old, and was buried in great pomp at Winchester. Foreign-born, he had been one of the best kings of England since Ecgbert.

HAROLD I [1035–1040]

The empire of Canute broke up on his death. He left two sons, Sweyn and Harold by his first wife, and one, Harthacanute, by his second wife, Emma. Sweyn succeeded to the kingdom of Norway, but was shortly afterwards driven out by supporters of an older line of rulers. Harthacanute was elected king of Denmark, and the English Witan elected Harold as king of England.

Harthacanute, however, was not satisfied with one Kingdom, and he came to England to fight for Harold's inheritance. Godwine, the powerful earl of Wessex, supported him, and after a few indecisive battles, Harold and Harthacanute divided the kingdom between them.

Both of Canute's sons were quite unlike their father; they were cruel, unprincipled and cared nothing for religion or justice. Worse, they hated each other, and soon broke the arrangement for sharing the country. Harold drove his brother out of England and reigned until 1040, when he died.

HARTHACANUTE [1040–1042]

When Harold died, Harthacanute crossed the North Sea from Denmark and claimed the English crown, backed by a vast army of Danes which he brought with him. His troops behaved with considerable cruelty and arrogance, and alienated any affection that the English might have felt for him, as a son of his revered father.

He retained his army in England and raised heavy taxes to clothe and feed it, using methods of which .his father would have sternly disapproved. When the people of Worcester rose in rebellion against the taxation, he marched to the city, took it by storm and burnt it to the ground.

In June 1042, he was attending the marriage feast of one of his followers when he suffered a stroke and collapsed. To the relief of the nation he did not recover, but died a few days later. Canute's line was now extinct, and the Witan turned again to the house of Alfred for a new king.

EDWARD [*The Confessor : 1042–1066*]

The heir to the house of Alfred, when Canute's line died out with Harthacanute in 1042, was Edward, son of Aethelred the Unready. As a child he had been taken out of the country to Normandy when Canute became king, and had spent his life at the court of Richard, Duke of Normandy, brother of Emma, his mother. Thus he had almost forgotten what England was like, and hardly remembered any words of the language.

The Witan elected him king when he was forty years old. All they knew of him was that he loved the church, had led an honest life and was incapable of knowingly committing an unkind or unworthy act. Given sound advice, there was no reason why he should not govern well. Pious and well-meaning as he was, however, Edward was not equipped to manage affairs of state, and for a while the government was administered by Godwine, Earl of Wessex, and the rest of the Witan.

This suited the king well, for he was more concerned with the church and with architecture. He endowed monasteries richly, took a keen personal interest in the development of teaching within these communities, and strove to keep up the

The funeral cortege of Edward the Confessor approaches Westminster Abbey

standards set by Dunstan among the clergy. He swept away many of the abuses that he found. He organised the building of churches, the most famous being Westminster Abbey, which was designed in the Norman style of Architecture and was larger than anything hitherto built in England. Later kings added to it, but some of Edward's foundation can still be seen today.

After a time, Edward, who had married Godwine's daughter, fell out with the great earl, for the latter objected to the king's Norman favourites who were being given the highest positions of state. At first Godwine was tempted to organise a revolt, with the support of his followers in Wessex, but the king summoned the help of the other two great earls, Leofric of Mercia and Siward of Northumbria, who were jealous of Godwine's power. They compelled him to retire abroad. The Norman favourites now took over the government, but in a year had made themselves so unpopular that the English were begging for Godwine to return.

He brought a fleet up the Thames and was welcomed with tremendous rejoicing. He was restored to his place as head of the Witan, and the Norman officers were banished. Then he made up his differences with Leofric and Siward.

When Godwine died in 1053, England had entered into a new age of prosperity. Small towns grew into larger ones, many new ones were built, and farming was expanded not only to meet the needs of the country but also to provide valuable exports. On the military side, a raid from North Wales, under the prince Gryffyd, was put down by Harold, who had succeeded Godwine as Earl of Wessex, and the Scottish king, Macbeth, was defeated at Lumphanan by Siward who gave the throne to Malcolm, the eldest son of Duncan I.

Edward died at the beginning of January in 1066, to the great sorrow of his people, for, though he was not a leader of men, he was revered for his saintly and humble behaviour, which earned him the name The Confessor. His kingdom had been ably managed by Godwine and by Harold, and it seemed to be set for peaceful development with the approval of everyone.

Within twelve months this happy situation was completely changed. By the end of the year England was under the heel of a foreign invader who was to make the results of his conquest permanent.

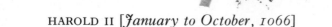

HAROLD II [*January to October, 1066*]

In Edward the Confessor's reign, Harold had been shipwrecked off France. He was given hospitality by William, Duke of Normandy, but when he wished to return to England he was not allowed to leave until he had sworn an oath to use his influence to get the Duke elected to the English throne as soon as Edward should die.

When Edward died, the Witan elected Harold as king, and he accepted, for he considered that his promise to William had been unjustly extracted from him. William immediately sent envoys to the English court to remind Harold of the oath, threatening invasion if he would not abdicate at once. Harold refused, and the Duke thereupon began to prepare a large expeditionary force.

Harold marshalled the levies of the south to stand in readiness for the invasion. Suddenly, he heard that his half-brother, Tostig, had invited the king of Norway, Hardrada, to invade the north. Immediately he marched to Northumbria and at Stamford Bridge, not far from the city of York, the two armies met in battle. By the end of the day, Harold's well-disciplined troops had completely routed the enemy, and both Tostig and Hardrada lay dead.

At that moment, news was brought to the king, while he was celebrating the victory, that William had landed at Pevensey Bay, in Sussex. The king gathered up his army and proceeded southwards, a journey that took several days. It was these days that were to prove fatal to England, for while Harold's men were tired out by the time they reached Sussex, William had had time to build a strong camp near Hastings and to get his men fit and ready for battle.

On the morning of October 14th, 1066, the sun shone in a cloudless sky. A gentle breeze rustled the falling autumn leaves on Senlac Hill (on which Battle Abbey now stands) where the king's army was arrayed behind fences of wooden stakes. In the centre of the line stood Harold, under the dragon-banner of Wessex, the flag of England. Near him were his bodyguards,

36

clothed in chain mail and armed with large-bladed axes. On either side were the shire levies, all of them on foot for they had not learned to fight on horseback, bearing a strange assortment of weapons, swords, clubs, choppers and even farming implements.

In the valley below William's army was assembled, the main body of Normans in the centre, flanked on either side by lines of mercenaries hired from many countries of Europe. Infantry and archers stood in the front lines, with the mounted troops behind.

The signal was given, and William's men charged up the hill, the archers pouring a deadly hail of arrows into the English lines. Time and again Harold beat off the attacks, until William withdrew to re-group, leaving the archers to keep up their barrage. The shafts gradually did what was expected of them, forced the huddled English to break rank and rush down the hill. At once William ordered his cavalry to swing into attack, and the disordered jumble of defenders were ridden down and killed, or driven off the field.

Meanwhile, Harold's bodyguard stood firm in an unbreakable ring round their leader. Wave after wave of the invaders flung themselves against the cordon, but were driven back with heavy loss.

Then, a Norman archer crouching behind a bush fitted a steel-tipped arrow into his bow and released the string. The feathered shaft sped through the air. For a moment there was silence, and then a great cry was heard from the bodyguards. The arrow had pierced the king through the eye, and he had fallen to the ground, dead.

The death of the king stirred the remaining English to fight on, but overcome by superior numbers, they were cut down without mercy. With Harold had fallen two of his brothers, and an uncle, many of the thegns, and nearly all of his gallant bodyguards.

It was the end of the battle. It was the end, too, of Anglo-Saxon England, for the Conqueror had wrought a defeat more complete than any since the overrunning of the country by Saxons and Angles several centuries before.

After the English had been defeated near Hastings and their king, Harold II, slain on that October day of 1066, Duke William of Normandy wandered over the battle-field looking at the thousands of dead Englishmen, and thinking deeply. What were his thoughts, and how did he feel, now that he was about to add the kingdom of England to his Norman dukedom?

He knew, of course, that although the English had lost the battle, they would still not accept his rule without resistance. His army was on enemy soil, and the town and country people would not like to see foreign troops walking about, giving orders, enjoying themselves and perhaps tormenting the shopkeepers or being cruel to the womenfolk. There was a grandson of Edmund Ironside still living, Eadgar, and perhaps there would be a move to give Harold's crown to him. This would mean that William would have to fight again, for he was absolutely determined to keep hold of the kingdom he claimed he had won by battle.

And so it was, for some of the surviving Saxon thegns offered the crown to Eadgar. When William heard of this he marched to Dover, took possession of its great castle and then set out on the road to London. Here and there he left detachments of soldiers to control the roadways so that Eadgar's supporters would find it difficult to keep in touch with each other. Then Eadgar and his followers gave up, went out to meet William and offered him the throne. On Christmas Day he was crowned William I in Westminster Abbey, and from that moment he set out on a programme of reform that was to change the face of England.

To begin with, he had more resistance to deal with in various parts of the country, but in five years he managed to put it all down. The most difficult rebel was Hereward, a Lincolnshire thegn who was a great warrior. For years he held out in a fortified camp in the marshes of Ely, but in the end he was betrayed and the defenders were taken. Hereward escaped, but soon afterwards was offered a pardon by William. He respected his courage and thought he would be a useful man to have in his army.

William then took measures to ensure that the English would not rise against him again. He built castles in various counties, and he began the construction of the White Tower (the largest building of the Tower of London) to guard the Thames. He garrisoned these fortresses with troops, but at the same time gave them strict orders not to ill-treat the English. He had a number of schemes he wanted to introduce and these would work much better if he had the co-operation of the people. To carry out these ideas he had a number of followers who were good soldiers, capable business men and experienced builders. Before we see what William and his Normans did, we should know something about the arrangement of land ownership in England and the rights and duties of the owners.

In Anglo-Saxon times, some of the land belonged to the kings. Much of it, however, was owned by the thegns. They were expected to serve the king in time of war,

as we have seen in Alfred's reign, but otherwise they had the same sort of power over their estates that the king wielded over England. Because there were no engines of transport in those days, it took a long time to get from, say, Bristol to Northampton, and so the king was not always able to see that the thegns managed their little "kingdoms" with justice.

The thegns could not manage or farm all their lands, and so they would let parts of it to local people, in return for certain services. These people were tenants, and sometimes, they, too, would let smaller parts to sub-tenants. The services usually consisted of providing the landlord with a proportion of the farming produce, and agreeing to serve him if he went to war. (This meant that if a thegn rebelled against the king, his tenants were expected to rebel with him.)

Below these tenants and sub-tenants were a class of people who were poor and who were not free. They were called villeins, and they were allowed to plough small strips of land to try to make a living out of them, but they also had to work certain hours every week on their lords' estates. They were supposed to receive protection in return, but often this did not

mean very much since they were virtually slaves.

The Normans knew about this arrangement in England and they had a more developed version of it. They called the estate a Manor and its owner a Lord of the Manor. The rights and duties of all on the manor were clearly laid down. When William became king of England, he decided to introduce this Norman system.

He began by stating that all land belonged to him. He kept some of it for himself, especially the great areas of forest, for he loved hunting. Then he distributed the rest. Some he gave to the Church. Four-fifths of the remainder he gave to his Norman followers, and the last fifth to those Saxon thegns who had agreed to work with him and not against him. When giving these estates to these lords, he set down terms. They had to fight for him if he demanded it. Their manors had to provide a fixed number of men, according to the value of the land. The men had to serve without payment for forty days.

He handed out these manors with some care. A lord might receive several manors, but they would be scattered in different parts of the country, which meant that if he wanted to rebel he would have difficulty

in collecting all his forces together. William would not allow the lords to build castles unless he had given special permission, and so most of the fortresses built in his reign were on the lands he kept for himself.

There was one more thing that he did. Every lord of the manor had to swear an oath of allegiance to the king, and his tenants and sub-tenants likewise. If a lord wanted to rebel, the attempt was not likely to succeed, as his tenants' loyalty was to the king direct.

This arrangement of ownership and its duties was called the Feudal System, and the Norman version of it lasted in England for many generations. It was largely due to it that, with few exceptions, the kings of England managed to control the nation and build up the monarchy into a strong central source of government.

William now turned his attention to the old Witan. This body of advisers had had great power; it had elected kings and it had deposed them if they ruled badly. It was made up of the wisest men of the land, usually thegns and bishops. The new king did not abolish it, but he altered it, and it became known as the Great Council. Its members were now his chief tenants, all of whom owed everything they had to him. They still had the power to elect kings, but it was not often that they gave the throne to someone other than the person whom the previous king had selected.

By these means, William made his power felt throughout the nation. When he had to visit his dukedom of Normandy, he left England under the charge of his lords, some of whom did not always behave well. In this case, when he returned, he confiscated their estates and gave them to other lords.

In 1085, by which the new system had had time to settle down, William decided to carry out a thorough survey of the country. He wanted to find out the size of all the estates, how much in them was arable or pasture land, how many cattle there were, the number of people who worked on them, and so on, and he sent out clerks to every district to get this information. The results of their enquiries were written down on rolls of parchment which were known as the Domesday Book, and which can still be seen in the Public Record Office in London. It was a great work, and it told the king, to a high degree of accuracy, how much everybody was worth, and how much, therefore, he could expect to get when he raised taxes. The Anglo-Saxon Chronicle records the thoroughness with which the clerks did their work. "Not even one ox, nor one cow, nor one pig escaped notice in his survey."

When he had thus learned the exact names, position and duties of all the landowners of England, and their wealth, he summoned them all to a great meeting at Salisbury to compel them to re-affirm their oath of allegiance to him. Of course, not every owner could come, but the attendance was remarkably high, so high that the meeting had to be held in the open, on Salisbury Plain.

William's love of hunting led him to take over huge areas of forest, the most famous of which was the New Forest in Hampshire. To preserve the woods and the game, harsh laws were imposed with cruel punishments for breaking them. For example, if a deer was killed, the offender would have his eyes put out.

The Normans were great builders. Apart from the White Tower, they rebuilt Durham Cathedral, with its huge cylindrical pillars and its vast round arches. There are many smaller churches in the country which were started in those times and which still have Norman remains. They also put up castles, and William himself laid the foundations of Windsor Castle, which succeeding kings improved.

In 1087, William quarrelled with the king of France, and he invaded his territory and laid siege to the city of Mantes. While his troops were setting fire to it, a blazing beam fell down near his horse, which reared and threw the king to the ground. He was taken to Rouen but died there almost at once.

When the Conqueror died, he left an England which, if it was not happy, was well-ordered and ruled by a powerful monarchy. It remained to be seen how his successors would manage to maintain the new system of government.

William II, known as Rufus because of his fiery red hair, was born in 1056. He was the second surviving son of the Conqueror, and he inherited the kingdom of England, while his elder brother, Robert, succeeded to the dukedom of Normandy.

William was a thick-set, rugged man, of medium height, powerful limbs and handsome appearance. He had all of his father's courage and ability, but his violent temper often led him to act unjustly. At the same time he was not as black as some historians have painted him, and he had three qualities not found in many rulers; he was a faithful friend, a generous enemy, and he had been consistently loyal to his father.

As soon as he came to the throne, William was faced with a revolt by the Norman barons. Outwardly claiming to support the grievance of Robert that he had not been given England, but in reality hoping to increase their own power, they declared war. William appealed to the native English to come to his aid, promising them that he would govern with a lighter hand than his father. The response was unexpectedly high, and in a short campaign he put down the revolt and drove the barons out of the kingdom.

He was not able to keep his promise of milder rule. Finding himself short of money, he had to increase the rate of taxation, and he extracted its payment with some harshness. He also enforced the forest laws, introduced by his father, which carried penalties of death or mutilation for anyone caught interfering with the large tracts of woodland set aside for the royal sport of hunting.

The death of William Rufus

William's military expeditions were crowned with success. He defeated Malcolm III of Scotland in 1092 and extended the boundary between the two countries. He invaded Wales, overran most of the south, and installed his barons as local lords. In the north, he built castles at Rhuddlan, Flint and Montgomery. In France he conquered the duchy of Maine, and in 1096 he unexpectedly obtained possession of Normandy, when Duke Robert mortgaged the duchy to him for enough money to pay an army with which he wanted to join the First Crusade.

By now William had maintained and increased his father's dominions, but the cost had been high.

William then disturbed the people by a fierce quarrel with the Church. In 1093 he had appointed Anselm as Archbishop of Canterbury, hoping that the latter would provide him with money from the rich sees and give his support in other necessary actions. He had misjudged Anselm, however, for he was a learned and pious priest who refused to give the king what he wanted. From that moment bitter enmity sprang up between the two men. Anselm resisted every attempt by William to get money from the Church, and he lost no opportunity of publicly condemning the king for his policies. William on his part would have put the archbishop to death, but Anselm escaped from the country.

William's death in 1100 was sudden and violent. Hunting in the New Forest on August 1st, with his friends, he saw a stag and cried out to Sir Walter Tyrrell, "Shoot, Walter, in the name of the Devil!" Tyrrell drew his bow and let loose an arrow. It missed the stag—and pierced the king through the heart. Tyrrell immediately fled into hiding, leaving the body of his dead master on the ground where a charcoal-burner came upon it and carried it on a cart to Winchester for burial.

Despite his faults, William had ruled successfully for all his reign, and his kingdom was as strong as it had been when he succeeded his father.

HENRY I [*Beauclerc: 1100–1135*]

Within forty-eight hours of hearing the news of his brother William's death in the New Forest, the Conqueror's youngest son, Henry, took advantage of Duke Robert's absence on the First Crusade and assembled a gathering of nobles at Winchester. There he persuaded them to elect him king, by making a number of promises of good government. He then moved to London and was crowned as Henry I.

Born in 1070 in Yorkshire, Henry became known as Beauclerc, that is, fine scholar, because he devoted his youth to learning. He knew Latin and French well,

and he studied law, religion and history.

Henry also inherited the qualities of his father, and these, coupled with his interest in law, enabled him to govern with as much strength and with more justice than his two predecessors. On the other hand, he was selfish, and at times he could be cruel and unmerciful.

After his coronation, he renewed his promises by issuing a charter to the nation in which he undertook to uphold the laws of England. He delighted the people by marrying princess Matilda, who was a descendant of Alfred the Great. He then granted a charter to the city of London, and this served as a model to his successors when they gave privileges to other cities and towns.

When Duke Robert returned to Normandy in 1100, he planned an invasion of England to secure the throne which he considered was his by right. Gathering support from powerful Norman barons in England, he set sail, but at Portsmouth where he landed Henry bought him off with a heavy bribe. The king then turned on the rebel barons, and, with the help of the English levies, crushed them.

Before long, however, Duke Robert

A travelling judge sets out on his circuit

again tried to unseat his brother. Henry invaded Normandy, and at Tinchebrai he defeated and captured Robert, sending him to Cardiff Castle for the rest of his life —some twenty-eight years. Henry thus won Normandy and he managed to keep it, governing there as firmly as in England.

He completed the conquest of South Wales and established colonies of Englishmen in the counties. With Scotland he maintained peaceful relations, which allowed the Scots to advance in civilisation and wealth.

Meanwhile he continued his policy of encouraging the Normans to live in peace with the English people, treating both as equals under the law. In time the two races intermarried, having been set an example by the king himself. He also developed the administration of law, and introduced the system whereby judges travelled about the country to try cases in the shire courts.

In 1120, Henry's son, William, was drowned at sea, and this meant that his heir was his daughter, Matilda. The barons were unlikely to elect a woman as their ruler after the king's death, but because he regarded their choice, his nephew Stephen, as a weak, unreliable man who would be unfit to govern, he compelled them to swear an oath that they would accept Matilda. He then arranged for her to marry the courageous, handsome and sport-loving young count of Anjou, Geoffrey Plantagenet, and their son was one day to become king Henry II.

For the rest of his reign he ruled with a firm hand, and the condition of England improved. Trade flourished, fine buildings were raised, and the Normans and English settled down to living together at peace.

At the age of sixty-five Henry died, in December 1135, while on a visit to his daughter.

As soon as Henry I died, his worst fears were realised. The barons, meeting in London, forgot their oath and offered the throne to Stephen. Despite his personal promise to Henry that he would not stand in Matilda's way, he accepted. At Christmas he was crowned, amid the cheering of the crowds with whom he was popular. It was not long before they had cause to regret their rejoicing.

Stephen was the son of the Count of Blois and his wife Adela, the Conqueror's youngest daughter. He had spent most of his life at the court of his uncle, Henry I, and he had seen the extent of his power. He had also witnessed the difficulties with which even the strongest king had to contend. It is extraordinary, therefore, how little he appeared to have learned.

He had the courage of his Norman relations, but that was all. Kind-hearted, generous to the point of extravagance, never able to refuse a friend's request, constantly changing his mind, he was quite unfitted to rule men.

The barons soon took advantage of his weakness. Openly supporting the claim of Matilda—which they had conveniently ignored when Henry I died—they rebelled. By 1138 nearly every magnate in the land was up in arms. At that moment, however, David I of Scotland, Matilda's uncle, invaded England on her behalf, but his soldiers committed such atrocities in the north that the barons supported Stephen's efforts to expel him.

Once David had been checked, the barons returned to their opposition to Stephen, and he made matters worse by constantly giving in to them. They fought amongst each other, built castles and fortresses up and down the country, and oppressed the common people in a manner far worse than the followers of the Conqueror.

Stephen then ruined his cause by a quarrel with the Church. He threw the bishops of Lincoln and Salisbury into prison because they would not assist him, and earned the enmity of the whole clergy. This was Matilda's hour, and she landed in Sussex with a strong force, marched up to Lincoln and challenged Stephen to pitched battle.

On the field Stephen's courage asserted

itself. He fought like a lion, slashing left and right with his sword. When it was broken a soldier gave him a mace, and he swung it round with the fury of a wild boar, until he was hit on the head and taken prisoner. Matilda had triumphed. She was proclaimed queen, but was never crowned, for within a short while, her arrogant and revengeful behaviour turned everyone against her, and she was driven out of the country. Stephen then continued to rule as king.

Barons and criminals alike enjoyed the disorganised state of the realm. For ten years or more, though Stephen was king in name, the country was wracked with lawlessness and seemed to have no government. Lords of the manor seized anyone who appeared to have money, locked them in dungeons and tortured them. Armed gangs of robbers raided towns and villages, smashing shops, taverns and houses, throwing the goods and the contents into the streets.

Finally, in 1153, peace was made at Wallingford. The terms were that Stephen should continue to reign for his life, but that his successor should be Matilda's son, Henry.

A few months later, the harassed and luckless king died, leaving his country in a most desperate condition.

HENRY II [*Curtmantle: 1154–1189*]

On December 19th 1154, Winchester cathedral was packed with nobles, clergy, and a throng of the people of England. The great doors opened, and in came a procession, its members gorgeously clothed, bearing swords of state, banners and royal regalia. Towards the rear walked a young man of twenty-one.

Suddenly, trumpeters blew a fanfare, and a herald summoned the young man to his coronation. He read out his titles, and it was an impressive list. "Henry, Duke of Normandy (this through his mother), Count of Anjou and Count of Touraine (through his father), Duke of Aquitane (acquired by his marriage to Eleanor of

Aquitaine), Lord of Brittany . . ." So the list went on.

Now he was to add the kingdom of England, war-torn and miserable as it was, to a range of lands in France greater than those possessed by the French king himself.

The prospect of managing so vast an empire, and of dealing with so desperate a situation in one important part of it, might well have daunted one so youthful. But, as we shall see, Henry II brought to the problem a combination of talents seldom found in the history of British monarchy.

Henry, nicknamed Curtmantle because of the short cape he used to wear, was broadly built, with a freckled face, fierce grey eyes, and red hair cut short. He had a harsh, cracked voice, and was given to fits of ungovernable temper. His energy was untiring, and it was said that he never sat down except to meals which he ate hurriedly, and on horseback on which he travelled ceaselessly about his dominions.

Like his grandfather, Henry I, he was learned, and equally concerned with law reform. He never forgot a face, he was quick to forgive an injury, and he seldom broke his word once he had given it.

As soon as he was crowned, Henry set out to restore order. He forced the barons to pull down the castles they had built in Stephen's time—some 350 of them. The bands of foreign troops, hired by the barons for their raids upon one another, were sent out of the country. Corrupt and inefficient officials were dismissed, and the weight of the king's authority was made to be felt in every corner of the land. In five years the country was at peace.

Thereafter, Henry devoted his energies to four main problems, the improvement of the legal system, the relations between Church and state, the invasion of Ireland, and the protection of the empire's boundaries.

He appointed as sheriffs men whom he could trust. He resumed the practice of sending judges to shire courts to try cases, which had lapsed under Stephen. He introduced the system of trial by a jury of twelve men, and, to begin with, most of the cases heard by these juries were disputes over ownership of land. This effectively stopped greedy barons and lords of the manor from seizing property from more unfortunate owners by force of arms, and it was a boon to thousands. Juries also tried other civil disputes and criminal charges, thus ensuring a much better chance of justice being done.

When Henry tried to extend his reforms to Church law, however, he met with bitter opposition.

Since the time of the Conqueror, the Church had had its own courts in which church offences were tried. By 1154, these courts were trying clerics accused of common law offences, such as murder, assault and theft. Punishments were limited to doing penance or to being forbidden to celebrate services. Henry thought this was unfair, and to put it right he appointed his friend and counsellor, the learned and fun-loving Thomas Becket, Archbishop of Canterbury, hoping that he would get the Church to agree. He could not have made a worse choice.

Becket, who had been an inseparable companion of the king, enjoying the same tastes and amusements, suddenly changed his whole way of life. He gave up all pleasures, wore shirts of hair next to his skin, and lived the life of the most austere monk. Determined to keep the Church free from state interference he opposed every suggestion put forward by the king. Even when Henry proposed that the

Church should continue to try clerics for common law crimes, but hand the convicted to the state for punishment, Becket flatly refused to agree. Henry exploded, and, terrified for his life, Becket fled from the country.

Six years later, they patched up their quarrel, and Becket returned. Immediately, he began to act in a most high-handed manner, and he provoked the king to one of his outbursts of temper, the results of which neither could have foreseen.

One day in December 1170, Henry was in council with some of his barons in Normandy when news of yet another of Becket's insults was brought to him. Leaping up from his chair, shaking with anger, he cried out: "I have given that man everything, and this is how he behaves. Will none of you who sit at this table rid me of this meddlesome priest?"

Four knights, Reginald FitzUrse, Hugh de Murville, William de Tracey and Richard le Breton, left the chamber at the end of the meeting, rode to the coast, crossed the Channel and galloped along the road to

Canterbury. They reached the cathedral at eventide, burst open the doors and rushed inside. There was Becket, preparing to take evening service. Drawing their swords, they struck him down and killed him.

When the news spread, the whole nation, indeed all Europe, was horrified, but no one was more shocked than Henry. At once he sent messages to the Pope saying that he had not given orders for Becket to be murdered. He was absolved, but all the same he did penance at Becket's grave at Canterbury and allowed himself to be flogged by the monks.

After the murder, Henry gave up the attempt to reform Church law. Meanwhile, the activities of one of his vassal lords in Ireland, Richard de Clare, nicknamed Strongbow, commanded his attention.

In 1171, encouraged by the Pope to bring the Irish Church back into obedience, Henry crossed the sea from Milford Haven to Waterford with a large army, to assert his authority over Ireland. He marched to Dublin, and the size of his forces compelled both the English lords and the Irish princes, especially the overlord, Roderic O'Connor,* to pay homage, and to accept his claim to be "Lord of Ireland," a title which succeeding English kings adopted. Henry had no difficulty, either, in getting the Irish Church to give up their old customs and acknowledge the supremacy of the Pope.

When he returned from Ireland, he was met with revolts in his other dominions. To his great distress, most of them were stirred up by one or other of his sons, Henry, Richard and Geoffrey, who, it seemed, were impatient to have the territories that they would inherit on their father's death. One by one Henry put them down, and in every case he treated not only his sons but also their followers with great mercy. No one was executed, and no estates were confiscated.

By 1175, there was peace in all his dominions. Abroad, Henry was considered the greatest king in Western Europe.

*See Rulers of Ireland, page 226.

Princes came to him to settle differences between themselves. Nations sought his alliance. At home, he continued with his law reforms. He led his advisers and attendants an exhausting life as he made them follow him all over the countryside on his many visits to cities and towns, to see how his new programme was working. There he would hear court cases and complaints, attempting to give justice to all who sought it.

At this time an increasing amount of land came into the ownership of smaller farmers and growers, and this resulted in an amazing growth of agricultural produce. Trade, especially exports, expanded and made the country richer than it had ever been. Corn, cattle, butter, tin, lead and a host of other things crossed the channel in unending streams to the markets of Europe, and in return came fine cloth, furs, timber, spices, and gold, all enriching the national life. A careful check on royal and government spending, together with a fairer system of tax collection, filled the coffers of the treasury.

Despite these prosperous times, the last years of the reign were sad for the king. His son Henry died of fever in 1183, and Geoffrey was killed in a tournament in 1186. Richard, unable to wait for his inheritance, once again rebelled, and this time he was joined by John, the king's youngest and most adored son. When Henry heard that John had turned on him, he was stricken with grief. Already ill from overwork, he now no longer wished to live. "Let things go as they will," he cried to his physician, one sunny morning in July, 1189, "I have nothing to care for in this world now." And he turned his face to the wall and died.

So ended the lawgiving king Henry, first of the dynasty that later ages called Plantagenet, after a sprig of broom (planta genista) which his father always used to wear as a badge. He had found the kingdom rent with civil war, lawless and poverty-stricken; he left it ordered, rich and united to a large empire.

48

When Henry II died, his empire passed to the elder of his two surviving sons, Richard, and the barons duly elected him king Richard I. John, who had so basely betrayed his father, received nothing, but Richard made him Earl of Cornwall.

The stories of Richard's gallantry and military leadership, which earned him the nickname Coeur de Lion (Lionheart), are so popular that they have covered up the fact that as ruler of England he was a disaster. Much of Henry's work was undone, and there was continual trouble in the dominions in France.

Born in Oxford in 1157, the third son of Henry II, Richard grew up to be a tall, handsome and athletic man, with long arms and legs which gave him a considerable advantage in close fighting in battle. He had immense personal courage and great charm of manner. Unfortunately, the family vices in him outweighed his virtues. He was rebellious as a son, faithless as a husband, inconsiderate as a ruler, and he was capable of extreme cruelty and injustice.

On his accession, he immediately began to prepare to join the Third Crusade to the Holy Land. This required a great deal of money, but with no care for the welfare of England, he sold a large number of privileges to individuals and to communities that would ordinarily have had to earn them. His friends paid highly for offices of state, and cities and towns obtained charters in return for enormous contributions to the war chest. He is supposed to have said: "I would sell London itself if I could find a buyer rich enough."

Richard left England at the end of 1189, and, collecting extra forces from his French dominions, he joined Philip Augustus, King of France. Together they sailed for the Holy Land. On the way, Richard landed in Cyprus, conquered the island, and then in great pomp and splendour married Berengaria, daughter of the King of Navarre, who had come out to join him there.

The two kings then set off for a point near Acre. There, some of the Crusaders who had already arrived, were under attack by the Sultan of Egypt and Syria, Saladin. Richard and Philip drove the Sultan off, captured Acre and began the march to Jerusalem.

Suddenly, Philip announced that he was returning to France, taking part of his army with him. Richard proceeded alone down the coast and defeated Saladin again at Arsouf. He pushed on to within a few miles of the Holy City, and stood ready to take it by storm. At that moment, the army leaders quarrelled among themselves and the attack was delayed. When they were ready again, the French troops refused to move. They were exhausted, they said, from the continual search for water and the shortage of food.

Richard had not enough men to go on alone, and in despair he turned back towards the coast. At Jaffa he defeated Saladin again, and made a three-year truce with him.

Leaving his army in the hands of his generals, Richard took sail for England in a private ship. It was wrecked in the Adriatic Sea and he had to continue overland. On his journey he was seized at Vienna by Duke Leopold of Austria, with whom he had quarrelled, and sold to the Emperor of Germany, Henry VI. Henry imprisoned him and demanded of England the huge ransom of £100,000.

Taxation to provide the money for the Crusade had already crippled the country, and it was some time before the ransom money was collected and paid. When Richard finally returned, he found his kingdom in disorder.

During his absence, his ministers had ruled with such arrogance that a rebellion had broken out, led by Prince John. The rebels captured a number of royal castles and dismissed the ministers. Then John, who heard of his brother's capture, seized the chance to take the throne for himself. Within weeks of Richard's return, however, John was defeated and exiled.

Instead of remaining in the country to re-establish his authority, Richard went to France, from which he was never to return. For the next four years he was endlessly occupied with revolts by barons in his French possessions, most of them being supported by the French king, Philip Augustus. He managed to check the revolts, but it cost England dearly, for heavy taxation was again imposed.

The Lionheart, whose bravery was famed throughout Europe, was to die in battle. While laying siege to the castle of Chaluz in Aquitaine, he was wounded in the shoulder by a cross-bow arrow. The wound became gangrenous and for days his surgeons battled to save his life. It was no use, however, and on April 6th, 1199, Richard died, in his last breath enjoining the barons to accept his brother John as their king.

JOHN [1199–1216]

On the south bank of the Thames, near Windsor, lies the famous meadow of Runnymede. There, on the morning of June 15th, 1215, a host of the greatest barons of England, clad in chain mail and surrounded by soldiers and attendants, was drawn up in front of a colourful array of tents.

A little way along the opposite bank was another, much smaller gathering and in the middle of it stood the broadly-built, red-haired king of England, John.

Suddenly, the sound of the heralds' trumpets was heard, and within minutes the king's party crossed the river to meet the barons. Their leaders, Stephen Langton, Archbishop of Canterbury, and the army commander, Robert Fitzwalter, stepped forward and bowed to the king. Then they escorted him to a chair at the head of a long table. When the king sat down, Langton and Fitzwalter, and leading representatives of both sides, followed suit.

In front of the king was a sheaf of parchment documents, containing a long list of promises. This was Magna Carta, and it became one of the most famous charters in English history.

The king, already aware of the nature of the promises, glowered at the impressive lines of barons ranged against him. It was clear that they meant to get his agreement. Reluctantly, he took up the royal seal, held it for a moment, and then affixed it to the charter. By doing so he agreed to observe a number of liberties for all classes of people.

There were sixty-three clauses in Magna Carta. Among other things, they ensured that the church would be free from interference, that taxes would not be raised without the consent of the Great Council, and that justice would not be sold, refused or delayed to anyone.

Presenting the charter was an attempt by the barons to curb the king's power which, they claimed, he had abused over and over again. He had quarrelled with his vassals in France, with the Church, and in the end with his barons at home.

John was born in 1166, the youngest son of Henry II. Like his father, he was hot-tempered, and because his mother spoiled him he became lazy and irresponsible. At the same time, he was clever, and he had a lively sense of humour.

His first job was a failure. Sent to Ireland by his father to receive the homage of the native princes, he insulted them by laughing at their long, trailing beards, and he had to be brought home.

We have seen that he rebelled in his brother Richard's absence on the Crusade, for which he was banished. Later on they made their peace, and Richard left the English throne to him in his will.

As soon as he became king, John's troubles began in earnest. He had already shocked the nation by divorcing his first wife, Isabella of Gloucester, because he was tired of her. Divorce was not unknown in royal families, but to get rid of his wife for this reason seemed totally unjust. Worse was to follow, however, for in 1200 he wooed and married Isabella of Angouleme,

although she was engaged to one of his vassals in Poitou, Hugh de la Marche.

In revenge, de la Marche, assisted by John's nephew, Prince Arthur of Brittany, led an army into Aquitaine and besieged the fortress of Mirabeau. John marched swiftly across country to the city, raised the siege and captured many of the leading rebels, including Arthur. This was one of the few occasions when John showed his skill as a general.

Arthur was murdered a few months later, and although to this day no one knows who really killed him, it was believed at the time that John was guilty.

The remaining rebels continued the war, and they asked Philip Augustus to help them drive John out of the English dominions. Within four years, Normandy, Anjou and Touraine were conquered, and John had to retire to England. The great empire of Henry II had almost gone.

At home, John provoked the Church by arranging for his friend, the Bishop of Norwich, to succeed Hubert Walter (who died in 1205) as Archbishop of Canterbury. The Pope, Innocent III, however, would not recognise this, and appointed an English cardinal living in Rome, Stephen Langton, in his place. John was furious at this interference in English affairs, and he would not allow Langton into England.

The Pope replied by putting England under an Interdict (March 1208), which meant that churches were closed and people could not be buried in cemeteries.

This interdict lasted five years, and it was a sad time for the people, for they took their religion seriously. By 1213, The Pope had still not been able to bend the king to his will, and so he announced that John was no longer king of England, and he instructed Philip Augustus to invade the country to depose him. John realised that the Pope meant to enforce his will, and he gave in. Langton was admitted to his office, and the Interdict was then lifted.

Although most of his reign was occupied with wars against the barons and arguments with the church, John found time to interest himself in architecture and town-planning. He organised the building of Beaulieu Abbey in Hampshire, and a wide bridge across the Thames near the Tower of London. He was the first person to see that Liverpool, then a small town, would make an excellent port, and he granted it a charter, urging the inhabitants to develop it. He also gave charters to other towns and encouraged the growth of local government.

In 1214, he tried to recover his dominions in France, but the campaign was a failure, and the heavy taxes raised for the war were completely wasted.

By now, the barons had had enough of the king, and they drew up Magna Carta and forced him to agree to it.

When he put the royal seal on the charter, however, he had made up his mind not to keep the promises. He sent a messenger to the Pope begging him to release him from his oath of agreement. Surprisingly the Pope, the same one that had put England under the Interdict, agreed, and he rebuked Langton for taking sides against his king.

The barons now took to arms. Offering the throne to Louis, son of Philip Augustus, they invited him to England to lead them against the king. Louis landed in Kent and soon became master of eastern England. But he found that he was ruler of only part of the nation. Many barons had joined John rather than serve a foreigner. John, who was in the north at the time, was encouraged by this unexpected support, and he marched southwards, capturing a number of castles belonging to followers of Louis.

While his army was crossing the river Wash, however, it was overtaken by a high tide, and all his baggage and treasures were swept away. Many of his troops were drowned.

This was a severe blow to the king, and before he could recover, he was taken ill. He retired to Newark and there, on October 18th, 1216, he died.

Simon de Montfort's first Parliament in 1265

HENRY III [*1216–1272*]

The reign of Henry III lasted for more than fifty years, and yet almost the only benefit England derived from it was the foundation of Parliament. Even that was the result of the king's bad governance.

The civil war, begun in John's last year, did not end at his death. Louis, the French prince, and his followers continued to fight for the crown which had passed to Henry, John's elder son, who was only nine years old. One by one, however, the rebel barons deserted Louis and joined the cause of the boy king, which was led by two able and powerful lords, William the Marshal and Hubert de Burgh. In twelve months Louis was defeated, and then driven out of the country.

William the Marshal governed as Regent until his death in 1219, and his successor, Hubert de Burgh, continued until 1227. Both men ruled well. The last remnants of rebellion were stamped out, Magna Carta

was re-published and its terms in the main carried out.

In 1227, Henry came of age, and soon showed himself to be a strange mixture of good and bad. He was handsome and courteous, kind to his friends, and after he married Eleanor of Provence in 1236, he proved to be a good husband and father. He was intensely interested in the arts and in building, and he surrounded himself with a brilliant collection of craftsmen and artists. He started the construction of Salisbury Cathedral, and he rebuilt Westminster Abbey—perhaps his greatest achievement.

His faults as a ruler, nevertheless, were numerous. He was a spendthrift, especially where his wife's many relations were concerned; he was unable to keep his word; he would not take advice; he would not concentrate on one subject at a time. All the same, he was neither cruel nor oppressive, which explains why his subjects stood his mistakes and also his extravagance for so long.

For the first years, he allowed Hubert de Burgh to act as his chief adviser, but in 1232, with awful ingratitude, he dismissed and imprisoned him for trying to prevent him embarking on an unnecessary war with France. From then on he decided to manage his own affairs, and he acted as his own chief secretary, chief justice and treasurer. As a result, the business of government became hopelessly disorganised. He tried to recover some of the dominions in France lost by his father, but he was defeated and had to make an humiliating peace.

An event in 1257 brought the country's patience to an end. The Pope, Alexander IV, offered the vacant throne of Sicily to Henry's second son, Edmund, on condition that Henry would lead an army to Sicily to enforce the claim. Henry eagerly agreed, and speedily began to make preparations.

This needed money, however, and he summoned the Great Council, demanding from them an enormous sum which, he calmly said, he had promised to supply. The barons were furious; the king had no right to pledge English revenues to the Pope without their consent. They refused to grant the money and, instead, forced him to surrender the government of the country into their hands.

The leader of the revolt was Earl Simon de Montfort, a wise, honest and very popular noble who was married to the king's sister, Eleanor.

For some years the new arrangement worked well. Special committees looked after finances, superintended the dispensing of justice, and directed the nation's foreign policies.

In time, Henry grew tired of the control of the barons, and resisted them. At Lewes, an army of de Montfort's defeated the king's forces, in 1264, and Henry was captured with his elder son, Edward.

In 1265, de Montfort summoned the first parliament in English history that included representatives of the towns and boroughs as well as nobles and bishops, and this marked the beginnings of the parliamentary system we have today. Its members confirmed the acts of de Montfort.

The good earl's rule did not last. Prince Edward escaped from his captors, and fled to the West Country where he enlisted the support of barons who were jealous of de Montfort. They declared war, and at Evesham, in August, 1265, de Montfort's army was beaten on the field, and the earl was slain. His ideas and his work survived.

Thenceforth, Henry ruled with the aid of the council, in which his son Edward played the leading part, preparing himself for the responsibilities to which he was soon to succeed.

In November 1272, the king died peacefully in his sleep, and he was buried in his beloved Westminster Abbey. The nation had forgiven him his misrule and it mourned his passing.

EDWARD I [*Longshanks : 1272-1307*]

One day in 1278, John de Warenne, Earl of Surrey, and a great landowner, stood before a panel of commissioners of the king, Edward I. The chairman looked up and spoke:

"By what right do you hold these lands?" he asked, thrusting forward a bundle of documents describing vast estates scattered over the country.

Surrey glowered at the panel, and then, from behind his back produced a rusty old sword and threw it on to the table.

"Here are my title-deeds," he cried. "My ancestors came over with the Conqueror and won their lands with this, and with it I will keep them from anyone who tries to take them from me."

He turned on his heel and stalked out of the room. He was not going to account to the king for his properties, despite the order *Quo Warranto* (By What Authority) which had just been sent out to discover who owned what in England.

The order, issued by Edward because he wanted to know how estates belonging to the crown had got into private hands, was one of the many reforms that he introduced into the English legal system, reforms which have earned him the fame of being one of the greatest lawmakers ever to sit on the English throne.

When his father died in 1272, Edward was away in the Holy Land on the Seventh Crusade. Nevertheless, he was immediately proclaimed king, and it was the first time that the crown had been passed by strict hereditary succession without the procedure of election by the Great Council. It was nearly two years before he came back to England, but when he arrived he received a tumultuous reception.

Standing well over six feet tall (he was nicknamed Longshanks), Edward looked splendid. His reddish hair, the long hooked nose, the flashing eyes, and the muscular limbs, all commanded attention and wonder wherever he walked. He had all the gifts of his family. He was just, proud, unselfish, hardworking, fearless, and once he gave his word he never broke it. His knowledge of law was matched by his skill as a general, and both these qualities were put to the test many times in an eventful reign.

Edward's legal reforms, most of which were carried out in the earlier years, were devoted to strengthening the monarchy and keeping the barons and the church under firm control, and at the same time to widening the liberties of the ordinary people. Enthusiastic about de Montfort's new conception of parliament, Edward summoned a number of them during his reign because he believed that "what touches all should be approved by all."

By the Statute of Mortmain he regulated the amount of land that could be held by the church, for as landowners, clerics had not been paying a fair proportion of the kingdom's taxes. The order *Quo Warranto* returned to the crown some of the lands taken by powerful barons during the civil wars in Henry III's time, though the Earl of Surrey, the rusty-sword wielder, was one allowed to keep his estates.

Edward also agreed that no taxes should be raised without the consent of the Lords and Commons assembled in Parliament. This was an important step. By the Statute of Winchester he rebuilt the national army, laid down new terms of service and detailed what armaments each person should provide for himself. The statute also set up local police forces for dealing with outlaws and highway robbers. Main roads were not to have hedges or ditches nearer than fifty yards or so from the edges, which helped to prevent highwaymen springing surprise attacks on travellers.

Apart from his close personal concern with law and government, Edward spent a good part of his reign in military exploits, and it was Wales that first demanded his attention.

Wales was still divided into two. The south and the centre, known as the Welsh Marches, were ruled by English barons (called Lords Marcher) who had long before settled there. One of their duties was to keep the unruly Celts in the north within their territories of Merioneth, Caernarvon, Anglesey, and parts of Montgomery and Denbigh. Over this land, which was called Gwynedd, an overlord prince ruled, with under-princes as local governors. We shall see, in the chapters on Princes of Wales, that the system of rulership was very confused, and that the princes were frequently fighting each other for supreme power.

In Edward's reign, however, one man had established himself as undisputed ruler of Gwynedd, and this was the lively and fearless Llywelyn. On several occasions Edward ordered him to come to his court to pay homage, as earlier Welsh princes had done to his ancestors, but every time Llywelyn refused. Accordingly, Edward decided that force would be necessary, and he raised a great army, invading Gwynedd in 1276. Llywelyn and his followers took refuge in the mountains of Snowdonia, but after a few months were forced to surrender. He then agreed to pay the homage.

Seal of Edward I

Six years later, Llywelyn threw off his allegiance and brought his band of warriors into English territory, harrying the countryside with fire and sword. Edward retaliated at once and defeated the Welshman again in Snowdonia. Llywelyn escaped southwards, but near Builth Wells he was surprised by an English patrol and killed. His brother David took over the princedom, but he was captured and executed at Shrewsbury. As an independent kingdom Gwynedd ceased to exist.

Edward now reorganised the kingdom on the English model. He built castles at Conway, Beaumaris, Caernarvon and Harlech, and encouraged English people to build towns there and settle. By the Statute of Wales, of 1284, English law was made to operate in north Wales, though some of the older Celtic customs were allowed to remain. To make them feel part of the new arrangement, Edward gave offices of state and civil service to native Welsh people.

Not long after the settlement of Wales, Edward, who believed passionately in a united kingdom of the British Isles, had an opportunity to bring Scotland into the union.

The Scottish king, Alexander III, had died in 1286, leaving the throne to his four-year-old granddaughter, Margaret. In 1290 she died, and the Scottish council of Regency found themselves in a quandary. There was no other person left in the direct royal line. Immediately, a number of distant relatives all began to make claims to the throne. The Council put the matter to Edward to suggest a new king, and he agreed on condition that he should be acknowledged overlord of Scotland. Desperate to have one monarch and so avoid civil war by the various claimants, the Council accepted. Edward then put forward John Balliol, a great-great-grandson of David I. The only other claim worth considering was that of Robert Bruce, grandfather of the famous victor of Bannockburn, also a descendant of David I.

Balliol was crowned at Scone in 1292 and at once did homage to Edward. The new king managed well for a time, but when Edward began to assert his authority in Scotland more directly, the Scottish nobles objected, and persuaded Balliol to form an alliance with France, the enemy of England. Edward ordered Balliol to change his attitude, and when he refused, the English king invaded Scotland with a large army, captured Berwick, and then defeated Balliol at the battle of Dunbar in 1296. One by one, the big towns surrendered, Edinburgh, Perth and Stirling. Edward accepted Balliol's resignation and took on the title King of Scotland himself. As governor of Scotland he sent John de Warenne, who had resisted the statute *Quo Warranto*. It seemed that Scotland had been conquered and settled as effectively as Wales had been.

This was an illusion. A year later, rebellion broke out, led by Sir William Wallace, a tough, brave and ruthless knight who could command the most fanatical loyalty from his followers. He crushed an English army sent against him at Cambuskenneth, near Stirling, and then led his

Caernarvon Castle

victorious men across the border into Northumberland. Edward marched northwards, drove Wallace out, and at Falkirk, in Stirlingshire, defeated the Scottish hero. Wallace escaped and fled to the hills where for some time he kept up guerilla warfare against the English, harrying their fortresses and cutting off their supplies.

In 1303, Edward, exasperated by Wallace's activities, assembled yet another army, led it to Scotland and once more defeated him. Again Wallace escaped, but shortly afterwards he was betrayed, hanged, drawn and quartered.

Another revolt occurred in 1306, this time under Robert Bruce, the grandson of the Bruce whose claim to the Scottish throne had been considered in 1292. Edward, now an old man of nearly seventy, once more marshalled his troops and took them to the obstinate Scottish dominion, but he was a sick man. At Burgh-on-Sands he died, having urged his son, Edward, to continue the expedition.

The great king was carried all the way to Westminster, where he was buried. On his tomb was inscribed: "Here lies Edward the First, the Hammer of the Scots." Although he had failed in his dream of a permanent union of England with Scotland, he had accomplished much in England and Wales. He had given them sound government, set an example to Europe by his legal reforms, and made the monarchy a source of justice to barons, clergy and people alike.

57

Edward of Caernarvon, Prince of Wales, succeeded Edward I when he was twenty-three years old. He was different in every respect from his brilliant and majestic father. Indeed, it was only in appearance that any similarity lay, for he, too, was tall, erect and strong-limbed, with the same bright eyes and hair.

Born at Caernarvon in 1284, he was held up as a baby before a crowd of Welsh people by his father who wanted to honour them by showing them their future king. In 1301, Edward I bestowed the title Prince of Wales on the boy, a title which has ever since been given to eldest sons of English monarchs.

Even in his youth Edward was a disappointment, for he showed no interest in his father's great legal and governmental work, nor in his military campaigns. He developed into a lazy, unreliable, extravagant and pleasure-seeking man who surrounded himself with unworthy friends.

The Battle of Bannockburn

These qualities stayed with him for the rest of his life, which was to end with horrible tragedy.

As soon as his father was safely buried, Edward II disbanded the great army which was poised for a crushing blow on Robert Bruce in Scotland. He then returned to his palace and settled down to a life of hunting, gambling and gaiety with his favourites, the worst of whom was a young upstart knight from Gascony, Piers Gaveston. Edward paid no attention to government and passed all state matters over to Gaveston, who was equally unfit to manage them.

Before long, the nation was tired of the favourite, and the barons attacked him in Parliament, urging the king to dismiss him. Edward gave in at first, but when a few months later he brought Gaveston back, the barons rebelled. At Scarborough Gaveston was captured and put to death.

In Scotland, Robert Bruce was continuing his campaign against the English almost uninterrupted. Cities and fortresses fell, and by 1314, the great stronghold of

Stirling was under siege. Edward stirred himself at last and assembled one of the largest armies hitherto seen in England—nearly 100,000 men. Marching northwards, he encamped at Bannockburn, about two miles south of Stirling. In front of his lines was a bog, and behind that a small hill, on which Bruce's much smaller force was drawn up. Bruce's men had dug pits in front of their ranks and covered them with brushwood, as traps for the English cavalry.

When the signal was given, Edward ordered his army to move forwards across the bog. Weighed down with their armour, hundreds of them began to sink into the mud, at which moment Bruce's troops let loose a hail of arrows and spears. Those that got through the bog struggled up the hill to storm the Scottish lines, but were beaten back. When the English cavalry made its charge the horsemen fell into the covered pits and lay jumbled on the ground, a sitting target for another hail of arrows and spears.

Another wave of Scots came over the hill and rushed into the melée, cutting left and right with hatchets and broad-bladed swords. The English were slaughtered in their hundreds. Edward panicked, broke his camp and fled from the field, leaving the army to its fate.

The result was a crushing victory for Bruce. The English had to withdraw from Scotland altogether, and Edward I's work was completely undone.

The barons, led by the king's cousin, the Earl of Lancaster, now took over the government, but they ruled no better than Edward, as they were only interested in increasing their wealth and authority. Gradually, some of them deserted to Edward, notably Lord Despenser and his son, Hugh. With them, Edward defeated Lancaster at Boroughbridge in Yorkshire, in 1322, and the earl was put to death.

Edward's wife, Isabella, the daughter of King Philip of France, hated the Despensers, who at least were governing better than the Lancaster party. Seeing that her husband was under their power, she waged war on them. With the help of her lover, Roger Mortimer, Earl of March, she pursued them to the West Country, where both of the Despensers were caught and executed. Edward was roughly seized by guards and taken to Kenilworth castle. Then the queen summoned a parliament, in the name of her son, Prince Edward, and persuaded the members to depose her husband. He was transferred to Berkeley Castle in the summer of 1327.

One evening in September, frightful screams were heard ringing through the dark, stone-flagged corridors of Berkeley. The king's keepers were torturing him to death with red hot irons.

One night, at Nottingham Castle, in 1330, the seventeen-year-old son of Edward II, King Edward III, gathered a band of trusted followers, and crept quietly along the passages up to the rooms of his mother, Isabella. Reaching the door, he knocked and went in. There was his mother, seated by the fire, and standing by the window was her lover, Roger Mortimer.

There was a clatter as the followers drew their swords. Edward ordered Mortimer to go downstairs with them. Then he told his mother that her rule was over, and that he was taking the government into his own hands. She would be honourably confined at his pleasure. Mortimer was taken for trial, found guilty of organising the murder of Edward II, and immediately executed.

Edward had been king for three years, and now he meant to give England good government.

Edward III

The young king was tall, handsome, with bright golden-red hair and penetrating eyes, and he looked every inch a king. He had charming manners, ready wit, extraordinary energy and determination. Above all, he was chivalrous, and when he founded the Order of the Garter in 1348, it was because he believed in the idea of a gathering of noble knights, richly dressed, colourfully armed, fighting with the honour and bravery associated with the legends of King Arthur and his Round Table of Knights.

His first military adventure was an attempt to reconquer Scotland. At the battle of Halidon Hill, in 1333, he defeated the Scots under Lord Archibald Douglas, who was Regent during the minority of Robert Bruce's son, David II. He then gave the crown to the son of John Balliol.

His greatest fame as a soldier, however, rests with his campaigns in France where he began what is called the Hundred Years War. This was a struggle fought, with short intervals, for nearly 120 years, for the purpose of winning the French crown. Believing that he had a better right to the French throne than the existing holder, Philip VI, Edward went to war in 1337 to assert it. He was the nephew of the previous French king, Charles IV, whereas Philip was only a cousin.

He invaded France with the help of the Flemings, people from a territory that is now Belgium, but his first campaign was unsuccessful. The only exception was his great defeat of the French navy at the port of Sluys, in which nearly all the enemy vessels were sunk or captured.

Edward returned to England, having used all the money granted to him by Parliament which had been keen to support his claim. When he asked for more to make another attempt, the members were not so enthusiastic. They made him accept certain conditions, to allow a committee to keep a check on the accounts, not to raise any additional taxes other than those that they granted, and to choose his advisers only with their agreement.

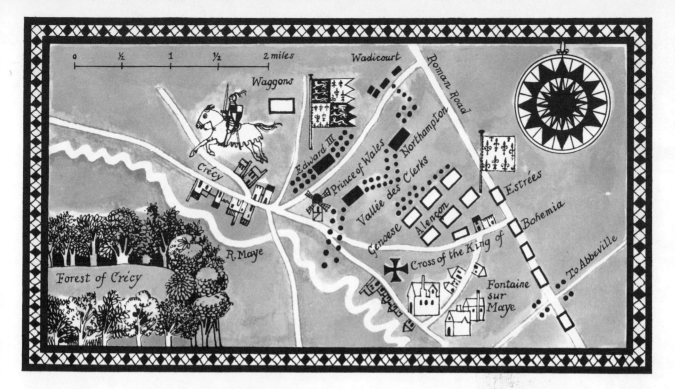

Edward consented, and in 1346 he led another invasion force across the channel. The French believed that he would make for Bordeaux, but in fact he landed near Cherbourg. With him were about 20,000 men, half of whom were archers carrying a relatively new weapon, the long bow. This long bow, invented by the Welsh, was over seven feet tall. It had a range of more than 300 yards and its arrows could pierce chain mail or sheet armour. A good archer could shoot six arrows a minute with deadly accuracy, which was much more effective than the crossbow.

Edward pushed across France and reached the town of Crécy, where he found the army of Philip VI, three times the numerical strength, ready to fight him. Edward placed the main part of his forces halfway up a hill overlooking the town, with the archers right out in front. His reserves were held at the top of the rise. One of the commanders on his main front was his sixteen-year-old son, Edward, known as the Black Prince for the dark, shining armour that he wore.

The first infantry regiments of the French army moved towards the English lines and when they came in range they were greeted with a shower of well-aimed arrows, flying thick and fast. Hundreds fell, and were followed up by the second and then the third French groups. Still the slaughter continued. Then the French sent in the cavalry. The archers aimed at the horses, and when the unseated riders fell to the ground the English men-at-arms charged in for the kill. It was a massacre, and by the evening, the enemy was routed.

The victory made Edward the most feared monarch in Europe, and when the news of it reached London, there was tremendous rejoicing. Edward then raced on towards Calais, and after besieging it for some months, compelled the inhabitants to surrender. He now had a vital port on the French mainland—and it was to remain in English hands for two hundred years.

The victors returned to England and received a warm welcome. The king rewarded his officers and men, and gave the signal for a holiday of feasting and celebration. He founded the Order of the Garter, and appointed twenty-six knights, one of whom was his son, the Black Prince, who had fought courageously at Crécy. Here was the opportunity to create that round table of chivalrous knights, sworn to great deeds and courteous behaviour. It seemed as if the legend of Arthur had come to life.

Then, amidst all the celebrating and jousting, the splendour and the pride, death struck, and struck hard, knowing no class barriers, confined to no limits. It was the Black Death, a plague which came sweeping through Europe from the East. Beginning with black swellings, it felled its victims within two days, ending with high fever and violent sickness. Nearly half the population of England was cut off within twelve months. Entire communities in monasteries perished, whole families from the eldest to the youngest died, villages and towns were emptied of the living. Even the king himself lost a daughter. It was the worst plague in recorded history.

In England, the Black Death gave hope to the surviving lower classes. Labour became scarce so labourers could demand more money. Though the government introduced a statute to restrict wages to what they had been before the plague, it was often impossible to enforce it. Many lords of the manor paid the higher rates, for they were desperately short of workers.

Despite the Black Death, it was a period of great building activity. Wonderful improvements were made to many cathedrals and churches, such as Lichfield, Wells, Bristol and Exeter. At Salisbury, the great spire, which is today a landmark, was being erected. Windsor Castle was enlarged. Houses were more solidly constructed, more roads were planned.

After the capture of Calais, a temporary truce was made between England and France, and since the French had suffered as badly from the Black Death, they were not for some time ready to win back their losses. In 1355, Edward suggested a more lasting settlement. He offered to give up his claim to the French throne if he could have Aquitaine as an English possession, free from interference. The new king of France, John, (Philip had died in 1350) refused and so Edward asked Parliament for another grant to prosecute the war.

With his soldier-son, the Black Prince, Edward crossed again to France and began to ravage the countryside. He had to return hurriedly because of a crisis in Scotland, and the prince was left in command. Young Edward swept through central France with a small but hardy force of some 8000 cavalry and archers, and outside Poitiers he ran into an enormous army, led by king John, nearly eighty thousand strong. At such odds it seemed foolhardy to risk battle, but the gallant prince formed his lines in a position similar to that at Crécy. Once again, the English archers with their deadly longbows carried the day, and the French were driven off the field. Nearly eight thousand were killed, among them scores of the highest nobles and knights of the kingdom. King John and his son were captured.

A treaty was signed at Bretigny, in 1360, at which Edward's original terms of 1355 were agreed. His fortunes were now at their highest. Surrounded by his grown-up sons, children of his adored wife, Philippa, whom he had married in 1329, he looked forward to a prosperous close to his reign. And wealth there was, for trade with Europe was growing. The valuable wool industry was bringing rich returns, weavers from Belgium were settling in East Anglia and Wiltshire, and producing export revenue. Merchants were expanding their businesses, and in the city of London the companies of craftsmen were rapidly building up their industries.

In spite of this prosperity, the last years of the king were but a shadow of his former glory. When his wife died in 1369, he fell into the hands of unscrupulous favourites. Some of his sons, given responsibilities of government, were not showing the promise expected of them. John of Gaunt, his fourth son, anxious to win laurels on the field of battle like his great brother, the Black Prince, succeeded only in losing much of Aquitaine in a number of defeats. Then at home, Gaunt ruled harshly, exacting heavy taxes and trampling on justice, working in the name of his father who had become senile and hardly knew what was happening around him. It was a sad spectacle, this once great king, the terror of Europe, beloved of his people, the paragon of chivalry, now reduced to a wreck.

In the summer of 1377, Edward III died at Richmond, not as he would have liked, surrounded with glory and affection, but deserted by his friends and despised by his people who had forgotten his former greatness.

Edward, the Black Prince

The Black Prince had died a year before his father, the old king, Edward III, and so the throne passed to the prince's son, Richard, who was only ten. The country was ruled by a council of regency, headed by Richard's uncle John of Gaunt. We have seen how Gaunt wished to imitate his elder brother's military exploits and how these resulted in failure. Now he continued to fight in France but was again defeated. He was not to be put off, and he asked Parliament for more money to carry on the struggle. In 1379, a new kind of tax was raised, the poll-tax, whereby every man had to pay a sum according to his wealth. Dukes, for example, were assessed at over six pounds, and ordinary labourers or villeins had to pay four pence. This tax, which was raised again the following year at a different scale, proved to be very unpopular indeed.

At first sight a few pence may not seem much to pay, but the villeins were so poor that fourpence meant much more to them than did six pounds to a duke. They had other grievances, and in 1381 they rebelled in what is called the Peasants' Revolt. What were these grievances?

In the country there were still many villeins who were not free men. They spent some of their days trying to earn a living on the strips of land allowed them by the manor lords, and the rest of their working hours on the lords' farms. They wanted more money, and they also wanted the freedom to move to other areas where they might earn it, but because they were villeins they were not allowed to go. The free labourers also had complaints. They objected to the taxes which they had to pay the lords, and they hated the lawyers who kept lists of what they owed. The townsfolk, too, quarrelled with their employers. When the poll taxes were introduced, then, it was the signal for revolt.

They received a great deal of encouragement from minor clergy who went up and down the country, preaching about the equality of man, a theory that was not likely to be understood or welcomed by employers or landlords. One of these priests was John Ball, and his favourite text was the rhyme:

> "*When Adam delved and Eve span,*
> *Who was then the gentleman?*"

In the middle of June the revolt broke out. Thousands of peasants rallied at Maidstone under Wat Tyler, a builder's mate, and then marched to London. At the same time another mob in Essex, led by Jack Straw, set out for Hampstead. On their way, both mobs sacked the houses of the lords and the gentry, seeking out in particular the manor rolls on which were written down the duties and the debts of the peasants. Risings erupted in other districts and a number of government officers were murdered.

In the Tower of London, where the young king had his court, the Council reviewed the position. The capital was surrounded by peasants, so the gates were locked and messages were sent to the leaders asking their demands. They answered that they wished all villeins to become free men at once, that they should be able to rent lands, that poll taxes should be stopped, and that a free pardon should be given to all taking part in the rising.

While the Council considered these demands, the king decided to act on his own. With great courage, for he was only fourteen, he set off on horseback to Mile End with a procession of officers and clerks. There he came upon a mob of thousands of angry, shouting rebels, who were waving all manner of weapons. He pulled up his horse and raised his hand to still the noise.

"Good people, I am your King. What is it that you demand?"

The leaders came forward, greatly impressed by his boldness but a little disturbed at the gathering behind him.

"We wish that you will make us all free men, ourselves, our heirs and our lands."

"I agree to your demands," answered the king. "If you will go home, I will see to it that your grievances are put right. In the meantime, I will have pardons written for

Richard II at Mile End

you now," and he waved his hand to the clerks who straightway started to write them out on pieces of parchment. The peasants eagerly grasped the precious bits of paper and turned to go home.

Meanwhile, Wat Tyler and some of his mob had burst through the gates of London and had begun to pillage the great houses. John of Gaunt's palace in the Strand was burnt down, though he was abroad at the time, and even the Tower was besieged. Again the king agreed to meet the rebels, and this time at Smithfield he came face to face with Tyler. The leader moved towards Richard and raised his hand. One of the king's attendants thought he meant to strike him and at once cut Tyler down, killing him on the spot. At this a howl of anger went up from the mob.

With great presence of mind, Richard moved forward: "You have lost your captain," he cried. "Follow me, and I will be your leader." And so they did, down the streets and out of the city, where they set off for their homes.

Unfortunately, the king was not as good as his word. As soon as he got back to the Tower, the pardons were cancelled and warrants were issued for the arrest of the leaders. Many were caught and executed, including John Ball.

Though the peasants failed initially in their bid for justice, they had so frightened the lords that as time went on conditions gradually improved. In time, too, villeins became free men, and when this happened, it was the end of the Feudal System.

When he was eighteen, Richard decided

65

to rule for himself. He filled the court with his friends and appointed some of them to high office. They proved to be incompetent, and before long a rising broke out, led by another of Richard's uncles, Thomas, Duke of Gloucester. At the battle of Radcot Bridge, the rebels triumphed, and some of the favourites fled abroad. Others, including Tresilian, the Chief Justice, and Sir Simon Burley, the king's tutor, were executed.

Gloucester and his supporters now took over the government, but within a year had showed that they were no better than their predecessors. In 1389, during a meeting of the council, Richard suddenly asked his uncle how old he was. The duke said that he was twenty-two. "Then I am old enough to manage my own affairs," snapped the king, and forthwith dismissed Gloucester and his friends.

The young king was tall, with reddish hair and deep blue-grey eyes. He was an intelligent man, he could write poetry and music, and he knew a great deal about art and architecture. But there was something about him that was odd. He was loyal to his friends, but he was capable of nursing revenge against anyone who offended him, for long periods of time. He had fits of childish temper, and sometimes his actions were quite unpredictable.

He ruled well to begin with, and 1389 to 1397 were prosperous years for England. The war with France was halted and commerce with the French revived. Much building was undertaken, and Richard himself sponsored the reconstruction of Westminster Hall.

During his reign a movement had grown up, which had been started in his grandfather's time by a priest called John Wycliffe. This learned man had been thundering against the riches and the high living of the bishops and the senior clergy, and he had gathered a considerable following of priests who lectured throughout England, urging a return to a simple life, such as that which Our Lord lived, according to the New Testament. His followers were called Lollards—a name once given to a community of people in Europe who tended the sick and the dying. Wycliffe had died in 1384, but the Lollards went on with their work. Although they attacked the very foundations of the established church, Richard was content to leave them alone. (His successors were not so merciful.)

In 1397, Richard suddenly decided to wreak vengeance upon his uncle Gloucester and his supporters who had retired to their estates after their dismissal eight years earlier. Gloucester, Lord Arundel and the Earl of Warwick were arrested and imprisoned. Arundel was tried and executed, Warwick was banished for life. Gloucester died mysteriously, and it is believed that he was murdered. Richard then sent his cousin, Henry, John of Gaunt's son, into exile for ten years.

The king began to rule like a tyrant. He raised forced loans from rich men, and so avoided the need to call Parliament. He maintained a large standing army with which he threatened anyone who dared to oppose him. When John of Gaunt died early in 1399, Richard seized all his estates and refused to allow Henry to inherit them. This was the signal for Henry to return to England and in the summer he landed at Ravenspur, in Yorkshire, when the king was away in Ireland.

As soon as he arrived, Henry found that the nation wanted no more of Richard, and they flocked to his banner. So he marched inland and prepared to attack the king when he landed from Ireland. Richard was held up by rough weather and when he did reach North Wales, he was captured at Flint by the Duke of Northumberland's soldiers, who delivered him to Henry.

In London, a parliament was hastily summoned and Richard was compelled to abdicate, agreeing to hand his crown to Henry. Then he was taken to Pontefract Castle, in Yorkshire. There he was said to have been murdered, and Shakespeare, in his play *Richard II* actually describes the scene. But, in spite of a great deal of enquiry, no one has yet been able to say exactly what happened to him.

HENRICVS IIII

Henry of Lancaster was elected King Henry IV by a Parliament filled with his supporters, but he soon found out that these allies were only going to let him stay on the throne on their conditions. Parliament chose his ministers, it kept tight control of his income and expenses, it did not hesitate to criticise him if he stepped out of line, and it ensured that the towns and the shires were properly represented at its assemblies. Henry seems to have been happy enough with this arrangement, for it guaranteed that the country would not be ruled by a tyrant, the very reason for his deposing his cousin, Richard II.

Henry was a brave and energetic man, thickset, good-looking, and gentle mannered. He began his reign, as far as the people were concerned, with an advantage: he could not be worse than Richard, and rumour had it that he preferred the company of ordinary folk, merchants, farmers and artists, to the aggressive barons who had voted him to power. He increased the pension of the great poet Chaucer, he put up new ideas of business and trade management to merchants, he carried out many re-building schemes, including the reconstruction of the great central tower of York Minster, which had collapsed, and he gave his patronage to lesser arts and crafts throughout the country.

His reign, nevertheless, was troubled with rebellions. The worst was a rising in Wales, under a gentleman-farmer, Owain Glyndwr, who claimed to be a descendant of Prince Llywelyn. Glyndwr was a cunning, ruthless and able leader of men, and in a short time he drove Henry's forces out of the castles and towns in North Wales. Then, in 1403, the Duke of Northumberland, and his son, Henry Percy, known as Hotspur for his speed and energy, rose in revolt, on the grounds that they had not been rewarded enough by the king. They planned to join forces with Glyndwr.

Henry was too quick for them. He hurried across country to Shrewsbury where Hotspur was commanding his father's army, waiting for Glyndwr to arrive. There he defeated him in a great battle, in which Hotspur was killed. Glyndwr, hearing the news as he was approaching Shrewsbury, retired to the mountains of Snowdon, and there kept up an irritating guerilla war against the royal troops for some years.

To keep the richer bishops on his side, Henry had to agree to their demands that Wycliffe's followers, the Lollards, should be ruthlessly put down. He signed an order of Parliament stating that anyone found guilty of heresy was to be burned at the stake. This was an opportunity for the Church to single out those of its members who had been preaching against abuses in high places and as a result many Lollards were martyred.

For the last years of his reign, Henry was crippled with illness, and he had to leave the government to his son, Prince Henry, who was a very popular man. While visiting Westminster Abbey in March, 1413, the king was taken ill and in a few days he died.

It was October 1415. A small English army of six thousand men-at-arms and archers, led by the handsome and swashbuckling Henry V, was approaching Agincourt village, by the Calais road, not many miles from Crécy. At the village, Henry came upon the French army, arrayed across and on either side of the road, in three columns, one behind the other. Numbering over thirty thousand, cavalry, foot-soldiers and crossbowmen, it contained the pick of the troops of France. At its head was the Constable, Jean D'Albret.

The Constable's front column was manned with armoured troops, mixed with knights, also heavily clad, who had been ordered to dismount. In front of them the fields were sodden with the October rains.

Henry drew up his little force in a single line, of several blocks of men. Pointed stakes were driven into the ground at an angle before them, and behind these crouched the archers, gripping their longbows, hands at their quivers.

The enemy front column moved forwards and soon began to slither into the mud, weighed down with their armour. When they came within range, the English archers opened fire, and within minutes wrought frightful havoc among the struggling, earth-caked knights. Then Henry ordered the advance. Lightly clad in tough leather jackets, they pressed across the fields with ease, and cut down the remnants of the first French column. When the second column came on, again the archers fired, and again the slaughter followed. Then the English began to run, on and on through the second column to its rear.

The third column wheeled away to attack the English in the back, but when the troops saw the dreadful massacre in the boggy fields, they broke and fled.

The battle was over, and lying dead on the ground were the Constable, the Duke of Brabant, and many barons and knights. No less than nine thousand French were killed, for the loss of only a few hundred Englishmen. It was an astonishing victory, and by it Henry achieved as much as his

Henry V's archers at Agincourt

great-grandfather, Edward III, had done in his hard campaigning seventy years before.

Henry was born at Monmouth in 1387. As a child he was quick to learn and loved outdoor activities. By the age of ten he could play the harp well, and he had a library of books, all of which he had read. As he grew older, his sporting exercises took up more time, though he never lost his interest in music and literature. He could run faster than almost any man in England, he had a splendid record of success in jousting, and he was an expert in military training and weapons. At the age of sixteen, he had his first taste of warfare, when he commanded a wing at the battle of Shrewsbury.

When he came to the throne in 1413, he was well versed in the arts of war, and he also had a sound experience of government.

We have seen that the conquests of Edward III and the Black Prince had been all but lost. Henry, anxious to restore to England its feeling of national pride, re-opened the question of the claim to the French throne. He invaded France in the summer of 1415, and captured the port of Harfleur, at the mouth of the Seine. Then he turned northwards and destroyed the French army at Agincourt.

This victory, together with more successes in Normandy, enabled him to compel the French to accept terms of his choosing. The French king, Charles VI, had been insane for some years, and Henry now proposed that he should take over as Regent of France, with the condition that when Charles should die, the throne itself should pass to him. To confirm the agreement, he married Charles' daughter, Catherine, and when their son Henry was born, he became heir to two thrones.

The agreement was signed at Troyes in 1420, and it put Paris and most of northern France into the direct government of England. It seemed at last as if France would become a province of England, and Parliament in London granted Henry more money to complete the conquest.

By 1422, he had won most of it, but, to the dismay of his army and of his people at home his health began to give way. He contracted a severe chill and was unable to throw it off. In this weakened state he caught dysentery, and died, at the end of August, aged only thirty-five.

The reign of Henry VI, which began when he was only nine months old, was the most tragic in English history. All his father's conquests in France were lost, his own kingdom was then rent with bitter civil war, his throne was taken away from him, and finally he died in the Tower of London, probably by violence. Yet none of these things was his fault.

On his accession, a council of regency was formed, and the two leaders were his uncles, John, Duke of Bedford, and Humphrey, Duke of Gloucester. Bedford, a wise and popular man, who had great gifts as a soldier and a statesman, was made Regent of the English lands in France. Gloucester, the Regent of England, was not so able, and he was also reckless, unreliable and quarrelsome.

To begin with, England was ruled well, and in France more victories brought more land under English dominion. Then, in 1429, the tide began to turn.

The English successes had been largely due to the want of leadership from the French monarchy. When the mad Charles VI died in 1422, his son, Charles VII, proved to be an idle and incompetent man, completely in the power of unworthy favourites. He seemed to be content to rule only part of France, and even when the great city of Orleans was under siege by the English he showed little interest in its fate.

Then an extraordinary thing happened. A young girl of seventeen, daughter of a peasant farmer from Domrémy, obtained an audience with the king. Her name, she said, was Jeanne d'Arc (Joan of Arc), and she announced that in a vision some angels had told her the English would be driven out of France, and that she would command the forces that did it. The king laughed at first, but she was so insistent that eventually he believed she might be able to inspire his troops.

Jeanne was given a suit of white armour and a splendid horse, and a small troop of soldiers. In April, 1429, she entered the besieged Orléans, and took over command of the garrison. Within a few days she drove off the English. This was the first of many victories which she won, with an increasingly large army, as the dispirited Frenchmen found new hope and flocked to her standard.

Charles VII, who had not yet been crowned, since by the Treaty of Troyes the king of England was also king of France, was persuaded to come to Rheims by Jeanne, and there in great splendour he received his crown.

The next year, still leading victorious troops, Jeanne was captured by some Burgundian troops, and handed over to the English. Bedford regarded her not as a divinely inspired leader but as an evil witch, and after a trial she was condemned to death. In May, 1431, in the market place at Rouen, she was burned alive at the stake. Her work, however, had been done; the French were filled with a sense of patriotism, and nothing could now stop them from getting back their lands.

Paris was captured in 1436, the year in which Bedford died. Normandy held out for some years more, but the battle of Formigny, a terrible defeat for the English, gave the whole province back to France. By 1453, the English were driven out altogether, and the town of Calais was their only French possession.

Back in England, serious trouble had been developing. The barons, already rich, had been seeking to increase their wealth. They fought amongst each other, raising private armies, ravaging the countryside, and making England as unsafe and as unhappy a place to live in as it had been under king Stephen. There were two main parties, one led by Cardinal Beaufort, a grandson of John of Gaunt, and his two nephews, Lords Somerset and Suffolk;

the other party was led by Humphrey of Gloucester, supported by another descendant of Edward III, Richard, Duke of York. They were helped by the richest family in England, the Nevills.

The Beaufort party wished to end the war in France, but the Regent was anxious to continue it, and he blamed the English defeats on the Cardinal. In and out of Parliament the two parties bickered, and the council grew weak and divided. Eventually, the Beauforts won the king to their side, and Gloucester retired.

The rule of the Beauforts was harsh. Nothing was done to stop the private wars among the nobles. Gloucester was arrested on a trumped-up charge of treason and died under mysterious circumstances. This angered the nation, as he was popular, despite his faults. The English forces in France did not get proper support. Finally, a rebellion broke out in Kent, led by Jack Cade, an army veteran, who demanded the dismissal of the Beauforts and the restoring of law and order. It was put down after severe fighting and heavy loss of life.

When the English abandoned France in 1453, the nation had had enough of the Beauforts, and they were disgraced.

What had been happening to the king in these times? He grew up in an atmosphere of bitterness, watching his father's work being undone and the order of his kingdom breaking up. Pushed around by self-seeking ministers, forced to sign this and that Act of Parliament, treated as a halfwit, this pathetic monarch endured continual misery. Humble, inoffensive, gentle-mannered, he yet had none of the qualities of kingship. He was devoted to studies and to religion, in which he found his only happiness. By 1443, when he was at last old enough to rule, events proved to be too strong for him.

Henry was a great builder. He founded Eton College, and King's College, Cambridge, with its vast and magnificent chapel. He encouraged other arts, too, and in his time sculptors, poets and musicians produced works of great beauty. The book

Le Morte d'Arthur (The Death of Arthur) by Sir Thomas Malory, dates from this time.

In 1445 he married Margaret, daughter of the Duke of Anjou, a pretty but determined woman who soon bent him to her will. The last years of his life were completely dominated by her ambitions.

When he was stricken with a fit of madness in 1453, Parliament chose the Duke of York as Protector of the realm. In a few months the king recovered and his wife, who hated York, persuaded Henry to dismiss him and bring back the Beauforts. Immediately they made plans to crush their rivals, and this was the signal for the outbreak of what is known as the Wars of the Roses.

These wars, so named because a white rose was the emblem of the Yorkists, (the Duke of York's party), and a red rose that of the Beaufort party, (called Lancastrians because of their descent from John of Gaunt, who was Duke of Lancaster) lasted, with intervals, for thirty years. They were fought with great cruelty and bitterness, and there was none of that chivalry so typical of the days of Edward III. Prisoners were usually slaughtered, and treachery and deceit were rife. All the same, the fighting was confined to the nobles and their private armies. For the most part the people looked on, hoping that whichever side won it would at least provide good government.

There were several battles, and first one side won and then the other. In 1460, at Wakefield, the Lancastrians routed the Yorkists and the Duke of York was slain. The next year, York's son, Edward, with Richard Nevill, Earl of Warwick, turned the tables and defeated the Lancastrians at Towton. Henry VI, his wife and his little son, Prince Edward, fled to Scotland.

Edward of York was proclaimed king Edward IV by a hastily summoned Parliament, and for some time there was peace. The government was well run by the energetic Earl of Warwick. Henry VI, meanwhile, had ten more years to live.

Arms of Warwick the Kingmaker

EDWARD IV [*1461–1483*]

The victor of Towton, Edward Plantagenet, Duke of York, became king Edward IV at the age of eighteen. He took on a throne that had been won with blood, and began a reign that was to see the shedding of more ere it was over.

Edward was six feet tall, slim and extremely good-looking in his younger days. He had courteous manners, an excellent brain and a strong sense of humour. He had already proved his ability as a commander at Towton, and later on he was to show his worth as a statesman. There was one bad flaw in his nature, however, and that was an excessive love of pleasure, in the pursuit of which he would often neglect his royal duties.

We have seen that his chief supporter was Richard Nevill, Earl of Warwick, his cousin, and the greatest landowner in England. When Edward was crowned, he handed the business of government to him and retired for a while to enjoy feasting and other pleasures. Warwick, a brilliant and courageous man, jovial and popular, loved work and enjoyed power, which for the most part he used well.

Though Towton brought Edward a crown, it took four years of skilful leadership for Warwick to stamp out the embers of resistance. By 1465, he reported to his king that his country was in order, and that a favourable treaty had been made with the Scots. He now felt that the king should cement an alliance with France by marrying one of the French princesses.

To his dismay, he heard that the king had already married—secretly—because he knew his advisers would not approve his choice. His bride was a widow, Elizabeth Woodville, whose family, though rich, did not belong to the nobility. After his marriage, Edward showered the Woodvilles with titles and lands, and seemed to be building them up as rivals to Warwick's great power. There was a reason for this. Edward knew that if Warwick could win him a throne, he could also take it away. If they should quarrel, a rival power dependent upon him would protect him against the great earl.

Warwick was furious about the marriage, especially as he had already begun negotiations with the French and had even invited top representatives to London to meet the king. For a while, he carried on with the government, though it was no secret that the two men were now enemies. Then, in 1467, Edward suddenly dismissed all Warwick's ministers from office, and made an alliance with Burgundy, France's enemy. The earl retired to his estates and plotted rebellion.

He won over the king's brother, George, Duke of Clarence, who married his elder daughter, Isabel Nevill. Then he formed a league with some rich barons who hated the Woodvilles, and in 1469 he struck. He defeated the king at Edgecote and captured him. Warwick released him a few months later, and Edward turned the tables by driving Warwick out of England.

Warwick now made overtures to Henry VI's wife, living in France (her husband had been captured in 1467 and put in the Tower), and together they planned to invade England and restore Henry VI to the throne. They landed in Devonshire and within weeks gathered enough support to force Edward to fly from the kingdom. Henry was released from the Tower and in great pomp restored to his throne.

Caxton demonstrates his printing press to Edward IV

Edward was not the kind of man to rest idly in these circumstances. He returned to Yorkshire where he had a large following, and marched towards London. At Barnet, in March 1471, he completely defeated an army under Warwick, and the great earl, known to history as "The Kingmaker" was killed on the battlefield. Henry was sent back to the Tower. Six weeks later, the remnants of Warwick's party were crushed at Tewkesbury, where Henry's son, Edward, was slain, and his wife captured. Edward had won back his throne and he was not to lose it again.

At the end of May, the tragic Henry VI, still grieving the loss of his son, and suffering the most degrading treatment at the hands of his gaolers, died in his cell in the Tower. He was said to have been taken ill, but people believed otherwise. A triumphant king could not afford to keep alive a rival any longer, even if he was in prison, and so he had Henry put to death.

The rest of Edward's reign was undisturbed at home. He ruled well, and since he had confiscated the enormously rich estates of the Kingmaker and his allies, he had little need to ask Parliament for money. When he wanted it, he raised what he called "benevolences," that is, forced loans from the rich.

Industry and agriculture, which had suffered grievously from the war, slowly began to rally. It was also a time of great progress in learning, art and civil service. William Caxton brought to England for the first time a printing press and began to print books. Histories were written, textbooks on law were compiled, and portrait painting became popular. Edward also introduced a system of postal services, whereby relays of horses stationed at twenty-mile intervals conveyed letters and documents across country at the rate of 100 miles a day.

Edward's eating and drinking brought his life to an early end. He died in April, 1483, aged only forty-two, but already grossly fat and sometimes hardly able to move.

When Edward IV died, he left two sons, Edward and Richard, who became known to history as the Princes in the Tower. Edward, the elder boy, was aged twelve and he succeeded as Edward V, under the guardianship of his uncle, Richard, Duke of Gloucester, who was appointed Protector of the Realm.

Within weeks, Edward V was deposed and, together with his brother, sent to the Tower from which they never came out alive. They are said to have been murdered on the orders of their uncle Richard, who wished to usurp the throne.

Parliament had declared that they were both illegitimate, and therefore not in the line of succession. This was because evidence was presented to the members that Edward IV, before he married Catherine Woodville, had already been betrothed to another woman, and this engagement was considered as good as marriage itself. Parliament then elected Richard of Gloucester as King Richard III.

The mystery of what happened to the two princes will probably never be solved. While many historians say that they were murdered on the instructions of their uncle, there are some who believe that they lived into the reign of Henry VII and then were despatched by him. Certainly, during the short reign of Richard III he was never accused of their murder, and since the Tower was a royal residence as well as a prison, it is always possible that they lived there quietly, out of sight, for they were too young to be given any position of state.

Edward V and his brother Richard enter the Tower

On the morning of August 22nd 1485, the sun rose over a large, sloping field outside the town of Bosworth in Leicestershire. At the top of the hill, on a magnificent white charger, which Shakespeare called "White Surrey," sat Richard III, king of England. Round him was his army, drawn up and ready for the signal to charge. At the other end of the field, arrayed in battle order, was another army, at the head of which was Henry Tudor, great-great-grandson of

Richard sent for reserves, waiting at the side of the field under the command of Lord Stanley. Spurring his horse, Stanley brought his men down into the fray. To the king's horror, he charged the flanks of the royal army, throwing them into confusion. He had betrayed his king and gone over to Henry Tudor.

When Richard saw that all was lost, he jabbed his spurs into White Surrey's sides, and catapulted into the centre of the fight. Hewing and slashing left and right with his

John of Gaunt, and leader of the Lancastrians.

Suddenly, the trumpets blared forth, and Richard's cavalry leapt forward into action. Down the slope they rushed, waving their swords and axes, followed closely by infantry and archers. On and on the horsemen and foot-soldiers pressed, headlong into the thick Lancastrian ranks, where both sides fought desperately—for the crown of England was at stake. Gradually, the king's troops began to be worn down.

great battle-axe, he cut down all that came near him. Fighting with the courage of despair, and resolved to die as King of England, he pushed onwards towards his adversary, whom he could see near the Lancastrian rear.

And then, a blow from behind felled him to the ground. Immediately, his enemies bent over him, stabbing and cutting. Pierced by many wounds, Richard died, a soldier's death, on the field of battle. It was the end of the House of Plantagenet, which had ruled England for more than three hundred years.

What kind of man was this fearless soldier, this desperate king, and why was he fighting for his throne?

Richard was the youngest brother of Edward IV, and had fought at Barnet and Tewkesbury, where, aged only sixteen, he had proved to be a fine leader of men. He had then gone north to manage his estates and to govern that part of England for his brother. When Edward died, he willed that

The death of Richard III at Bosworth

Richard should be guardian to his children.

Richard was described by later historians as a monstrously deformed man, with a hump back, a withered arm and the features of a devil. This was perhaps to show that a man with such deformities was the more likely to have murdered his own nephews. It was some years after his death before he was said to have committed so wicked a crime. Portraits painted of him in his lifetime show him to have been good-looking, with a kind face, thoughtful eyes and a firm jaw. It seems that if he had been so monstrous in shape, someone would have written it down during his reign.

Of his abilities not even his bitterest critics have denied him the credit. There was more. He was well-read, intensely interested in law (several hundred good Acts of Parliament were passed at his encouragement), and he continued his brother's patronage of the arts.

Richard married Anne Nevill, in 1472. She was the Kingmaker's younger daughter, and it was a most happy match. They lost their only son, Edward, through illness in 1484, and this was followed very soon after by Anne's own death.

Richard was particularly loved in the north, and in the records of the city of York, there is an entry, written just after his death at Bosworth, which says: "This day was King Richard, late mercifully reigning upon us, piteously slain and murdered, to the great heaviness of this city." On the other hand, he was not understood in the south, from where much of Henry Tudor's support was drawn.

Shortage of money made him raise the same kind of "benevolences" as his brother, Edward IV, had done. And while the nation disliked the Woodvilles, they were disturbed at the way he executed two of them without fair trial.

The Lancastrian party, though quiet in the time of Edward IV, rose again during Richard's reign, for they had a leader of great merit, Henry Tudor. He landed in Wales from France and brought an army across country to Leicestershire, and there at Bosworth he triumphed.

Historians have said that when Richard died, the Middle Ages also passed away. It is true that the new king was a very different sort of man from his predecessors, as we shall see, and the new spirit of adventure in Europe, which was carrying mariners like Columbus and Vasco da Gama to new lands, by sea, opened up a whole world of riches. Certainly this gave the rulers of Europe a new outlook and altered the conditions of society.

When Richard III fell at Bosworth, his crown slipped off his helmet and rolled along the ground to a near-by hawthorn bush. There, Lord Stanley picked it up and, carrying it slowly to the victor, Henry Tudor, offered it to him, amid the cheers of his supporters who saluted him as Henry VII. It was a symbolic gesture. Henry had won the crown by right of battle, for he had the slenderest claim to it by right of descent.

He was the son of Edmund Tudor, a Welsh noble who had married Lady Margaret Beaufort, great-granddaughter of John of Gaunt. Most of his youth had been spent in exile, his family had fought for the Lancastrians, and had been disgraced when the Yorkists triumphed. In his wildest dreams Henry could never have imagined that he would one day be king of England. There were many more direct descendants of Edward III, but when Richard III became king, these dreams would not have been so fanciful. But even when Stanley put the diadem on his head, there were still Richard III's nephews, the Earl of Lincoln and the Earl of Warwick, both of whom had better claims.

The nation, however, was exhausted from the wars, and though it had liked the last Plantagenet, it accepted the new king in the hope that he would give England permanent peace. When he married the sister of the Princes in the Tower, Elizabeth of York, in 1486, people regarded it as a union between the houses of Lancaster and York.

Like so many of his forerunners, however, Henry was pestered with rebellions. He put them all down with vigour. Then he decided to break the power of the barons once and for all. By the Statute of Livery and Maintenance he forbade them from having private armies, and he punished them, if they were caught, where it hurt most—their pockets, for he would fine them huge sums of money. The Earl of Oxford, one day, entertained him, and Henry noticed that the earl had a large body of men, all wearing his badge. The king ate his dinner, but as he left, he turned to his host and said: "You have disobeyed my laws about private armies; my lawyers will be seeing you about this in due course." The surprised Oxford was duly fined several thousands of pounds.

Henry confiscated all stocks of gunpowder in private hands, and made it a rule that the government was henceforth to be the sole supplier of it. He introduced a Court of Star Chamber—so called because its members met in a room with a ceiling decorated with stars—and in this tribunal he and his advisers would try cases of law-breaking or violence by the barons.

These acts humbled the nobility, already weakened by their losses in the Wars of the Roses. Then, to make them even more harmless, Henry gave high offices of state to middle-class people, gentry who would owe everything to him. These men were often great organisers and businessmen and they could be depended upon to carry out unpopular work. Two of them, William Empson and Edmund Dudley, were his chief tax gatherers, and over the years became the most hated men in England. This suited the king, for while he got the money he needed, he did not suffer the unpopularity.

Having strengthened his own position, Henry now decided to make allies of countries in Europe. His eldest son, Arthur, was married to Catherine of Aragon, daughter of the King and Queen of Spain, and when Arthur died soon afterwards,

Catherine was married to his brother, Prince Henry, later Henry VIII. His daughter Margaret married James IV of Scotland. Henry VII then made a commercial treaty with Flanders, called the Great Intercourse, which allowed free entry of English goods into Flanders, and vice versa, and which stated that both countries would combine to keep the seas free from piracy, a dangerous menace at that time.

Henry Tudor was the first of a dynasty of monarchs who sprang from a different background than that of their predecessors; they lacked the nobility of the earlier kings, but they more than made up for it with their hard business sense and their wisdom. Henry was a tough, practical civil-servant type of man, who preferred trading to warfare and technical details to grand theories. He was an accurate accountant, and the account books of the royal exchequer of his time can be seen today with his initials on the columns. In looks he was commonplace, having none of the handsome features of the house of Anjou. As a father, he was stern but fair, though as a husband he was neither affectionate nor generous. Nonetheless, he was never unnecessarily cruel.

His reign saw tremendous advances in learning and discovery. While Columbus and Vasco da Gama were making their famous voyages for the kings of Spain and Portugal, respectively, Henry encouraged the Cabots, father and son, to make their great expedition to North America, where they discovered Newfoundland and opened up the fisheries there. Caxton continued to produce books, Dean Colet founded St Paul's School, Sir Thomas More began to write his famous book, *Utopia*. Education was extended to more people, as schools began to admit pupils whose parents were poor.

In 1509, Henry VII died, leaving behind him an ordered kingdom, with a tamed baronage, a prospering middle class and, packed away in his treasury, the enormous sum of £2,000,000 in cash.

HENRY VIII [1509–1547]

One day in 1530, Cardinal Wolsey, Archbishop of York, and until recently Lord Chancellor of England, was reading in his study at his palace in York, when there was a knock at the door. A servant came in, and in trembling tones, said:

"My Lord, there is a squad of armed men at the front door, demanding to see you."

The cardinal raised his eyebrows, then closed the book and got up from his chair.

"Very well," he said, quietly, "I will go and see them."

He walked out of the room and there, in front of the main door, he saw a number of soldiers, an officer in charge at their head. The officer withdrew a scroll of parchment from his pocket and unrolled it. Looking at Wolsey, he said: "My Lord, I have a warrant for your arrest, in the name of the King. You are to accompany us to London."

When Wolsey enquired on what charge, he was told he was accused of conspiring with the King of France, to the detriment of the realm of England. Wolsey knew that the king, Henry VIII, meant to have his head for quite different reasons, and that he had trumped up this false charge.

The troop mounted and bade Wolsey do the same. Then they set off on the road to the capital. During the journey, Wolsey, who had been unwell for some time, begged to be allowed to stop for a while, and at Leicester Abbey he was given a room. A few days later, his illness worsened and it was clear he had only hours to live. He turned to those around him and said: "I see the matter against me how it is framed. If I had served my God as well as I served my king, God would not have abandoned me in my old age." Then he closed his eyes, and died.

The man who had governed England for the first fifteen or more years of Henry's reign, and had guided the nation's foreign policies with signal success, had come to this dismal end. It was but one example of the ingratitude that Henry VIII showed towards his ministers.

When Henry succeeded in 1509, he was received with tremendous enthusiasm. As Prince of Wales he had been very popular. He was large, powerfully built, handsome, athletic, and at the same time he was well read, could speak four languages, could play the lute and the organ, and had composed music. He had a fresh complexion, with auburn hair, and deep-set eyes, inherited from his mother, Elizabeth of York.

To court the people he dipped heavily into the rich coffers left by his father and gave them fine pageants and tournaments. He also spent vast sums on his own and his courtiers' entertainment, and soon the money began to run out.

So that he could spend time on his pleasures, he entrusted the government to Thomas Wolsey, son of an Ipswich butcher, who had entered the church. He picked well, for Wolsey was an energetic, able and learned man, who loved management. His promotion was rapid. Privy Councillor in 1511, Archbishop of York in 1514, he became Lord Chancellor a year later, when he was also made a cardinal by the Pope. His success went to his head, and he behaved in a most arrogant manner, surrounding himself with a vast train of servants and living like a king. He even built himself a palace of royal dimensions— Hampton Court. Wolsey was hated for this, but the king endured it because the unpopular measures that had to be taken would be blamed not on himself but on the cardinal.

Wolsey governed well. He made treaties abroad which kept England at peace for years without loss of prestige. He closed some of the smaller monasteries and used the money to build new schools and colleges, notably Christ Church at Oxford. He upheld the teachings of the Church which were then being attacked by the leaders of the Reformation in Europe. In this he worked with the king who published a pamphlet attacking the Reformers and was rewarded by the Pope with the title Defender of the Faith.

Henry's wife, Catherine, had failed to give him a son and heir, and he grew tired of her. He fell in love with a maid of honour at court, Anne Boleyn, and wanted to marry her. He therefore instructed Wolsey to begin talks with the Pope for a divorce, on the grounds that he should never have been allowed to marry Catherine in the first place, because she was the widow of his brother. Unfortunately, the Pope, even if he had been ready to grant this desire, could not do so. Rome had just been sacked by the troops of the Emperor of Germany, Charles V, and the Pope was his prisoner. Moreover, Charles was the nephew of Catherine, and he was not going to allow her to be insulted in this way.

With base ingratitude, Henry blamed Wolsey for the failure and stripped him of all his offices. Then he had him arrested on a false charge and planned to put him to death. After Wolsey died at Leicester, the king tried again to get the divorce, but still meeting with refusal, he lost patience. He appointed a learned but weak man, Thomas Cranmer, as Archbishop of Canterbury, and ordered him to try the issue in an English church court, without reference to the Pope. Cranmer meekly pronounced the marriage at an end, and the king straightway married Anne Boleyn in 1533.

The Pope declared the marriage illegal. Henry replied by ordering his subjects to disobey papal orders and renounce the supremacy of the Pope. By another act, the Act of Supremacy, he had himself declared Supreme Head of the English Church. Anyone who refused to acknowledge him as such was deemed to be guilty of high treason. Sir Thomas More, who had succeeded Wolsey as Lord Chancellor, and Bishop Fisher of Rochester, were two of the leading men of the day who did refuse, and they were executed at the Tower of London.

For the sake of his love for Anne Boleyn, Henry had broken with Rome. It was a momentous decision, and it had sad results. The people were in a quandary. The king, while setting up an independent church in England, nevertheless kept most of the teachings of the church of Rome. Those who believed in the reforming ideas of Luther and his followers (they started the split in the old church, and became known as Protestants) were treated as heretics by the king and punished severely, often by burning at the stake. Equally those who still accepted the Pope as God's Regent on earth, were also regarded as heretics, and they were similarly persecuted.

These difficulties did not worry the king in the least. He was much more concerned about the low state of his treasury. To fill it again, he resorted to a disgraceful act. He ordered first the smaller monasteries, and then the larger ones, throughout the kingdom, to be dissolved, and the incomes, rents and capital to be paid into the royal exchequer. Hundreds of innocent monks and nuns were, overnight, made destitute, and the buildings in which they had spent their lives were plundered.

By 1536, Anne Boleyn, who had given Henry a daughter, later to become Queen

Dissolution of the monasteries

Elizabeth I, had yet failed to give him a son. Like Catherine, she was thrown aside, arrested on a charge of misconduct and executed at the Tower. Henry then married Jane Seymour, the daughter of a Wiltshire knight, and she gave him a son, Prince Edward, but the strain of childbirth was too much for her and she died two days later.

The king's chief adviser, Thomas Cromwell, a low-born adventurer of some ability, and the man who had carried out the hateful programme of sacking the monasteries, now persuaded Henry to marry a German princess, Anne of Cleves. It would, he said, strengthen his alliance with the Protestant parties in Germany, and, of course, she would bring with her a large dowry. The king agreed, though he had not yet met her. When she did arrive in England, the king was appalled. She was plain and stupid. He went through with the marriage, but almost at once divorced her, and pensioned her off to retirement. For this mistake, Cromwell paid with his head, in 1540. He was another of the king's servants, ready to carry out unpopular measures, only to be rewarded with ingratitude.

In the same year, Henry married Catherine Howard, a cousin of Anne Boleyn, but within eighteen months she, too, was charged with misconduct and executed. Finally, he married Catherine Parr, a beautiful and intelligent widow of twenty-six, who caused him no trouble and who nursed him through the illnesses of his last years.

Having wasted all the riches of the monasteries and squandered a great deal more besides, Henry now debased the English coinage. He issued gold sovereigns containing one sixth of copper, and silver shillings that were no more than half their weight in the same metal. The gold and silver left he kept for the exchequer, but his subjects soon found, to their dismay, that their money, until then regarded as the purest in Europe, was no longer acceptable to continental merchants. They demanded higher prices for their goods, and at once the cost of living in England rose, bringing widespread poverty.

At the beginning of January 1547, Henry, now fifty-six years old, a shadow of his former self and gripped by a revolting illness, entered the last stage of his life. He had become unbalanced, believing that everyone was plotting to kill him. He even suspected his blameless wife, but before he could raise a hand against her, he died on January 28th.

Henry had come to the throne in an atmosphere of the greatest popularity. When he died, he was mourned by none. He had impoverished the nation, torn its religion apart, made a mockery of its laws, and behaved with the utmost cruelty on numerous occasions. His earlier encouragement of the arts, his enthusiasm for learning, his sense of national pride—and all of these had been very great—were now all forgotten. People were only relieved at his passing.

EDWARD VI [1547–1553]

King Edward VI, son of Henry VIII and his third wife, Jane Seymour, was nine years old when his father died. He had been a delicate boy since birth, and his illnesses so weakened him that he never lived long enough to reign without a council of regency. Two heads of this council, first, Edward Seymour, Duke of Somerset, the king's uncle, and then, John Dudley, Duke of Northumberland, were responsible for the main events of the reign.

Somerset was a kind, generous and well-meaning man, anxious to do good, but he was muddle-headed and unwilling to take advice. He had sound ideas but he nearly always blundered in carrying them out. He wanted to make England completely Protestant, a desire shared by a great many people. He arranged for the publication of a new prayer book, in English, called the *First Book of Common Prayer*, and much of it was written by Cranmer. This was received well.

Unfortunately, Somerset believed that

The Duke of Somerset on the scaffold

making England Protestant meant removing as many traces as possible of the old religion, and he ordered the destruction of church ornaments and furniture, carved woodwork and beautiful stained glass windows. This offended the nation deeply, and people were further enraged when some bishops who protested about it were thrown into prison.

He was faced with two rebellions, in 1548 and 1549, and he handled both of them clumsily. The first, a small Catholic rising in Devonshire, was put down with unnecessary cruelty, for it was not dangerous. The second—and much more serious one, led by Robert Ket in Norfolk, and which aimed to destroy the whole order of society, was met with attempts to make terms. The rebels refused, and soon all East Anglia was behind them. In the end the revolt was only crushed by a full-scale military operation, led by John Dudley.

This John Dudley, son of the Edmund Dudley who had helped to run the nation's finances in the time of Henry VII, was a tough, ruthless, clever man, who, from the very day he was appointed to serve on the regency council in 1547, set out to overthrow Somerset and take the Protectorship for himself. The revolt of Ket gave him his chance. When it was crushed, he persuaded a number of fellow councillors to vote Somerset out of office, send him to the Tower, and give the Protectorship to himself. Then he went to the king to announce the take-over.

Young Edward viewed these proceedings with some interest. He was a highly intelligent boy (he knew several languages and had learned much about history and religion), and he appeared destined to be a great man. He was, however, for his tender years, remarkably hard and unsympathetic.

The new Protector was very different from Somerset. He feared no man on earth, and he cared nothing for popularity. He held on to the reins of power by never hesitating to strike down all those that dared to oppose him. Despite his abilities, he ruled no better than Somerset. Continuing a war with France that had begun earlier on, he was defeated and had to make peace. At home, he tried to reform the coinage, but succeeded only in bringing misery to the poorer classes by not giving them a fair value for the old coins which he took back in exchange for new ones.

Somerset was released from the Tower and invited to sit again on the regency council, and he began to build up a party that acted as a check to some of the Protector's schemes. His popularity with the people never waned, notwithstanding his mistakes, and now it grew rapidly. Dudley, who had made himself Duke of Northumberland, was alarmed, and he had Somerset arrested on false charges of high treason. In the New Year of 1552, Somerset was executed at the Tower.

As the crowds espied the dignified figure of the former Protector walking towards the block, they took off their hats and lowered their eyes. The axe was raised, and when it fell, there was a great cry from the people. Then the foremost ranks rushed towards the block and feverishly pulling handkerchiefs from their pockets dipped them into the fallen man's blood, to carry away a memento of one whom they had loved.

The young king was not so stirred: he noted in his diary "This day the Duke of Somerset had his head cut off, between eight and nine o'clock in the morning"—heartless feelings for his own uncle who had done him no personal harm.

Edward's health was getting worse, and by 1553 it was obvious that he had only months to live. Northumberland's position was in danger, for the king's heir was his half-sister, Princess Mary, daughter of Henry VIII and Catherine of Aragon. She was a devout Catholic and it was extremely unlikely that she would continue to employ a Protestant statesman.

To avoid this possibility, Northumberland persuaded the sickly king to make a will leaving the crown to his cousin, Lady Jane Grey, a great-granddaughter of Henry VII. Then the Duke married her to his son, Lord Guildford Dudley. If the arrangement should work, his power would be supreme.

Edward died in July, before he had the

chance to rule by himself. From what we know of him he would very probably have been an excellent king. Immediately, Northumberland proclaimed his daughter-in-law queen.

LADY JANE GREY [*July 9th to 19th, 1553*]

Known as the "Nine Days Queen," Lady Jane Grey was but seventeen when the throne was put into her unwilling hands. She loved her husband dearly, she was devoted to her books, she was meek and inoffensive, but had no interest in affairs of government. She agreed to become the prop of her father-in-law's schemes because she knew no better, and for this the pathetic girl was to pay with her life.

As soon as she was proclaimed in London, Northumberland ordered his men to arrest Princess Mary, the rightful heir. Mary escaped to Suffolk and there the people rose to her support and saluted her as queen. The Duke followed her with an army, but no sooner had he left the gates of the capital when the Londoners rebelled and declared for Mary. As he marched towards Suffolk, he found that his army was deserting him along the way, and by the time he reached Cambridge he had only a handful of followers left. The Earl of Arundel, one of Mary's military leaders, arrested him and brought him back to London where he was tried for high treason, convicted and executed.

Mary was heralded as Queen Mary I, and Lady Jane and her husband were thrown into prison.

MARY I [1553-1558]

Northumberland's schemes had so angered the nation that when Princess Mary defeated him and came into her rightful inheritance, the people went wild with joy. They could not have known anything of her nature, nor could they have foreseen the terrible results of her ideas.

In 1553, Mary was a hard and embittered woman of thirty-eight. Forced to live in lonely country houses after her mother had been divorced from her father Henry VIII, twenty years before, closely watched by servants of the king, and then, in her half-brother Edward's reign, never allowed to come to court, she had grown up miserable, suspicious and unwanted. She was now prematurely grey-haired, with sunken cheeks, a thin, cruel mouth, and eyes that were ever filled with hatred.

One thing had kept her going, her devout belief in the Catholic faith, and this devotion was to guide everything that she did as queen. She began by overthrowing the newly-established Protestant religion. Cranmer was dismissed, along with many other bishops and clergy. The new prayer book was banned. The Latin Mass was restored. She planned to bring the nation once more under the supremacy of the Pope, and even threatened to give back to the church all the monastic lands taken by Henry VIII.

Then she had another idea. Her heir was her half-sister, Elizabeth, Anne Boleyn's daughter. Mary loathed her, refused to recognise her and determined to marry and have her own child. She picked on Philip II, King of Spain, son and heir of the Emperor Charles V, the most powerful monarch in Europe. The latter welcomed the idea as it would bring England into his already vast dominions. The Spanish king, however, was not so enthusiastic. He was twelve years younger than Mary, handsome and pleasure-loving, and he had little affection for the English. He did not look forward to marrying so old a bride, but, as his father insisted, the betrothal was announced, in 1554.

In England, trouble followed at once. Nobody wanted a Spanish king-consort; that he was a champion of Catholicism only made it worse. A dangerous rebellion broke out, led by the Duke of Suffolk, Lady Jane Grey's father, and by Sir Thomas Wyatt, a Kentish knight who was a great leader of men. They aimed to depose the queen, and offer the throne to Elizabeth, who was at this stage kept in complete ignorance of their plans.

Unfortunately, Mary was not ignorant of their plans, and when Wyatt's force of some ten thousand men reached London, she was ready for them. A running fight took place in the Charing Cross–Fleet Street area and Wyatt was defeated. He, Suffolk and the rest of the leaders were caught, tried and executed. It was then that Mary decided to dispose of Lady Jane Grey and her husband, who had been languishing in the Tower since the previous summer.

On the morning of February 12th, Lord Guildford Dudley was led from the round chamber in the White Tower to the block. In the meanwhile, his wife was preparing to meet her end the same morning. As she gazed out of the window, a handcart was trundled along the green. On it lay the mangled remains of her husband. She

Coronation of Mary I

burst into tears, and then quickly recovered. Half an hour later she herself was led out to the scaffold.

In July, Mary married Philip at Winchester. The Spaniard tried to fit in with the English, studying their habits closely, even drinking English ale, which did not agree with him. But, the climate upset him and he suffered from a continual cold. England would not welcome him.

A parliament was summoned in the autumn, and under pressure it voted for a return to the Papal fold. The nation now had to accept the supremacy of Rome. Immediately, harsh laws against all those who would not adhere to the new arrangement were put into operation, and the penalty for disobedience was death at the stake. In two years some three hundred people were martyred. Among them were Hugh Latimer, Bishop of Worcester, and Nicholas Ridley, Bishop of London, who were burned together at the same stake in the city of Oxford. Even Cranmer did not escape, for, though he changed his mind

and agreed to accept the Catholic faith, it was clear that Mary was bent upon destroying him. So, at the last, he changed back again to his Protestant beliefs, and was tied to the stake. As the flames licked around him, he thrust his hand into them, the one with which he had signed the agreement to accept Rome.

Throughout this persecution, Mary never wavered. She believed it was her duty to God to destroy all those who had offended Him by following the Protestant cause. Her cruelty was stimulated by her own personal miseries. She had failed to produce a child, and her husband had deserted her for the happier atmosphere of his native country. She relapsed into self-pity and, worse, was stricken with Bright's Disease, a slow but incurable killer.

Her marriage to Philip led to England being dragged into a war against France, in which England lost her last French possession, the port of Calais. In November 1558, Mary died of Bright's disease, loathed, feared and neglected.

November 20th, 1558, was cold and misty. Members of the privy council of England had wrapped themselves well as they rode swiftly along the road from Westminster to Hatfield, in Hertfordshire. There, in a big country house, Elizabeth Tudor, who had been proclaimed Queen Elizabeth I the day before, sat in front of a crackling log fire, deep in thought. She had inherited a kingdom but with it had come a host of problems. She would need the best advisers she could get.

Her reflections were suddenly disturbed when a servant announced the arrival of the privy councillors, chief among whom was Sir William Cecil. She bade them sit down at a table prepared for the meeting, at which the affairs of the kingdom were to be discussed. Then she spoke to Cecil.

"I wish it that you shall become my principal Secretary of State. This judgment I have of you, that you will not be corrupted by any manner of gift; and that you will be faithful to the State; and that without respect to my private will, you will give me that counsel which you think best."

It was a great honour for Cecil, a brilliant, practical statesman, and he said as much. Never was a sovereign's faith more completely justified by events. For forty years he devoted his life to his queen, and he succeeded in managing her kingdom and steering it through a most difficult period.

As the meeting went on, Cecil looked at her, thinking. This woman has the makings of greatness, but she will have to be guided carefully. It is a man's world.

What was she like? Handsome, red-haired, imperious like her father, proud, shrewd, witty, and yet sympathetic. Always magnificently dressed and bejewelled, a poet, a harpsichord player, perhaps the best dancer in England. Learned and keen to learn more, able to talk about many things. And at the same time, vain, ungrateful, mean, and often unable to make up her mind.

Elizabeth I

Her first problem was religion, but she resorted to no extremes. A course of compromise was the answer. England would be Protestant, but there would be

87

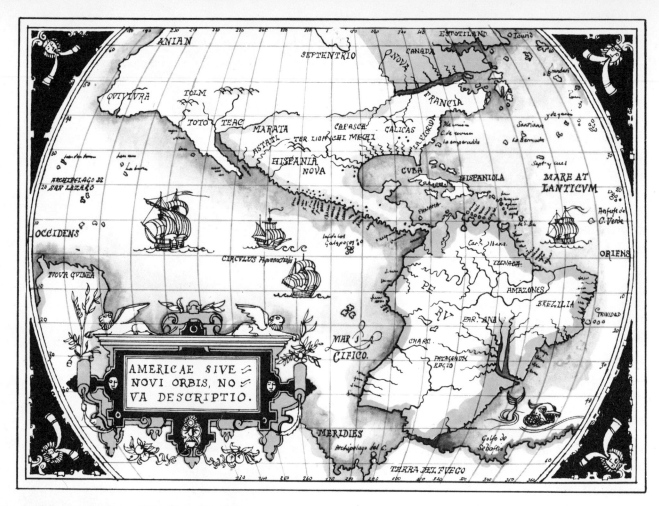

A 16th-century map of the New World

no persecutions against drifters. The prayer book of Cranmer would be revised and re-issued, and English would be the language used in church.

As to foreign affairs, the war with France must be ended. So it was, and out of the treaty she did well, receiving 500,000 crowns in exchange for leaving Calais permanently in French hands. At the same time she must be polite to Philip of Spain, whose offer of marriage she had turned down. England could not afford a war in that quarter just now.

Yet another problem was the succession to the throne. Her heir was her cousin, Mary, Queen of Scots, an ardent Catholic who was ready to work hard for her faith. England did not relish this possibility. With great tact, Cecil urged Elizabeth to choose for herself a husband. There were many suitable men who wanted to press their suit, princes from Europe, high

nobles in England. But to none would she give the answer yes.

There was one man she loved, Robert Dudley, whom she made Earl of Leicester, son of the hated Duke of Northumberland of Edward VI's time. He was believed to have murdered his first wife, Amy, in an Oxfordshire country house, and it would be dangerous to marry someone under that kind of suspicion. Yet she loved him still, and perhaps because of it, decided never to marry at all.

The nation, then, had a chance to repair the damage done to the economy in the past quarter of a century. The coinage was reformed, this time honestly, and trade began to thrive again. A new spirit of adventure and hard work spread throughout the land.

For centuries, England's main enemy had been France, but in Elizabeth's time that nation was so torn with civil wars over religion that it gave her little trouble. There was a new danger and this was the growing power of Spain. Spanish mariners had discovered new lands in the continent of America, which held vast treasures of silver and gold. Then the Spaniards had crossed the Atlantic to conquer and settle there, making a new empire. Swiftly Spain became the richest, and so the strongest, nation in Europe, and when in 1580 Philip II won Portugal, with its huge territories in South America and in the East, he had the largest empire the world had yet seen.

It was a Catholic empire, and Philip, who saw himself as a Crusader against the Protestant faith, stretched out his greedy hands for more dominions. One of them he wanted was England, and there were additional reasons for planning to conquer it.

English mariners dreamed of sharing in the wealth of the new world. Captains like Hawkins, Frobisher and Francis Drake set out on expeditions across the Atlantic where they would fight Spanish ships and sometimes seize the great treasure-loaded galleons and bring them home to their queen. This alone was reason enough for war, but Philip for years stayed his hand. His new lands needed government, and he had rebellions in Europe, in Holland for example, to deal with. So England and Spain remained at peace in theory, but in practice would irritate each other at every opportunity.

Elizabeth encouraged her captains in their piracy—for that is what it was—and she sent troops to help the Dutch in their fight for independence. Philip egged on the discontented Catholic nobles in England who more than once rose in rebellion. He also seized English ships when they ventured into what he claimed were Spanish waters, and dealt cruelly with their captains and crews.

Then in 1586 when Mary Queen of Scots, Elizabeth's prisoner for nearly twenty years, was found to be involved in a plot against her, and was tried and sentenced to death, Philip decided that the time had come for open war. Mary was executed in February 1587, and immediately Philip, to whom Mary had made over her rights to the English throne, prepared a great fleet of ships for the invasion of England. Every port in Spain and Portugal became a hive of industry; special troop transports were built, ships of war were refitted, and the finest soldiers and sailors of Spain recruited.

Cadiz was one of the main dockyards, and in the summer of 1587 Francis Drake, with incredible courage, sailed into it and burnt over ten thousand tons of shipping, returning to England unscathed. Elizabeth and the whole nation were delighted; it delayed the Spaniards for several months, valuable months for England to get ready to meet the invasion.

In July, 1588, the Spanish set sail in 130 ships, a fleet known as the Great Armada. They were to pick up extra forces under the Duke of Parma in Holland. Reaching Plymouth Sound, they were espied by the English who ran down to their ships, hoisted the sails and steered into the channel. Between Plymouth and the Isle of Wight, Lord Howard, the fleet commander, and Drake, his second in command, fought the enemy at close quarters, causing terrible confusion by sending in fire-ships, small craft which were unmanned but burning fiercely. Then they chased them up the channel as far as Calais and there wrought further havoc. By now the Spaniards, commanded by the Duke of Medina Sidonia, a soldier who had never before been to sea, lost heart, broke their squadrons and in twos and threes fled into the North Sea. Many ships were buffeted by the winds, driven round the north of Scotland and down the Irish sea, many of them being wrecked on the way.

The Great Armada was broken, and the threat of invasion vanished. Throughout the whole kingdom there was rejoicing and celebrating. Philip was by no means beaten, but he never again tried to conquer England on her own ground.

Elizabeth had fifteen years more to reign, but they were years free from rebellion and dangerous war. Cecil, whom she had made Lord Burghley, continued at the helm of state, and round him had gathered a brilliant collection of ministers: Walsingham the secret service chief and plot-breaker, Knollys the financial expert, Bacon the astute lawyer, Archbishop Whitgift, the manager of the church, and Raleigh, the poet and historian, who was also a navigator and one of the first colonisers in North America.

It was a wonderful period in other respects. Marlowe invented blank verse and wrote some of the best poetry in the English language. Shakespeare began to pen his plays; Nicolas Hilliard introduced the art of miniature painting; Byrd composed beautiful church music. Great country houses were built in a new style, many examples of which are standing today. Exquisite silversmiths' work was produced, and tapestries were embroidered. There was, indeed, a general upsurge in all kinds of learning and art, stimulated by the new feeling of national pride.

Towards the end of her life Elizabeth had one favourite who, in the end, betrayed her. This was Robert Devereux, Earl of Essex, a handsome but reckless and not very intelligent young man. He tried to imitate Drake in raids on Spanish ports, but failed. Then she sent him to Ireland to deal with a rising, but he was equally unsuccessful. When he returned, he plotted to overthrow the government, for he wanted the highest position himself. He was arrested, tried, and executed in 1601, an end well deserved for such ingratitude to his queen.

Elizabeth's long career was now drawing to a close. Many of her contemporaries at home and abroad had already passed away. Philip II, ruler of the largest empire the world had ever known died in 1598; in his last days he was racked with illness, and grieved by the decline in his country's power and wealth. Burghley, one of the most faithful men ever to serve the Crown, died in the same year. Leicester, the only man whom Elizabeth had loved, had died some years earlier.

By the beginning of 1602, she was becoming weaker. She continued to hunt and dance—she amazed the courtiers with her energy, but it was short-lived. Her close friends and her opponents were gone, and her kingdom was at peace. There was nothing left to fight for, and so she brooded. And with this brooding came illness.

She bullied Parliament, and behaved with increasing imperiousness towards her ministers. Then her robust health collapsed. She began to refuse food and became a recluse, spending hours on her own. In the spring of 1603 she caught a severe chill. But she refused to see her doctors, and soon she could hardly eat or drink at all.

On March 23 the final crisis came. Elizabeth summoned up her strength, and struggled on to her feet. She stood quite still for a few minutes, and then sank to the floor. Imperiously, she signalled to her servants that she wanted to lie down among her cushions.

She fell asleep, and when she woke again, Robert Cecil, Burghley's son, was standing over her. "What are your instructions as to the succession, Madam?" She did not answer, so he asked: "The King of Scotland?"

Elizabeth motioned her consent, then lapsed into a sleep from which she never awoke.

She was the last of her line, an age had come to an end. The greatness of Britain was soon to evaporate under her cousin James I, and it was fifty years before the name of England was again to mean something in Europe and in the world.

Elizabeth had ruled England as an absolute monarch, and, in the main, the people accepted it. If they feared her, they also loved her. But they did not for long allow her successors to be so dictatorial.

The English scatter the great Spanish Armada with the help of fireships

James Stuart, King James VI of Scotland, was the son of Mary, Queen of Scots and her second husband, Lord Darnley. When she was executed, he became the heir to the English throne, and on Elizabeth's death, he was duly proclaimed King James I. Thus was brought about what Edward I had failed to do by warfare, the union of the English and the Scottish crowns.

The new king began his reign at a great disadvantage. Englishmen's minds were filled with memories of the Elizabethan Age. James was a foreigner, and he did not understand the English. His younger days had been very unhappy, for his father had been murdered, his mother had been put to death after many years as a prisoner in England, and in his minority his kingdom had been governed, for most of the time, by self-seeking and quarrelsome lords.

It is not surprising, therefore, that he grew up to be heartless and untrustworthy. He was also vain and arrogant. He was extremely learned and in his time wrote several important books, but despite his knowledge, he never seemed to be able to use it wisely. Worse, he had already begun to surround himself with worthless favourites in Scotland, and when he came to England, he continued with this unfortunate choice of friends.

James was not helped by the fact that in his personal appearance he was deformed. He was weak-kneed and fat, and he had a tongue too large for his mouth, causing him to stutter, which was a great embarrassment. To distract attention from these disabilities, he exaggerated his scholarly gifts, and nothing pleased him more than to be surrounded with toadying courtiers who hung upon every word of wisdom that he believed he uttered.

If such a man had not been a king, he would have earned a great deal of sympathy. But since he was called upon to rule, it was much more difficult to accept the faults in his nature, especially when they led to the making of many mistakes.

He began to rule by what he called

'Divine Right', that is to say, he claimed that he was entitled to ignore ordinary laws because he was answerable only to God. No one was allowed to criticise him, especially the elected assembly of people, Parliament. When they did take him to task, he would dismiss them and govern without them.

He continued the religious arrangement of Elizabeth, but he started to persecute any one who drifted away from the established church. Roman Catholics were harshly dealt with, and he was equally severe with the growing Puritan movement. This was a sect of people who believed in a return to a strict following of the words of the New Testament gospels. These Puritans objected to bishops and vestments, and even to simple things like wedding rings and the making of the Sign of the Cross at baptism.

In November 1605 a plot to blow up the king and his ministers as they sat in council in the House of Lords was uncovered. One of the conspirators, Guy Fawkes, was actually arrested in a cellar just as he was about to set light to some barrels of gunpowder. The ringleaders were hunted down and either killed or swiftly tried and executed, without mercy, Fawkes himself was grievously tortured in the Tower of London and then executed.

James angered the nation by making peace with Spain. He seemed to have forgotten that for fifty years Spain had been England's bitterest enemy. Meanwhile, his favourites, all of whom were extravagant, soon plunged the king into debt.

Two of these were particularly hated. The first, Robert Ker, whom James made Earl of Somerset, handled the government and raised all sorts of illegal taxes. He was disgraced when a severe critic of the king, Sir Thomas Overbury, was murdered in the Tower, for Somerset was believed to have been responsible. He was followed by George Villiers, Duke of Buckingham, and James fell under this handsome young man's influence completely.

For years, Buckingham did as he pleased.

He led the nation into many troubles. He went to Spain with the Prince of Wales, Charles, to arrange for the latter to marry the sister of the Spanish king, Philip IV, in the hopes that her dowry would help to pay off some of James's debts. Worse, Buckingham promised the Spaniards that James would allow Catholics in England freedom of worship, something he must have known the nation would not accept. Then, he behaved so rudely at the Spanish court that Philip called off the marriage talks.

Towards the end of the reign, Parliament began to assert its power, and it revived the right to accuse the king's ministers of misgovernment before the bar of the House of Lords. Parliament also demanded the freedom to say what it thought fit, whether or not its criticisms were directed against the king himself.

The reign, however, was not without achievements. A new translation of the Bible was carried out, and James himself took great personal interest in it. Trade

Map of the New Colonies under James I

expanded, and the first successful settlements of British colonists were made in Bermuda, Barbados, New England, and in places in Africa and India. Colleges and schools were founded in Britain, for James was always interested in all things to do with learning. Inigo Jones, one of the most famous of English architects, was employed by James to construct several new buildings, including the Banqueting Hall at Whitehall, which still stands today.

In the meantime, the unhappy and misguided James had been giving himself up more and more to his pleasures. He took to drink and turned away from the nation's business, leaving it in the hands of Buckingham and his friends. At the end of March, 1625, James died, leaving the throne to his son, Charles.

Largely, though not entirely, through his faults and unwillingness to employ the brains of able men, he had undone much of the work of Elizabeth and her great team of ministers. He had angered people of all classes, most particularly the members of Parliament, and he left the kingdom in a state in which revolution seemed unavoidable.

If you walk up Whitehall from the Horse Guards towards Nelson's Column in Trafalgar Square, you will see in front of it an equestrian statue of Charles I, the only king of England to be tried and executed. Every year, on the anniversary of his death, a group of people who revere his memory gather round the statue to pay tribute to one whom they think was grievously wronged.

Looking closer at the statue, you can see something of his build and appearance, for he was slight, thin, with fine features. Charles was almost beautiful to look at; a well-trimmed beard covered a delicate, pointed chin. He had deep, sad eyes, and a look that expressed his gentleness of manner, for, indeed, he was a courteous husband and kind father. There is something tragic that so kind-looking a man should suffer so dreadful a death, but we shall see that violent though it was it was not undeserved.

Charles came to the throne in 1625. It was soon clear that he thought just like his father. He kept the hateful Buckingham as his favourite and he demanded huge sums from Parliament to carry out vainglorious expeditions in France and Spain. When these failed, Parliament became extremely angry and demanded the trial of the favourite. Charles replied by dissolving the assembly.

In 1628, Buckingham was assassinated, to the joy of all England. Charles now had a chance to show the nation that the first mistakes were the faults of his favourite, but as it turned out, he took over the government himself and began to rule like a dictator. He called another Parliament and asked for more money. This time they presented him with a petition. It was called the Petition of Right, and it was an improvement on the Magna Carta. Desperate for money, the king agreed to accept it; a few months later, when he had got his money, he broke his word.

Parliament met again in 1629 and the members determined to bring Charles to book. Angry speeches were made, almost revolutionary in their words, and the king dissolved it. For the next eleven years, he ruled without Parliament, and he continued in the same high-handed manner. He appointed two able men to carry out his measures. They were William Laud, Archbishop of Canterbury, and Thomas Wentworth, later Earl of Strafford. Laud's task was to curb the growing Puritan movement, which now included several brilliant statesmen like John Pym, John Hampden and Oliver Cromwell. Strafford was to enforce the king's will in taxation

and government, with little regard for the laws of England.

In those years, people who criticised the king were imprisoned without trial. The Court of the Star Chamber was revived, in which all kinds of offenders were heavily punished. The Puritan lawyer, William Prynne, was fined £5000 and had his ears cut off for writing a pamphlet which was said to have insulted the queen, Henrietta Maria, Catholic daughter of a former king of France. More illegal taxes were raised. Huge districts of the country were put under forest law, notwithstanding that most of them no longer had any forests, and heavy fines were imposed for trespassing.

Then he raised a very unfair tax, Ship-money. This tax had been invented before the Norman Conquest, to be used for building ships to fight the Danes; it was only used in time of war and only counties with sea coasts had to pay it. Charles now demanded payments from inland counties as well, and when the country was not at war. Naturally, this gave great offence throughout the land.

One day in 1636 the Sheriff of Buckinghamshire, with a posse of guards, arrived at the home of John Hampden, the county's Member in the 1629 Parliament. He demanded from Hampden a small sum.

"Unless you pay me directly" ordered the sheriff, "I shall arrest you in the name of the King."

"Very well, then, you must arrest me" replied Hampden, "for I shall not pay it. This country is not at war."

He was taken to Aylesbury and charged, but he said that he would contest the king's right to raise the tax. He and his lawyers prepared a case and took it to the courts, but the judges had been bribed beforehand and a majority gave judgment for the king. Hampden was fined, but he had made his point, and he became the hero of the hour.

Charles then angered the Scots by trying to make them accept the High Church religion of England. They preferred their own version of Christianity, called Presbyterianism, which was similar in many ways to the Puritan idea. Their leaders resisted and Charles prepared to take military action. For this he needed money, and in 1640 he summoned a parliament. The Members were in no mood to grant him supplies; eleven years of dictatorship had driven them to the point where nothing but a complete change in his attitude would satisfy them. He thereupon dismissed them.

A few months later, he summoned another parliament, and this became known as the Long Parliament, for it was never officially dissolved until 1653. The Members began by ordering the arrest of Strafford and Laud. Strafford was tried and executed, in 1641, and Laud remained in prison until he, too, was executed in 1645. Then the members abolished the Court of Star Chamber, declared Ship-money and all other illegal taxes as void, and took over the power to appoint and dismiss judges of the courts. This was to ensure that judges remained in office only so long as they carried out their duties correctly, and not at the king's will.

Charles saw that it was useless to resist these measures and he accepted them. Then he changed his mind. He went down to the House of Commons with some soldiers and tried to arrest five leading Members, including Pym and Hampden. They had heard of his intention and they escaped to the City of London where a large band of soldiers had assembled, ready to protect them. Parliament was outraged that the king should try to interfere with its elected members, and this, together with other actions, caused them to declare war on him. Both sides then prepared to fight it out.

The story of the Civil War would make a chapter on its own, but we can only summarise it here. The nation was roughly divided in half in this war. Most of the nobles and the church were on the side of the king, and also the majority of people in the north and the west. London, Kent and East Anglia supported the Parliamentarians, and they were joined by the merchant class. This was to prove vital in the end, for shortage of money was one of Charles's main difficulties. He was so short, in fact, that on one occasion he had to ask the colleges of Oxford to let him melt down their gold and silver plate.

The Parliamentarians, called Roundheads because they wore their hair cropped short, were full of enthusiasm but, to begin with, were not well trained to fight. They had good leaders, however, in General Fairfax, Cromwell and Lord Essex. Gradually, a new kind of force was built up, chiefly by Cromwell, and this was called the New Model Army. It was different in that both officers and men were carefully trained, they studied the lessons of warfare and remained in regular service instead of returning to civilian life once a battle had been fought.

Two great victories were won by the Roundheads, at Marston Moor in 1644 and at Naseby in 1645. Cromwell was second-in-command at both engagements, and it was his skilful use of cavalry that carried the day both times.

Eventually, the king was handed over to the Roundheads who imprisoned him at Carisbrooke, in the Isle of Wight. Then they tried to come to terms with him. They were prepared to let him rule, so long as the rights and the powers of Parliament were not interfered with; in fact, they wanted what we call constitutional monarchy. Charles appeared to agree with these terms, but at the same time he was plotting with allies abroad to send help to restore him to his old position. When the Roundheads learned this, they decided that the king must be put to death. His word could not be trusted.

At the beginning of January, 1649, Charles was put on trial, on the grounds that he had tried to raise war against Parliament and the realm: they claimed that Parliament was the sovereign power in England. Charles refused to pay any attention to the court proceedings, as he thought they were unlawful.

Nevertheless the trial went on, and the king was found guilty. A warrant was then signed by fifty or more members for his execution.

On January 30th, with a dignity and courage that impressed everyone present, the king walked out of Whitehall Palace to a scaffold which had been hastily erected in front of the windows. There he laid his head on the block and with one blow it was severed from his body.

Cromwell's New Model Army

Shocking though it was to execute an anointed king, it must be remembered that Charles had driven Parliament and the nation to the limits of their patience. Had he agreed to the terms offered when he was at Carisbrooke, all would have been well, but his obstinacy and untrustworthiness, more than anything, made it inevitable that he would have to die.

THE COMMONWEALTH [1649–1653] AND THE PROTECTORATE [1653–1659]

The Long Parliament, which had been in existence for fourteen years, was dissolved by Cromwell in 1653. By then many of its Members had already died, or retired, and some of them had even changed sides in the course of the Civil War. The nation was tired of it, and so was Oliver Cromwell.

One day in that year, he came down to the Commons, accompanied by a troop of soldiers. Leaving them outside, he entered the chamber and took his seat. For a while he listened to the proceedings with obvious boredom. Then he got up and walked over to the despatch box. Banging his fist down hard, he shouted: "You are no Parliament. I say you are no Parliament. It is time that you went." He called for the soldiers, and with a clatter of arms they marched in, turning the astonished Members out of their seats. "Fetch him down," cried Cromwell, pointing to the Speaker, and the latter was carried out struggling.

Then Cromwell espied the Mace, the symbol of the authority of the Commons, and with a gesture of disgust he ordered a soldier: "Take away that bauble; it is not wanted here."

In one swift move Cromwell had dismissed the elected assembly of the nation; he had, in fact, done worse than the late king, Charles I, when he had tried to arrest certain Members. What justification was there for this behaviour? Cromwell regarded it as necessary, for the good governance of the realm. Of course it was illegal, and he knew it. But the country needed proper government and he was going to give it to the people.

After the Long Parliament was so abruptly dissolved, Cromwell had himself made Lord Protector of England, an office to be held for life, and one which carried with it many powers once held by the kings.

What kind of man was this country gentleman who had come to the pinnacle of power?

Oliver Cromwell was a most remarkable

man. In war he had proved himself as great a commander as Edward I or Henry V, and yet he knew nothing of soldiering until he was well over forty years old. He was a great statesman, too, for in a short rule of five years, he made England respected and feared all over the world.

Cromwell was nearly six feet tall, with grey eyes, and a large nose. Described by one of his enemies as 'of majestic deportment and comely presence' he had, for a stern man, a kindly expression. It is wrong to think of him as one who never enjoyed himself. He was fond of hunting and he loved a game of bowls. He liked music and always provided musical entertainment at his banquets. Above all, he was fired with religious zeal. He was a Puritan, and his fervour won the reverence of his soldiers who were made to believe they were fighting on the side of God.

After the execution of Charles I, an act which Cromwell always regarded as "cruel necessity," as he put it, there was no one leader of the nation for four years. The country, declared to be a Commonwealth, or in other words a republic, was managed by leading Members of Parliament. Most of their time was taken up in dealing with Royalist resistance which continued in England and in Scotland. Cromwell won two great victories against them. At Dunbar, on September 3rd, 1650, where he met the Scots, he spoke to his assembled troops before the battle began: "Now let God arise, and His enemies shall be scattered." And scattered they were. Exactly twelve months later, he routed an army under the executed king's son, Prince Charles, at Worcester, and forced the prince to flee into hiding, whence, after many adventures, he escaped to France.

In Ireland, Cromwell's policy was extremely harsh. The Irish had risen against the government and had taken the side of Charles during the Civil War. They were joined by many of the Catholic Anglo-Irish nobles, and they had had some successes. Now the war was over in England, Cromwell decided to punish the

Oliver Cromwell

Irish rebels who had not laid down their arms. He took a powerful army across the sea to Dublin and immediately began to conquer Leinster. Two towns suffered particularly at his hands, Wexford and Drogheda. There, the rebels had fortified themselves and waited the assault of the English. Cromwell stormed both places and when they fell, he ordered his troops to slaughter the garrisons to a man. It was a cruel order, and one which the Irish have never forgotten. But it broke their resistance, and soon the country was quiet.

The nation was then at peace, but the government was weak and ineffective because its members quarrelled among each other. It was then that Cromwell turned them out of the Commons and took over the reins of government.

In five years he accomplished much, abroad and at home. In a war with the Dutch, the English fleet, led by Admiral Blake, defeated their navy in more than one sea battle. In a war with Spain, English troops captured Dunkirk, and Blake raided the Canary Islands, seizing treasure-laden galleons and bringing them home. The superb discipline of both soldiers on land and sailors at sea earned the respect of all Europe. England became feared among the nations who eagerly sought her alliance.

At home, his measures were often unpopular, though he had sound ideas. People

Cromwell dismisses Parliament

could not overlook the fact that he had come to power with the support of the army, and they did not like it when he used troops to enforce some of his actions. He had to do this because he met opposition not only from those who regretted the passing of the late king, but also among the most ardent republicans, who never seemed to agree among each other.

Cromwell reformed the courts of justice, he granted toleration of all kinds of Protestant belief, and he administered taxation through a special council who advised him. But, when he called parliaments, they objected to his measures, and so he dismissed them. This was tyranny all over again, and a number of conspiracies against him were hatched. They were all detected and crushed, but he was never completely free from the danger of assassination.

Because he could not get Parliament to agree with him, he divided the country into twelve districts, and put each under the command of a major-general. Their job

was to keep order and supervise the carrying out of the Protector's reforms. The major-generals were unpopular; Englishmen have always hated rule by the army, and eventually, he gave up this scheme and restored limited power to Parliament.

The prosperity of the nation was growing, even if the contentment was not. Additions made to the expanding empire, included the rich island of Jamaica. Britain ruled the seas, and she could trade with foreign countries on advantageous terms.

On September 3rd, 1658, the anniversary of Dunbar and of Worcester, Cromwell died. Great though he had been, his death was not mourned. He had in many ways been out of touch with his people. His ideas were too advanced and they were made even more difficult to accept by being enforced under what was really a dictatorship. And yet, he put Parliament on the road to achieving what in the end it desired, government of the nation through the monarchy.

When Cromwell died in 1658, his son Richard was elected Lord Protector. He was a cheery country-gentleman, with no vices and with little interest in government. He had none of his father's abilities, and after a few months he resigned, and lived in retirement for more than forty years. The nation was then controlled by a group of ambitious men who could not agree among each other as to a leader. Then General Monck, one of Cromwell's best commanders, marched to London with an army and invited the exiled Prince Charles to return to England and accept the throne as Charles II, on certain conditions.

These were that he was to rule with the aid of a freely elected parliament, that lands obtained in the time of the Commonwealth were not to be confiscated, and that there was to be religious toleration. Charles agreed, and he was received with great rejoicing in the capital. The people were happy to be spared any more military rule.

Charles was, as a government circular issued at the time of his escape after the battle of Worcester said, "a tall man above two yards high, with dark brown hair." He had a tremendous sense of fun and his court was ever filled with gay and amusing people, writers, actors and actresses, idle "men about town"—and some clever though wicked statesmen, too. He was interested in all kinds of things, art, science, music, literature and the theatre. His young days had been exciting and often dangerous, and he had even hidden in an oak tree near Shrewsbury after the battle of Worcester.

We tend to think of him as an idle and pleasure-loving man, content to leave the government in the hands of ministers, but this was not entirely true. He was extremely shrewd. He knew how to get money out of foreign princes without carrying out the conditions of payment. He could make agreements without the least intention of sticking to them and yet get away with it. It is probable that he did not believe very strongly in any particular policy,

though he leaned towards the Roman Catholic faith and would have liked to re-introduce it into his kingdom. A number of unpopular measures were taken in his reign, but almost always it was his ministers who were blamed.

His first adviser was Lord Clarendon, who reorganised the Church. The old English prayer book was revised and church services had to conform to it. Priests who would not accept this were forced out of their parishes. The Puritans and believers in other new faiths, like Quakers and Baptists, were persecuted and the prisons were filled with these "nonconformists", one of whom was John Bunyan, who wrote *Pilgrim's Progress* while in his cell.

England went to war with the Dutch, but the results were not so glorious as they had been last time. Indeed, a Dutch fleet actually sailed up the river Medway, in Kent, and burnt the docks and the ships at Chatham. Peace was made in 1667, and by it, among other things, England kept the colony of New Amsterdam in North America. Its name was changed to New York, so named after the king's brother James, Duke of York.

It was during these first years that two fearful disasters overtook London. In 1665, a great plague, not unlike the Black Death, swept through the capital's crowded streets, killing thousands. In a few weeks, more than one hundred thousand are said to have died. The clergy fled from their parishes, the doctors refused to attend the sick and the dying. The streets were filled with handcarts on to which bodies were thrown and then trundled along to communal graves at Mile End and elsewhere.

As if that tragedy was not enough. the next year London was engulfed in a terrible fire. Half the city was destroyed in a few days, including St Paul's Cathedral and more than eighty other churches. Offices, houses, banqueting halls, all fell to the flames, and yet the Great Fire was a blessing in disguise. The dirty streets, which had been used to empty rubbish and which had no proper drainage, were cleared and new houses made of brick, and not of wood, were built. Best of all, it gave Sir Christopher Wren, one of the great men of English architecture, a wonderful opportunity to design and build splendid new churches and houses. The most famous was his St Paul's Cathedral, still the pride of London.

The royal court pursued one long life of luxury, and at the head of it was the king himself. He had married Catherine of Braganza, a Portuguese princess, in 1662, but they had no children. He had tired of her, and sought comfort with a string of mistresses, the most famous—and the most lovable—of whom was an actress called Nell Gwyn. Charles set a bad example of behaviour and the doings at court were often scandalous. And yet the age was brilliant. Milton wrote *Paradise Lost*, Pepys, for several years secretary to the Admiralty, composed his famous Diary which tells us so much about London of those days, Purcell was the king's organist and produced fine music. Charles himself

founded the Royal Society, a gathering of scientists, the most famous of whom was Sir Isaac Newton, the discoverer of the laws of gravity and the best mathematician since Euclid and Archimedes. The king enjoyed dabbling in chemical experiments and he sponsored a number of discoveries.

For the later part of his reign, Charles ruled with the aid of a succession of ministers, most of whom were cunning and dishonest, but also able men. Having made peace with the Dutch, he then formed a secret treaty with France in which he promised to help Louis XIV to destroy Holland. For this he received a gift of enough money to carry on ruling without calling a parliament for some time.

When the secret leaked out, the nation was angry. There were some, however, who approved. It was then that the two party system in Parliament began to grow. In 1679, opponents of Catholicism brought in a bill to exclude from the succession to the throne the king's brother and heir, James, Duke of York, a staunch Catholic. The bill failed but the division between pro-Catholics and anti-Catholics remained. The two parties gave each other nicknames which survived for generations. Those for the bill were called Whigs, the name of an unruly band of Irish brigands, and those against the bill were called Tories, a word once used to describe a fanatical Scottish religious sect.

One important act was passed in 1679. This was Habeas Corpus, and it said that no man was to be kept in prison without a trial. The law still applies today in Britain, but it is sad to relate that not every other country in the world provides such a safeguard for its people.

In 1685, Charles died of Bright's Disease. He maintained his good humour to the end, even apologising to those around him for taking so long to die! His last words were said to have been: "Let not poor Nelly (Nell Gwyn) starve." Of all his mistresses, she had been the only one never to interfere in politics, never to boast that she was the king's friend, and it is pleasant to record that his brother James took the instruction to heart.

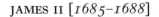

JAMES II [1685–1688]

Just before Christmas, in 1688, a small boat pulled away from the north bank of the Thames in London. It was dark and foggy, and the waterman had difficulty in steering a straight course to the other embankment. Crouched at the stern sat the muffled figure of James Stuart, King James II. As the boat moved slowly ahead, the king drew from his cloak a package and held it for a moment, thoughtfully. Then, with a chuckle, he threw it overboard and watched it sink. It contained the Great Seal of England, with which all government acts had to be stamped.

James had just lost his throne, and in a fit of childish petulance he threw away the seal, thinking that his successor would not be able to govern without it. He had forgotten that Englishmen will ignore such traditions if they have to, and after reaching the south bank and escaping to France, he was to see how wrong he was.

Why was the King of England escaping so furtively from his realm?

James was the second son of Charles I, and he, too, had been chased across the country, during and after the Civil War, and forced to go abroad. When his brother

returned as Charles II, he accompanied him, and soon received high office. For a time he looked after the navy, which he did well. He was a good administrator, and, while Duke of York, had been popular. But he was an obstinate man, vain and heartless. He believed strongly in the Divine Right of kings, just like his father and grandfather.

He succeeded his brother in 1685, and at once began on a course that was soon to cost him his throne.

One of Charles's illegitimate sons, the Duke of Monmouth, raised a rebellion in the West Country, seeking the throne. He was defeated at Sedgmoor—the last battle fought on English soil—and after a chase across Somerset and Dorset he was caught, tried and executed. Then the king acted with frightful severity. He set up the "Bloody Assize", a court under Judge Jeffreys, which was to try hundreds of people in the rising. More than three hundred were sentenced to death, over a thousand more were transported as slaves to the West Indies. The nation saw what it could expect from its new king.

James then showed his real intentions—nothing less than the complete restoration of Roman Catholicism in Britain. He

filled every kind of office with Catholics; sheriffdoms, mayoralties and judgeships. Then he issued a Declaration of Indulgence, an order which swept away all laws against Catholics, and he instructed that it should be read from every pulpit in the land.

Seven bishops, including the Archbishop of Canterbury, William Sancroft, begged the king to be excused from this duty, in as polite a letter as they could write. He replied by arresting them for disobedience, and he sent them to the Tower where they were all crammed into one cell. They were tried before the Court of King's Bench, but even the judges, who had been bribed, could not find them guilty. When they were acquitted, all England celebrated. There was dancing in the streets, bonfires were lit and feasting went on for days.

Up to that moment, the king's heir was his elder daughter, Mary, daughter of his first wife, Anne Hyde (Lord Clarendon's daughter). Mary was married to the Protestant Prince of Holland, William. Angry as the nation was with the king, it was prepared to wait for his death, believing that all would come right under Mary. But James's second wife (Ann had died in 1671) produced a son and heir a few days after the seven bishops were acquitted. The

news filled everyone with dismay; this boy would be brought up as a Catholic; he might be like his father and persecute all other believers.

It was not long before a conspiracy was formed to get rid of the king, and its leading members got into touch with William of Holland, offering him the throne if he would like to come to England and take it. He would have all the support he needed, they said, and so it was. William landed at Torbay in November, 1688, and immediately marched inland, gathering troops on the way. James was alarmed, and at once offered to change his policy, and even dismissed some of his more unpopular Catholic servants. But it was no use; the country had not forgotten the cruelty of the "Bloody Assize", nor would it take the king's word. One by one his friends and ministers deserted him, and his army which he summoned at Hounslow melted away. Soon he was alone. There was one thing left to do—escape—for his enemies were bent upon his capture and they would probably put him on trial. They might even do to him what had been done to his father.

Thus it was that he fled from England, but, though he never saw it again, it was not the last that it would hear of him.

WILLIAM III [*1688-1702*] &
MARY II [*1688-1694*]

When James II fled from England, the throne was offered to William of Holland and to his wife, Mary, under a special arrangement. They were to rule jointly as William III and Mary II, and they had to accept the Bill of Rights which stated that Parliament must be summoned regularly, taxes were not to be raised without its consent, freedom of speech was to be allowed in both houses, and no Roman Catholic was ever to sit on the British throne again.

William and Mary were happy together, though they were very different in nature. The Queen was a kindly, cheerful person, with considerable good sense; the king was a lonely man, difficult to get on with, shy and morose. He never really understood the English people. As a ruler he had many abilities. He was a cautious but brave soldier, and he was a most skilful diplomat. He was still ruler of Holland as well, and when he was in England, he always preferred to be surrounded by his Dutch friends.

Chief among the events of his reign at home were the foundation of the Bank of

England, in 1694, the reform of the coinage in 1695, when, for the first time, coins were milled round the edges which prevented "clipping", a practice which reduced the value of the coins, and the freeing of the press from government censorship. In 1701, the Act of Settlement was passed. This stated that, as William and Mary had no children, the throne was to pass to Mary's sister, Anne, and then, because Anne had no surviving children, it was to go on to the aged Protestant grand-daughter of James I, Sophia, Electress of Hanover, and then to her son, George Lewis.

William had to deal with two dangerous wars at the beginning of his reign; one, a revolt in Scotland to support the return of the exiled James II, and the other, a civil war in Ireland in which James came over from France and directed the military operations against William. In Scotland, the rebels defeated a government army at the battle of Killiecrankie in 1689, but their leader was killed and the rebels lost heart. In Ireland, the struggle was more pro-longed. Londonderry was besieged by

106

A siege during the war with France

James's army but it held out for over three months, under desperate conditions, until it was relieved. Then, in 1690, William himself came to Ireland and at the battle of the river Boyne he utterly defeated the Jacobites (the followers of James).

It was in Europe, however, that William's main energies were occupied. France, under the mighty and aggressive king, Louis XIV, was the strongest nation on the continent, and Louis had ambitions to add to his empire. For years before he had become King of England, William had resisted these ambitions when they were directed at Holland. Now he sought to break the power of the French, and to do so he built up an alliance of European nations, England, Holland and Spain being chief members.

The English fleet won victories at sea, and this prevented Louis XIV from attempting an invasion of England. On the mainland of Europe, however, things did not go so well. It was a war of sieges, directed against a chain of fortresses between France and what is now Belgium. William was defeated on several occasions, but almost always the French failed to take full advantage of their successes. By 1697, they were exhausted, and at the Treaty of Ryswick she gave up most of her conquests.

Then an extraordinary thing happened. The king of Spain, Charles II, who was both sickly and half-witted, had no direct heir. Unbelievable though it may seem, William III and Louis XIV plotted together to decide who should inherit the Spanish throne, with its dominions including Belgium, some Italian states, and its vast empire in America. After a lot of arguing, they agreed that it should be divided between the son of the Emperor of Austria and the Dauphin, Louis's eldest son.

Half-witted though he was, it is not surprising that Charles was absolutely furious. His wife was even more angry and in a fit of violent temper she smashed all the furniture in her drawing room. Charles died in 1700, and left all his possessions to the son of the Dauphin, Philip. This suited Louis XIV very well, but William was seriously alarmed. With all that power, France would be able to dominate Europe, and perhaps the world, for years to come.

Louis now felt strong enough to make war again. The exiled James II had died in 1701, and Louis immediately recognised his son, James Edward, as king James III of England. This was a deliberate act of provocation, and William negotiated a new alliance, called the Grand Alliance, and prepared for war.

Before any fighting began, however, he died. He was out hunting one day in 1702 when his horse stumbled on a mole hill and threw its rider to the ground. The king never recovered from his injuries and died. After he died, some of those in England who had not liked him used to drink a toast "To the little gentleman in velvet" —that is, to the mole whose hill caused the king's horse to stumble. One of the last things he did was to appoint John Churchill, later the first Duke of Marlborough, as Commander-in-chief of the armies of the alliance.

ANNE [1702–1714]

When William died, his wife's sister Anne became queen. She was a plump, good-natured woman, with simple tastes, but she had neither will-power nor brains. Her husband, the genial Prince George of Denmark, was much the same, and he was said to have been the most stupid man in Europe. They were devoted to each other and they had several children, all of whom died before their mother. They would probably have managed a farm with some success; that they were ever given England, Scotland and Ireland to rule is a matter of the utmost amazement.

Anne was dominated for years by a lady-in-waiting, Sarah Churchill, the wife of John Churchill, a professional soldier who had fought at Sedgmoor and in Ireland, and who was to become Duke of Marlborough in 1704. He was the greatest general that England has ever produced. He never commanded a big army until he was well over fifty, but thereafter he never lost one battle, nor did he fail to take any place to which he laid siege.

The best part of Anne's reign is really the story of Marlborough and his brilliant campaigns in Europe and of his wife's influence over the queen in her choice of ministers at home.

We have seen that war broke out over the Spanish succession matter, and that William formed the Grand Alliance just before he died. This group of nations included England, Holland, Austria, some German states, Portugal and Savoy, and against them were ranged France, Spain and Bavaria. In 1703 French armies marched down beside the Danube in the direction of Vienna, the capital of Austria, for it was Louis XIV's aim to force Austria to leave the Grand Alliance.

Marlborough saw that the French must be stopped, and he made a swift dash across Germany from Holland and reached Bavaria where he joined up with an army under Prince Eugene, the Austrian Emperor's most distinguished general. Together they took their forces along the Danube and succeeded in getting between the French and the Austrian capital.

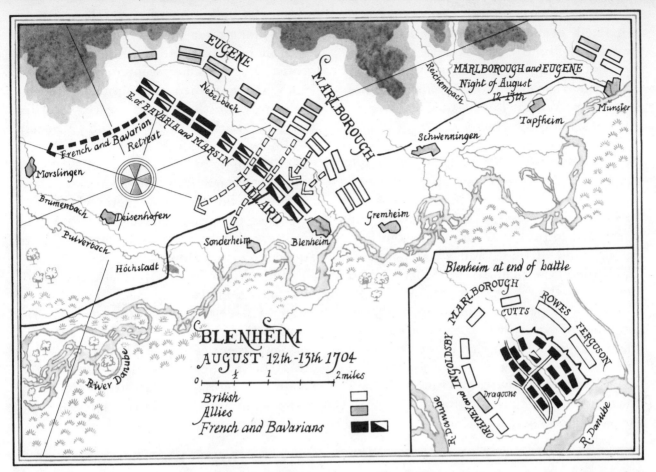

BLENHEIM
AUGUST 12th-13th 1704

British
Allies
French and Bavarians

Blenheim at end of battle

The French commander, Marshal Tallard, had his army drawn up near the village of Blenheim, on the Danube, facing a small stream which ran through marshy ground. Marlborough and Eugene arrayed their forces on the other side of the stream.

Changes had taken place in warfare over the years, and by now armour was no longer effective against more modern bullets. Rifles had improved, and bayonets were fitted to their ends, thus taking the place of pikes. Heavy artillery was also more destructive.

On August 13th, 1704, in the afternoon, the battle began. To start with, the fierce charges of the allied armies and the heavy rifle fire made little impression on the French ranks. Then, Marlborough noticed that the weakest part of the French line was not, as expected, its wings, but at its centre. So he re-grouped and ordered a charge of great strength at a small point in this centre, and the impact broke right through. Pursuing the enemy in large numbers as far as Blenheim he cut them down. Meanwhile, Eugene successfully dealt with stragglers

on the wings, and by the evening, the French had been routed. Many thousands were killed, or were taken prisoner, including their commander, Tallard. It was a crushing victory, as great as Crécy or Agincourt, and it saved Vienna. It also dealt the French a blow from which they never really recovered.

In the following years Marlborough defeated them again and again; three great battles are forever associated with his name, Ramillies in 1706, Oudenarde in 1708 and Malplaquet in 1709. A grateful nation heaped honours upon him, and gave him the magnificent palace at Blenheim, just outside Oxford.

The Grand Alliance had other successes, too. Gibraltar was captured by Sir George Rooke and has remained an English possession ever since. Huge areas of Spain were overrun by Lord Peterborough. And then, just as Louis XIV was ready to end the fighting, the government in England changed. Its new ministers were all for ending the war, too. By the Treaty of Utrecht in 1713, the throne of Spain remained in the hands of Louis XIV's grandson Philip, but Austria obtained Spanish dominions in Belgium and Italy, and Britain got control of valuable colonies in the New World. The balance of power in Europe had been corrected.

Meanwhile, important things had been happening in the British Isles. Although England and Scotland were united through the accession of James I in 1603, it was a union of crowns only. Both countries had continued to pursue separate paths in law, religion and in trade, and when James II was exiled, the majority of Scots wanted his son as their king. In 1707 an Act of Union was passed, which formed the kingdom of Great Britain, with one Parliament, in which Scotland was given a number of seats. The Scots were allowed to keep their own law and church—which they still have in substance today.

Europe after the Treaty of Utrecht

Not long after Marlborough's victory at Malplaquet, his wife fell out of favour at court, and with her went many ministers who had governed since 1702. The new ministry, which wanted peace, was led by the Earl of Oxford and Viscount Bolingbroke. They had taken a dislike to Marlborough whom they believed was becoming too ambitious—he is said to have wanted to be Captain-General of England, an office that would have given him great military power—and they persuaded the queen to dismiss him.

Bolingbroke was a brilliant statesman, but also a knave. He was a Tory and he wanted to see as Anne's successor James II's son, James Edward, despite the 1701 Act of Settlement. He was planning to bring this about when Anne died, and a privy council meeting decided to adhere to the act and invite George of Hanover to take up his new throne.

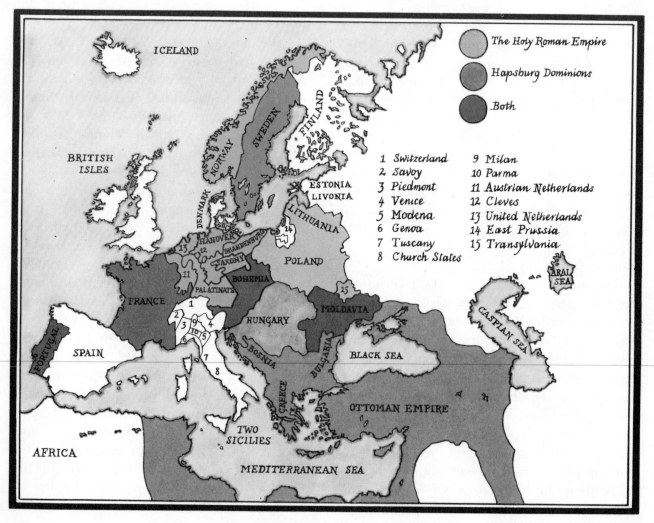

The Holy Roman Empire

Hapsburg Dominions

Both

1 Switzerland	9 Milan
2 Savoy	10 Parma
3 Piedmont	11 Austrian Netherlands
4 Venice	12 Cleves
5 Modena	13 United Netherlands
6 Genoa	14 East Prussia
7 Tuscany	15 Transylvania
8 Church States	

Battle of Sheriffmuir

GEORGE I [*1714-1727*]

By the time that George Lewis, Elector (or king) of Hanover, the son of the aged Sophia mentioned in the 1701 Act of Settlement, came to the throne of Great Britain as George I, Parliament had become all powerful. Kings could no longer rule as they pleased and they could not dismiss parliaments at will. Though his reign was short, it was very important.

He was fifty-four in 1714. He had spent nearly all his life in his native Germany, and he could not speak a word of English. Not many of his ministers knew German, and it is said that when he and his chief minister, Walpole, discussed matters, they talked in Latin, which neither of them could speak at all well. Because of this, and since he was also king of Hanover, he left the government of Great Britain in the hands of a group of statesmen who, about this time, first became known as the Cabinet. They were presided over by a Prime Minister, and the first of these was Sir Robert Walpole.

George was not happy in England. Although the Whigs were firmly in office (the Tories had fallen from power when Anne died) there were still many people who wanted to see James Edward as king. Not understanding anything about English politics, George felt his throne to be unsafe, and so it is not surprising that he preferred the atmosphere of Hanover. This meant that he had little influence upon the progress of Great Britain, which strengthened the authority of Parliament.

Up in Scotland, many people refused to accept George and in 1715 the first Jacobite Rebellion broke out. A Scottish army

under the Earl of Mar defeated the government troops at Sheriffmuir, near Stirling, but the Scots did not take advantage of their victory and soon the rising petered out. Some of its leaders were tried and executed, but on the whole the rebels were treated very leniently.

In 1720, the South Sea Company, a rich company in the Pacific and in South America, and in which thousands of people had invested their savings in order to make a profit, suddenly collapsed, and most people were ruined. At an enquiry, it was found that there had been some swindling and that senior members of the government were involved. The Postmaster-General, Craggs, committed suicide; Lord Stanhope died of a fit when he was asked questions about it in the House of Lords. Another minister was sent to the Tower.

The most able minister not involved was Walpole, a Norfolk squire who was a financial expert and a clever politician. George appointed him Prime Minister with directions to straighten out the muddle, saying that if Walpole could not make gold out of nothing, he could at least make it go a long way. Walpole began by making some of the people who had made money out of the South Sea company scheme repay huge sums. Then he gave high positions of state and in the church to people prepared to pay for them, though he did expect a high standard of ability as well. He reduced duties on imports and exports and this gave great encouragement to industry. It also made him very powerful.

George had been an indifferent king. He had not seen much of his British subjects and so they did not particularly regret his passing in 1727. At the same time, the reign was noteworthy for many works of art, as well as the gradual increase in material wealth. Daniel Defoe wrote *Robinson Crusoe*, Dean Swift wrote *Gulliver's Travels*, and Handel, a German organist and composer, became the director of the Royal Academy of Music, and wrote some of the most moving organ and church music of all time.

George II was forty-four years old when he succeeded his father in 1727. He was a fussy, bouncing little man, with great energy, but with a very bad temper. He understood English well, but he spoke it with a harsh, grating accent. He knew something of war, for he had fought like a lion in some of Marlborough's campaigns twenty years before. He had married Caroline of Ansbach in 1705 and until she died in 1737, he was almost completely under her thumb. There was a famous rhyme in those days which everybody knew. "You may strut, dapper George, but 'twill all be in vain; We know 'tis Queen Caroline, not you, that reign."

George hated his father, and for the last years they had hardly been on speaking terms. When he came to the throne he wanted to dismiss Walpole, whom his father had liked and trusted, but he found that there was no one else who could carry on the government. So Walpole continued in office for the next fifteen years.

Walpole's policy was to keep Britain at peace for as long as possible, so that the nation could advance in the prosperity which his financial reforms and the new engines of industry were bringing about. At the same time the whole tone of politics sank deeper and deeper.

The majority of members of Parliament were landowners, and some of them had what were called Pocket Boroughs. These were villages or towns in which they owned most of the land and which returned to Parliament the members of their choice. A particularly rich landowner, for example, might be able to control the votes in Parliament of a dozen or more members, and if the government majority was small, these votes could be decisive one way or another. The Duke of Newcastle was so wealthy that he had as many as fifty of these boroughs at his command, and for many years he managed to get a government post though he was really quite unsuited to administer it.

As a result, members were interested more in themselves and their possible chances of further enrichment than in their constituencies. Gradually, too, members were getting tired of peace, and to some extent they had cause. The Spanish had been interfering with English trading ships in the Americas. A Captain Jenkins claimed that his ship had been raided and his ear cut off. He even went to the House of Commons to show the ear, preserved in a jar. There was an instant demand for war, and Walpole had to give in. The English fleet was defeated more than once and in

Sir Robert Walpole

1742, Walpole's enemies, blaming him for the failures, succeeded in overthrowing him, and he had to resign.

In Europe, a war over the succession to the Austrian throne had broken out in 1740, and the new ministry in England joined in on the side of Austria. Once again, France was the main enemy. At Dettingen, George II himself led the British army into battle and won a great victory. It was the last time that a British king personally fought in battle. Two years later, the

George II leads his army at Dettingen

British were defeated at Fontenoy in 1745.

In 1745 there occurred the second Jacobite Rebellion, in Scotland, this time in favour of Charles Edward, son of James Edward, the Pretender who had failed in the 1715 rising. Charles, a handsome but not very able man, known to history as Bonnie Prince Charlie, tried to win the throne for his father and he actually succeeded in capturing Edinburgh, as most of the government forces were engaged in Europe. His success, though short-lived, had a remarkable effect. He was able to bring his army down through Scotland, across the border and as far south as Derby, meeting little resistance on the way. There he hoped to gather enough forces to march on London which, it was said at the time, would probably have fallen to him, so frightened were the government troops.

But his followers persuaded him to retire to Scotland and at the battle of Culloden Moor, in April, 1746, the Duke of Cumberland, one of George II's sons,

soundly defeated him. Cumberland's reputation was ruined, however, for the massacre of the prisoners which he ordered afterwards, and the wholesale ravaging of the neighbouring countryside which followed. After a hair-breadth escape, Charles reached Europe.

At this time, Britain, who had settlements in North America and in India, ran into trouble with the French, who had also founded colonies there. There were disagreements as to boundaries, and a number of engagements had been fought, with varying success to either side.

By the 1750s these quarrels had become very serious, and when in 1756 Britain joined Prussia in a war in Europe against Austria and France, it was the occasion for full scale war in the colonies as well. In North America, Admiral Boscawen captured the Isle of Cape Breton, and in 1759 General Wolfe won the battle of the Heights of Abraham, which overlooked Quebec, the capital of French Canada, and the whole colony fell into British hands. Wolfe was killed in action. He was a great soldier, and he was only thirty-two when he died. Somebody complained to George II that Wolfe was mad, when the king made him a general. "Mad, is he?" replied the king, "Well, then, I wish he would bite some of my other generals."

In India, the genius of Robert Clive, a civil servant who became a soldier, succeeded in defeating the French and also some barbarous natives in a number of skirmishes, the greatest being the battle of Plassey in 1757. Meanwhile, in Europe, the British defeated the French at Minden, in 1759, and Admiral Hawke, in the same year, destroyed a French fleet off Quiberon Bay. The year 1759 became known as *Annus Mirabilis* (the Latin for wonderful year) and the successes were largely due to a splendid prime minister called William Pitt, later Earl of Chatham.

Pitt became prime minister in 1757, when things had not been going very well for Britain, and there had been defeats in North America as well as Europe. He was a great war minister, rather like Churchill, and he, too, could inspire people to great deeds. He said, when he was appointed, "I believe that I can save Britain—and that nobody else can." He was as good as his word. He always picked first rate men, Wolfe, Hawke, Ferdinand of Brunswick (who won Minden), and he ensured that they had all the support that the government could possibly give them.

When the war was over, Britain did handsomely at the peace negotiations. Canada was confirmed as a possession, several islands in the West Indies were handed over, and the empire in India became a reality.

George II died in 1760, before the end of the war, but in the knowledge that Britain was already triumphant everywhere. He had enjoyed times of war, even if he could not always take part in them, and he must indeed have been proud of a nation that was foreign to him and yet one over which he had been appointed to rule.

Wolfe's troops scaling the Heights of Abraham

GEORGE III [*1760–1820*]

The reign of George III was the second longest in the history of British monarchy, and only Queen Victoria's was longer. It was also in many ways one of the most important and the most eventful.

George's father, Frederick, Prince of Wales, George II's son, had died in 1751. The young man who now became king had been brought up by his dominating German mother who used to say to him often: "George, when you become king, be a King!" And, unlike his two predecessors, he started with a determination to govern. Though German, he had been educated in England and he boasted "I glory in the name of Briton." He had many virtues. He was a good husband and a kind father, he loved hard work, adored hunting, and he was personally very brave. He was particularly keen on farming, and his interests earned him the nickname "Farmer George." On the other hand, he was obstinate, with the blindness of a well-meaning man who thinks he would be doing wrong if he changed his mind,

having once made it up. All the same, he was enormously popular, and he remained so, despite many troubles, all the days of his reign. His reign was so packed with events and new ideas, so illuminated with famous names, that we can only summarise them. The main things were the loss of the American colonies, the effects of the French Revolution, the career of Napoleon, the Industrial Revolution, and the individual exploits of some of the great people of the age.

George understood that the failure of his grandfather and great-grandfather to get on with the British people was largely due to lack of trying. He also saw that this had given the ministers of government very great power. He was going to put a stop to all that, and he began by forming his own party, called the "King's Friends." They were mainly Tories, who hated the Whigs for being in power for so many years, and they were ready to let George have more direct control over affairs, including the selection of ministers. The first to go was the great Earl of Chatham, some time before the war was over. There followed a succession of prime ministers who thought much like the king, and so were responsible for the mistakes of those days.

The English settlers in North East America had helped government forces to win Canada from the French, but instead of rewarding them George and his ministers exacted heavy taxes from them. At the same time, they refused to let them be represented in Parliament. There were other grievances, too, and in 1774 the colonists decided to break away from the mother country. War was declared and in what was called the American War of Independence, the British were defeated again and again. The American leader was George Washington, soon to become the first President of the United States of America, and he won independence from Britain in 1783.

In that year, by which time the nation was tired of the succession of defeats, a new prime minister was appointed. He was only twenty-four, and his name was

William Pitt, the son of the great Earl of Chatham. Everybody laughed at this appointment, and said it would not last for more than a few weeks. As it happened, however, Pitt was prime minister for eighteen years without a break, and in that time, like his father, he performed valuable services for his country.

By now, George had given up taking an active part in the government, and Pitt headed a Cabinet that was to govern in the king's name. He was not always clever at picking the right man for the job, but to him we do owe the advancement of Nelson, the greatest admiral in history, and of Wellington, the foremost British army commander of his time. We shall see what they did for Britain.

France was still the most powerful nation in Europe, despite its defeats at the hands of Marlborough and again in the time of the Earl of Chatham. The country was living, however, under a system that was out of date. The French king had absolute power, the barons were as rich, as greedy and as difficult to control as ours had been centuries ago. Feudalism, which had disappeared in England nearly five hundred years earlier, still lingered on. But a number of writers had been attacking this system, among them Voltaire and Rousseau. They had observed the American War of Independence, and encouraged the French people to win their freedom from absolute rule. In 1789, revolution broke out in Paris, though no one at first could have imagined the results.

It proved to be a far-reaching revolution, for it affected all Europe. In France, the lords were driven off their estates, and in many cases dragged off by the mobs to execution on a new instrument called the guillotine, a heavy steel blade in a wooden frame that slid down two rails and cut off the victim's head in one blow. Then the king, Louis XVI, a mild-mannered and well-meaning man, and his wife, Marie Antoinette, were captured after an attack on their palace, and put to death on this awful contraption. The whole order of society was upturned in France. Titles were abolished, peasants were freed from slavery, great houses were plundered. New laws were made, and even the calendar was changed. The French nation became a republic.

The revolutionaries could not agree among each other, and a young, brilliant and ambitious general, Napoleon Bonaparte, seized power and made himself head

of the state. Later, in 1804, he had himself made Emperor of the French. Napoleon re-organised France, gave it good government and introduced a system of law which has survived. Then he began to dream of conquering his neighbours. It was this that brought Britain into war with him.

What did George III think of all this? Of course, he feared that the same thing might happen in England, and his fears were not removed when certain Members of Parliament began to say, in the House of Commons, that there was something to be said for the aims of the French revolutionaries. He need not have worried, for Pitt, much as he cared about the liberties of the British people, preferred to correct grievances by peaceful means and not by violence. So Britain went to war with France, to stop Napoleon's ambitions. At sea, it was a succession of victories. Admiral Jervis defeated a French fleet off Cape St Vincent in 1797 and a year later, Horatio Nelson, the gallant Norfolk-born captain, who had already lost an arm and an eye in battle, smashed another French fleet at the battle of the Nile. Three years later, when Napoleon tried to persuade the Danes to join him, Nelson destroyed their fleet off Copenhagen. He seemed invincible. Napoleon then planned to invade England, and the ports of France were ordered to prepare troop transports and supplies. Getting them across the channel, however, depended on having the mastery of the sea, and in 1805, at the great battle of Trafalgar, on October 21st, the brave admiral Nelson once more inflicted a crushing defeat on the French. To the intense sadness of all Britain, he was mortally wounded by a bullet in the spine and he died at the moment of victory. Britain had lost her finest sailor, but he had crippled the French navy, and the threat of invasion was removed. Nelson's body was brought home to England and it was conveyed by land and river to St Paul's Cathedral, where it was buried with great pomp.

On land, however, Napoleon was everywhere successful. He won battle after battle against all who came near him, Austerlitz, Ulm, Jena, Wagram and many more. Then he put his relations on the thrones of the countries he had vanquished. By 1809 he had an empire that included, either as direct subjects or as dependent states, France, Spain, Holland, Western Germany, part of Poland and most of Italy.

The British viewed this with great concern, but the nation continued the fight. An expeditionary force under Arthur Wellesley, later Duke of Wellington, landed in Portugal and slowly began to fight its way to France. By 1812, all Portugal and much of Spain was in his hands. In that year, Napoleon, having quarrelled with the Czar of Russia, decided to invade that enormous nation. With an army numbering six hundred thousand men, many of them the best troops in France, he marched across Europe, broke through the Russian defence lines but when he reached Moscow, he found it abandoned and in flames. The Czar had withdrawn his forces into the interior and refused to give in. Napoleon had to retire, and on his retreat, during which he had to fight off raids by Russian guerillas, his army was struck by the terrible cold of the Russian winter. Tens of thousands died from exposure and cold. When he reached France, he had less than a tenth of the men with which he had set out. It was the beginning of the end for the French emperor.

Meanwhile, Wellington pushed onwards in Spain, and in 1814 he was ready to cross the Pyrenees and invade France. He went over the mountains, forged ahead and captured Toulouse. By this time, Napoleon had abdicated and gone to the Mediterranean island of Elba. The next year he returned to France and managed to gather up an army for the final attempt to assert his power. At Waterloo, on June 18th, he met Wellington, commanding a combined force of English and Prussians and after a bitter struggle lasting all day, he was driven off the field.

It was the end of the war. Now the

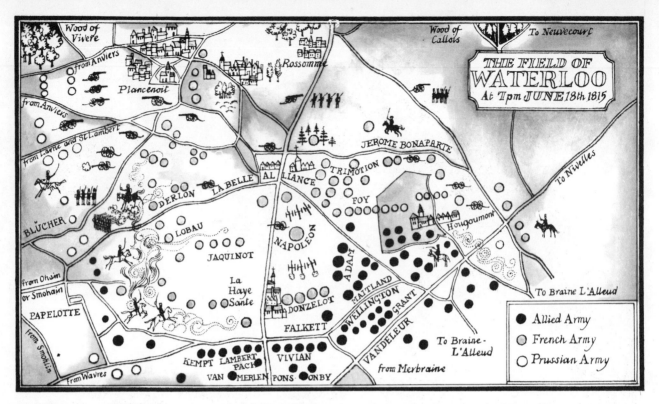

The map shows labels including: Wood of Vivere, Wood of Callois, To Neuvecourt, THE FIELD OF WATERLOO At 7pm JUNE 18th 1815, Rossomme, from Anviers, Plancenoit, from Anviers, from Lasne and St. Lambert, JEROME BONAPARTE, To Nivelles, TRIMOTION, AL LIANCE, LA BELLE, FOY, DERLON, Hougoumont, BLÜCHER, LOBAU, NAPOLEON, JAQUINOT, ADAM, To Braine L'Alleud, from Ohain or Smohain, La Haye Sante, MAITLAND, WELLINGTON, GRANT, PAPELOTTE, DONZELOT, FALKETT, VANDELEUR, from Smohain, To Braine-L'Alleud, KEMPT LAMBERT PACK, VIVIAN, from Merbraine, VAN MERLEN, PONS ONBY, from Wavres.

Legend: ● Allied Army, ◐ French Army, ○ Prussian Army

nations had to pick up the pieces of their shattered countries and put them together again. For Britain, it was a crowning success for her efforts. She became the dominant nation in Europe; her armies and navies were regarded as the most powerful the world had yet seen.

What had been happening in Britain during these long years of war?

Despite the men and the money needed to fight Napoleon and the French, the country had been reaping the benefits of the Industrial Revolution. This is the name given to the change when Britain became increasingly industrialised, and the most advanced country in the world.

Up to the eighteenth century, Britain had been, like all other nations, an agricultural community. But now she had begun to develop engines for the production of goods, and she was the first to do so. Many things were no longer made by hand; machines did the same work, and much faster. Hargreaves invented a spinning jenny with which one person could operate several wool-spinning wheels at one time. James Watt invented the steam engine for pumping water, and for driving machinery doing other work. Wilkinson set up the first iron blast furnace to increase the production of iron and steel. The Duke of Bridgwater and James Brindley carved miles of canals across England so that goods could be carried from one city to another in great loads. Roads were improved by McAdam, a Scotsman, who invented a new surface for them that is still remembered by his name. The railways were invented, providing quicker travel for both passengers and goods. Farming methods were improved, for the fields still had to be worked to provide the nation's food.

These and many other inventions and ideas made Britain the foremost nation of the world, and other countries sent inspectors to see the results so that they could help to industrialise their nations. But, new machinery made production cheaper, as one engine could do the work of many men. Before long, unemployment spread, and great misery resulted for the working classes. Riots took place and they were put down with severity. Many people starved. When they could find work, the conditions were barbarous; eighteen-hour days for just enough money to keep the wolf from the door. So the Industrial

James Watt and his steam engine

Revolution brought with it widespread unhappiness, but it also led to a new development. Working men, seeing that their labours were bringing profits to their employers, began to seek rights and privileges for themselves, something they had not done before.

In 1811, the king, who had been very much interested in the industrial progress of the nation, was taken ill with insanity, and it never left him for the rest of his days. His eldest son, Prince George, became regent, and acted as monarch in his father's name. For George III it was a tragic way in which to pass his last years, even if he was not aware of it himself. He had seen so many glorious things happen, and he had personally encouraged the greatest advance in science and engineering yet attempted. It had also been an age of brilliant achievement in art; painting by Gainsborough, Reynolds and Lawrence; furniture-making by Chippendale, Hepplewhite and Sheraton; literature from Gibbon (the *Decline and Fall of the Roman Empire*), Johnson (his great dictionary), Goldsmith, the witty playwright, and many others.

In 1820, the old king died, and although he had disappeared from public life nine years earlier, he was still mourned greatly. It was a reign that few would forget.

One of Brindley's canals where it crosses over a river

It was July 19th, 1820. In London the sun was shining, and the streets leading to Westminster Abbey were packed with people. They had come to see the procession that was soon to emerge from the abbey, a royal train, in the middle of which would be walking the newly crowned king of Great Britain and Ireland, George IV.

Suddenly there was a commotion at the entrance to the great church. A carriage had drawn up and out had stepped a woman, richly dressed, and accompanied by ladies-in-waiting. It was Queen Caroline, the wife of the king. She walked up to the doors, hammered loudly with her fists and demanded to be let in. Soldiers standing guard inside refused her entry; the king would not permit her to be present at his coronation. So she turned away and went back to her carriage.

When the crowds began to understand

Royal Pavilion at Brighton

what had happened, they cheered her as she set off down Whitehall. A few minutes later, the abbey doors opened and out came the royal procession. As soon as the king appeared on the steps, the people jeered at him, shouting abuse and shaking their fists. It was not a good start to a reign.

George had already made himself hated for his extravagance as a young man—he had spent so much on enjoyment and gambling that Parliament had threatened to refuse to pay his debts unless he reformed—and when he was prince regent the government had passed a number of acts which dealt severely with poor people who protested about the hardships stemming from the Industrial Revolution. These acts made him personally unpopular because he did nothing to stop them, and even appeared to approve them. When he refused his wife permission to attend his coronation, the nation was horrified. It was no secret that George and Caroline had been quarrelling for years, but this behaviour was not what people expected from a man who had once been known as "The First Gentleman of Europe."

In 1822, a new ministry took office and it consisted of men who sincerely wanted to do something about the misery of the working classes. They introduced measures which helped a great deal. Workmen were allowed to form trade unions, and they were once again allowed to strike (a right which had been withdrawn in the time of Pitt). Duties on imports and exports were cut and this lowered the cost of living. Perhaps the greatest measure was the reform of the criminal law, by the Home Secretary, Sir Robert Peel. Hunger had driven men to crime, but until then punishments for stealing were savage. Theft of a sheep or picking a pocket led to a death sentence, and many lesser crimes were punished with transportation to the colonies as a slave. Peel abolished the death penalty for all crimes except murder, treason and forging a Bank of England note. Transportation and long prison sentences were used much less.

In 1830, George died, regretted only by his friends who were as extravagant as himself. It was sad that he had wasted his life, for he was an able man. He was fond of the arts, and he had encouraged the building of many beautiful houses and streets. Some of the finest examples were the Regent's Park terraces, built by John Nash, and the Royal Pavilion at Brighton.

123

WILLIAM IV [1830-1837]

George IV had no son, and his only daughter had died in 1817. The throne therefore passed to his brother, William, Duke of Clarence. William was nicknamed "Silly Billy" for he gave the impression of being simple-minded. But he was not by any means as stupid as he appeared. He had had an interesting career in the navy, and he was known to be a supporter of parliamentary and social reform. He was a kindly, good-natured man, and it was largely due to his popularity that the great Reform Bill of 1832 was eventually passed with less civil riot and bloodshed than might have been expected, since the nation was deeply divided on the issue.

We have seen that in the eighteenth century, most members of Parliament of were landowners, and that some of them could control votes in both Houses of Parliament. This position was the same in the 1820s, but by then the population had increased. Many people had moved from the country districts to the small towns which were becoming great cities by virtue of the new factories that were going up and using the engines of the Industrial Revolution. These cities in many cases could not send any members to Parliament at all, and so the grievances of the industrial workers were not voiced in Parliament as they should have been. Centres of industry like Birmingham, Leeds, Manchester and Sheffield had no representatives, but many little towns like Lyme Regis, King's Lynn and Cricklade had two, and some, even, had more than two. Power then still rested in the hands of a few people, and bribery at election times was practised on a wide scale to keep it that way. The picture was even worse in Scotland and Ireland. It was a situation that could not go on for ever.

In 1831, the prime minister, Lord Grey, who was a Whig—the party that stood for reform—introduced a Reform Bill. It was to re-arrange the distribution of seats throughout the country. Pocket Boroughs were to be abolished. The right to vote was to be extended to a much wider section of the people. The bill was passed in the

Commons—by one vote—but was thrown out by the Lords. At once riots broke out in London and in many provincial cities.

Lord Grey presented the bill again, this time with the active support of William. He had promised that he would create enough peers in the Lords to guarantee that it would be accepted there. As it was, a number of the more conservative peers did not vote at all, and the bill was passed. This was a landmark in our parliamentary history, though it needed several more such bills before Britain arrived at the parliamentary state of today.

Other acts soon followed. The Factory Act of 1833 stopped children under the age of nine from working in cotton or wool factories—the owners had been making great profits by employing child labour—and hours of work for older children and adults were limited. Borough and town councils were to be filled with members freely elected by the people, as a result of the Municipal Corporation Act of 1835.

These measures were supported by William. It was not that he was a king who willingly fell in with the ideas of his ministers, but rather that he saw that there were grievances which should be put right, and he often said so. When he died in 1837, he was much mourned, for people had regarded him as "their king."

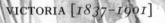

VICTORIA [1837–1901]

One day towards the end of the reign of William IV, people in London were stopped in the streets by news vendors and canvassers who handed them a leaflet. On one side was a picture of a young and beautiful princess, Alexandrina Victoria, daughter of the king's next brother, Edward, Duke of Kent, and on the other side was a drawing of the ugly and cruel features of another of William's brothers, the Duke of Cumberland, who was the most hated man in Britain. As they looked at the two pictures and studied the slogans underneath them, they thought about what it all meant.

Princess Victoria was the heir to William (her father had died in 1820) but it was feared that Cumberland would make a bid for the throne and was only waiting for his brother to die to put his plan into action. So the leaflet explained, and the dread was felt by everyone in the land. Cumberland had made himself loathed for his cruelty,

his arrogance and his opposition to all ideas of reform. If he had succeeded, there would probably have been rebellion. But, as it was, with the government and the people behind her, Princess Victoria became Queen Victoria immediately her uncle William died in June 1837. Her proclamation stopped the hated Duke, and he retired to Germany.

By 1837, the monarchy of Britain possessed influence rather than power, and it was the prime minister, his cabinet and the government which ruled. It was accepted that a sovereign would agree with government policies, whatever his or her personal feelings, and in turn would give advice to a prime minister or other ministers if they asked for it. It was a good arrangement and it still applies today. There have been several occasions when the sovereign has offered wise counsel and so prevented mistakes being made. Once, Queen Victoria and her husband re-worded an angry letter written by Lord Palmerston to the government of the United States of America, and it is said that this revision prevented the two nations going to war.

The eighteen-year-old queen, then, began a reign that was to last for sixty-three years, in which tremendous things were to happen.

Her first prime minister was Lord Melbourne, a gentle-mannered and experienced man who taught her the business of state. Then, in 1841, Sir Robert Peel came to power as head of a Tory government. His ministry carried out a great programme of reform; it introduced income tax for the first time on a regular basis, it reduced duties on several hundreds of goods so that the cost of living fell, and it passed the Bank Charter Act which controlled the number of bank notes issued.

Peel was a very great man, a fine orator, an untiring worker and an excellent manager of parliament. He fell from office in 1846, over troubles in Ireland, which are explained in the Rulers of Ireland part of this book.

Although Peel's reforms helped to make

Britain more prosperous, the wealth was not shared by the working peoples; indeed, their hardships got worse because a succession of bad harvests had raised the price of bread, and the factory owners were paying them only just enough to live on. Worse, they still did not have the right to vote, as the 1832 Reform Bill had given the vote to a limited range of people. So it was not long before they got together and demanded improvements in their condition. A People's Charter was drawn up which asked, among other things, that everyone over twenty-one should have a vote and that they should be able to vote in secret (this would mean that if your landlord or your employer was standing for Parliament you could vote against him without fear of losing your home or your job).

When in 1848 rebellions of working people in many European countries broke out all at once, it was feared that the same thing would happen in Britain. There were riots and demonstrations, and even a march to London, but this was stopped by the Duke of Wellington at the head of some troops. On the whole, however, there was little violence, and in time the workers got their demands.

The queen had married Prince Albert of Saxe-Coburg in 1840 and he became known as the Prince Consort. It was a very happy match. They had many children, one of whom, Prince Edward, born in 1841, became Edward VII sixty years later. Another was Prince Arthur, who was born in 1850. The Duke of Wellington, by now a very old man, was his godfather. Prince Arthur, who became Duke of Connaught, went into the army and in time he became a Field Marshal.

Victoria and Albert took the business of monarchy very seriously. They studied carefully all the documents and letters brought to them in the shiny red despatch boxes by various ministers and they asked questions about anything they did not understand. From time to time they advised ministers on this and that, especially Albert, who was a most intelligent man.

Victoria learned much from him, and when he died in 1861, only a few days after the re-writing of the Palmerston letter to the United States, she was well able to continue on her own.

Another of Queen Victoria's ministers who has left his name in the history books was Viscount Palmerston, known as "Pam" to his friends. He was an aggressive sort of man, with liberal ideas, and he was a great patriot. He believed that nations who wanted to advance in parliamentary reform, like Britain, should be encouraged, and he always put Britain forward as the champion of liberty. Sometimes he did things without consulting either the queen or his colleagues. Once, when he was foreign secretary, he congratulated Louis Napoleon, nephew of the great Napoleon, when he seized power in France and made it a republic again. He did this on his own, and he was promptly dismissed. When he became prime minister, he continued to uphold the prestige of Britain abroad though he was not much interested in social reform at home.

In 1854, Britain went to war with Russia in what is known as the Crimean War. Turkey had quarrelled with Russia, and as the Turks were our allies—their country and its empire was part of the land route to British India—the British feared that this route might be endangered. An army was sent to the Crimea to invade Russia. This war was a story of blunders. British troops had not fought in any major war since Waterloo—thirty nine years before—and the art of fighting had almost been forgotten. A number of battles were fought in which the losses were high on both sides. It was in this war that the famous Charge of the Light Brigade took place. Six hundred or more mounted British soldiers surged across a valley through a devastating barrage of Russian gunfire. Only a handful reached the other side. It was a glorious exploit, but it achieved nothing.

The hospital arrangements were very bad. Troops injured in the lines, who might otherwise have recovered from their wounds, were shipped to over-crowded and dirty wards, where many of them died from poisoning. It was then that Florence Nightingale, a nursing sister of great determination, came out to the Crimea to re-organise the hospitals and to ensure that the men received proper treatment.

The war came to an end, with a guarantee that Russia would not molest Turkey.

Soon after this, trouble occurred in India. The native soldiers in the army objected to a number of things. One was the introduction of a new rifle, the cartridges for which had to be bitten off at the ends before being put into the barrel. These cartridges were smeared in grease, and the natives believed that the grease was cow-fat. The cow was a sacred animal to them and they were not allowed by their religion to touch it. Using this belief as a reason, in 1857 they rebelled against their British officers in a number of garrisons and murdered many of them. The revolt

spread and soon all India was aflame. For more than a year the British, against overwhelming odds, fought to relieve the garrisons and put down the rising. Many acts of individual bravery were performed. In 1858 the revolt was quelled and order was restored.

When Albert and his wife were re-writing the Palmerston letter, in 1861, he was suddenly taken ill. He had contracted typhoid fever, and a few days later he died. The effect on the queen was terrible. She was distracted with grief, and she cut herself off from the nation for years. Retiring to one or other of the royal homes, she refused to appear in public. The nation resented this and in Parliament there was talk of overthrowing the monarchy altogether and setting up a republic. Then, in 1871, the Prince of Wales became seriously ill and the people's sympathy was stirred. It was during these sad days that another minister was to make his

Charge of the Light Brigade

Suez Canal

mark in history. He was Benjamin Disraeli.

Disraeli was of Jewish descent. He was an extremely gifted man; he wrote books, he had entered Parliament and made a name as a great speaker, and he was able to talk with knowledge about a variety of subjects. He became prime minister for a few months in 1868, and it was then that he became a close friend of the queen. He is said to have urged her to come out of retirement and show herself to her people again, and when she was attacked in Parliament he would visit her and assure her of his loyalty.

His ministry of 1874 to 1880 was full of achievement. Like Palmerston he upheld British prestige abroad, preferring to settle differences by discussion rather than by war. In 1875, he bought, on behalf of the government, a large number of shares in the Suez Canal Company which enabled Britain to control that most valuable short cut to India and the East. At home various bills improved conditions in the towns and the countryside. It was in the fast growing empire that he did great service. In 1877, the Queen was proclaimed Empress of India, a high-sounding title that, though it may not have pleased all Indians, showed the world that Britain was not going to allow interference in the great sub-continent. He made it known that all the empire peoples could look to the queen as the mother to whom they could turn in times of trouble.

In 1880 his ministry fell, and he died a year later, having been made Earl of Beaconsfield in 1876. The new government was headed by another famous man, William Gladstone, the only statesman to to have been prime minister four times.

Gladstone was a Liberal, the name taken on by the Whig party some years earlier. He was an expert on financial affairs, a keen reformer, and he was much more interested in home affairs than foreign policy. He never got on with the queen, who disliked him. He had a habit of addressing her as if he was making a speech in the Commons. Perhaps, too, she did not approve of his liberal ideas which were very advanced for the time.

In his first ministry, from 1868 to 1874, an Education Act had arranged for schools to be set up in every parish, and had given state grants to a number of existing schools. The Ballot Act of 1872 had made it possible to vote at elections in secret, one of the demands of the People's Charter twenty-four years earlier. An army act enabled a good soldier to become an officer without having to purchase his commission. In his second ministry, from 1880 to 1885, the vote was extended to an even greater range of people, the money a candidate could spend at election time was limited and education was made compulsory.

Like Peel, his career was to end over a dispute about Ireland, which is explained in the Rulers of Ireland section. In 1894 he resigned from office, when he was over eighty years old. He had served his country very well, and it is sad that the queen never thanked him for it. When he called to deliver up the seals of office, all she did was to enquire whether Mrs Gladstone was well.

The British Empire was growing rapidly, as we have seen, but it was not achieved without difficulty and unrest. There was trouble in Egypt and the Sudan, which threatened British control over the Suez Canal. A warlike tribe of savages, Dervishes, had overrun most of the Sudan, and it took some years to drive them out. Finally, in a great battle at Omdurman,

near Khartoum, in 1898, Sir Herbert Kitchener destroyed them, and brought nearly a million square miles of land under British dominion. There were difficulties, too, in South Africa, where the land had been colonised by British and by Dutch settlers (who were known as Boers). There had been quarrels, and at the end of the century a war had broken out, called the Boer War. For Britain it was, to begin with, a story of disaster. Several armies were defeated, and garrisons were beseiged. Then a great general, Lord Roberts, with Kitchener as his second in command, went out to take control. Within a few months the Boers were defeated, and South Africa became a dominion of the British Empire.

No story of the reign of Queen Victoria would be complete without some mention of the famous men of arts and science. There was a great revival of painting and sculpture, led by such men as Millais,

Rossetti, Burne-Jones and Watts. In literature, Charles Dickens wrote many novels which portrayed the bad conditions of the poorer classes and which helped to bring about many reforms. Macaulay, Ruskin, Thackeray and Trollope were among the leaders of the literary world. There were fine poets, like Tennyson, Swinburne and Browning, and towards the end of the reign there was a fast growing interest in opera and theatre. Gilbert and Sullivan composed their famous comic operas, and Oscar Wilde penned some of the wittiest plays ever to be written in the English language.

In the fields of science, Lister introduced the antiseptic system which has since saved countless lives from certain death through infection; Simpson first used chloroform as an anaesthetic, and the queen herself had this gas when she gave birth to Prince Leopold, her seventh child; Lord Kelvin

laid the first Atlantic cable; and Alexander Graham Bell invented the telephone.

Ships of war and merchant vessels began to be made of steel, and engines took the place of sail. Brunel built bridges, tunnels and railways. Faraday invented the electric motor and from that have stemmed all the machines powered by electricity in use in every house and factory. For the first time large blocks of flats were erected in towns, many of them by generous people who rented them to poorer people at very low rates.

In 1897 Victoria celebrated her diamond jubilee, and everyone, not only in Britain but throughout the world, celebrated it with her. She lived four years more, the most respected monarch in the world. When she died in 1901, she was head of the British Empire, which occupied almost a quarter of the land on the surface of the earth.

Lloyd George introduces his People's Budget

EDWARD VII [*1901–1910*]

Early in 1902, the people of Britain and its empire were getting ready to celebrate an important event, the coronation of the new king, Edward VII. It was to be an unusual one, for there were few people alive who remembered the last coronation of a British monarch—Queen Victoria's, as long ago as 1838. Court officials, heralds, service chiefs, all busied themselves with the intricate arrangements, and newspapers and publishing houses began to prepare the mass of booklets, special issues and souvenir programmes that would sell in great numbers.

Then suddenly, one evening, the news vendors' placards throughout London carried a horrifying announcement. The king was dangerously ill. People rushed to buy their copies and they read that indeed his condition was grave. He had appendicitis, which, in those days, was often fatal. For Edward it was particularly serious, for he was sixty, and though his physique was strong, he had led a most tiring life.

The greatest doctors in the land were called to give their opinions. Lord Lister, the pioneer of antiseptic surgery, was now an old man and too unsteady to perform the operation that he, among others, said must

be done at once. The coronation must be postponed, but this annoyed the king who said "I would rather die in the Abbey than put it off."

His doctors had their way, however, and he was prepared for the forthcoming ordeal.

The whole empire waited in suspense. Outside Buckingham Palace huge crowds gathered to read the latest bulletins on the king's condition, and every time an official came down to the gates with a fresh one, a strange silence fell upon everyone, as the foremost ranks strained their eyes to read it.

Then it was announced that the operation had been a success, and that Edward was going to get well. The people's relief was instant and widespread, and it was proof of the love that they had for their king.

Prince Albert Edward was born on November 9th, 1841, the second child and the eldest son of Queen Victoria and her husband, Albert, the Prince Consort. When he was a month old he was created Prince of Wales.

Edward's young life was hard in many ways, for his father was a strict man, deeply conscious of his duties as a father as well as those of a monarch's husband. The boy was given a rigorous education, but from an early age his affectionate and easy-going manner, which stayed with him all his life, rebelled against declining Latin nouns and learning the theorems of geometry. As he said in later life, he had not learned much.

When he was sent to Oxford University, he neglected the lecture rooms as often as he could for more exciting things, parties, dances, sports, and he appears to have enjoyed himself rather more than his father thought good for him. When he left Oxford to go to Cambridge University, he went on with the gay life, and he was taken to task several times by the Prince Consort for wasting his time. All the same, he made many friends, and indeed it was at this time that he developed his unique gift of friendship. Probably no monarch before or since has had so many acquaintances from such a varied section of the public.

After his father's death in 1861, Edward began to carry out royal duties, but he did not give up his gay life at all. He gambled at cards, he danced, dined and talked on into the early hours of the morning. He loved the theatre and made many associations with actors and actresses, something

that in those days was not considered as properly respectable for a prince of the royal blood.

In 1863, Edward married Alexandra, daughter of Christian IX, king of Denmark, who was a beautiful and talented girl. It was to be a happy marriage, despite Edward's pleasure-seeking activities, and his wife became adored by the nation for her great works of charity.

Queen Victoria kept in close touch with the nation's business, but she would not let her son share in these affairs until the very end of her reign. As a result, when he succeeded in 1901, he had not gained the experience that many previous Princes of Wales had had, but nevertheless he proved to be an excellent ruler. This was very largely due to his great personal popularity.

Edward's short reign was marked by many events, and by the rise to fame of several people who were to serve their country well. Two of these were David Lloyd George and Winston Churchill.

The Liberals were the governing party for most of the reign, and they brought in several reforms. Old people over seventy were given pensions, the rights of trade unions were strengthened, and labour exchanges were formed to find work for the unemployed. Lloyd George, as Chancellor

The Territorials in training

of the Exchequer, brought forward in 1909 what was called "The People's Budget," which, as he said, was meant to take money from the rich to help the poor. The rich did not like this at all, and as they were strongly represented in the House of Lords, the budget was thrown out by that house. The Liberals then called for a general election to support their reforms and to challenge the right of the Lords to reject bills connected with money. They were returned to power, and the Lords had to pass the budget. It marked the beginning of another struggle between Lords and Commons.

It was in foreign affairs that the king himself played an important part. Britain was frightened by the growing might of Germany, ruled then by a nephew of Edward's, Wilhelm II, the Kaiser, who was an aggressive man, determined to make his country the most powerful in Europe. France, too, was alarmed, but for many years the French government had been hostile to Britain. Edward took a personal interest in changing British policy and in 1904 the famous Entente Cordiale was established. This was an agreement of friendship with France, though it was not a treaty, and in time it led to the two

countries joining forces in the fight against Germany which broke out in 1914.

Edward also encouraged alliances with other countries, including Italy and Portugal, and though he may not have fully realised it, he was helping to build up in Europe a group of friendly nations that when the time came would stand together to resist the Kaiser.

In home affairs, Edward was particularly interested in modernising the army. The Secretary for War, Haldane, introduced the idea of the Territorial Force, which consisted of volunteers from many walks of life who offered to spend periods of time every year in military exercises and training, so that in the event of warfare the nation would have a reserve army upon which to call to support the regular army. Haldane's idea was resisted by the army chiefs, as they considered that the Territorials would be playing at soldiering; warfare was the business of professionals. But Edward spoke so strongly in favour of Haldane's scheme that it was carried through.

In 1910, the king was taken ill again, and his last days were ones of some suffering. At the beginning of May he collapsed altogether and died on the 6th.

Edward VII's eldest son, Prince Edward, died of pneumonia in 1892, and so his next son, Prince George Frederick Ernest Albert, became his heir. He was made Prince of Wales a few months after his father's accession in 1901, and when he became king George V in 1910, he was forty-four years old.

George was a man of great kindness and sympathy. He believed that the monarchy should come closer to the people, and in his reign he was to be seen in all kinds of places among them, to an extent that had not been the case for a very long time. He was loyal to his friends, strict but kind to his children, and he was generous with praise and with honours to people who served him well.

In 1893, he married Mary, daughter of the Duke of Teck, and they had five sons and a daughter, the eldest son becoming Edward VIII, and the next succeeding on Edward's abdication as George VI.

George entered the Royal Navy as a young man, for he loved the sea and was excited by the comparatively new ships of war which were powered not by sail but by steam. He rose through the ranks to become a commander, but when his brother's death brought him into the direct line of succession, he had to give up active service. He never lost his interest in naval affairs, and he was delighted when three of his four sons wanted to join the navy.

During his father's reign he undertook many royal duties, and he became immensely interested in the details of state and the procedures in which the monarch, in the increasingly complicated business of government, had to be involved. When he succeeded in 1910, government ministers found him to be a man of considerable wisdom and experience. It was as well, for almost at once the nation was plunged into political quarrelling, and he needed to steer a course of the utmost care through the difficulties.

The Liberals in the Commons wanted to curb the power of the Lords. Women, who were not allowed to vote, now began to demand this right. And there were agitations for giving Ireland Home Rule (see Rulers of Ireland). On top of all this, dark, threatening war-clouds were spreading over Europe.

The Liberals brought in a Parliament Bill. It said that any bill passed by the Commons in three succeeding sessions had

to become law, whether or not the Lords threw it out every time. The Lords were not to be able to throw out any money bill at all. Naturally, the peers were not inclined to pass the bill, so Asquith, the prime minister, went to the king and asked if he would create enough new peers to ensure its passage. George agreed, just as his ancestor William IV had done in 1832 over the Great Reform Bill. Asquith then told the House of Lords of the assurances given by the king. It would have meant making several hundred new lords, which would have been ridiculous, and so the Lords gave in.

The campaign for women's right to vote was understandable. While nearly every man over 21 could vote at elections, no such right belonged to any women. A great agitation for "Votes for Women" began and it was accompanied with some violence. The women's leaders, called Suffragettes (suffrage means vote), chained themselves to the railings in Downing Street, where the prime minister has his official home, and outside the House of Commons. Shop windows were broken, members of the government were attacked in the streets with whips and stones, and when these women were arrested and gaoled, they refused to eat, which meant that they had to be fed forcibly. One woman threw herself under a horse running in the Derby at which the king was present. Their campaign went on until it was interrupted by the outbreak of the First World War, in 1914.

This war, which began in the summer, involved nearly every nation in Europe. For more than four years millions of men were locked in a struggle to the death, and when it was over, the whole face of Europe was changed. Empires were broken up, monarchs forced off their thrones, and the boundaries of nations altered. And underneath the earth of the fighting areas lay the dead bodies of more than eight million soldiers.

The causes were complicated, but, by August 1914, Germany, Austria and Turkey found themselves ranged against Britain, France, Italy and Russia, and, later on, the United States, as the main combatants. The struggle was fought in France, Belgium, Italy, the Balkans, the Middle East, Russia and East Africa. It was fought at sea, and, for the first time, it was fought in the air. New weapons were used, such as the tank, poison gas and aeroplanes. Countless deeds of bravery were performed.

The Russian front collapsed when the Czar, Nicholas II, was driven off his throne and a new kind of government set up by millions of angry Russian peasants. A year later, in 1918, the allies defeated Germany, and both Austria and Turkey gave in as well.

The German Kaiser abdicated, so did the Austrian emperor. Their empires, as well as the Turkish, were split up into smaller states, many of them becoming republics with presidents as heads of state. Europe was indeed wearing a new look.

What did King George V think of all this? Naturally, he took an intense interest in the war, and he grieved as much as anyone over the huge casualty lists that were published in never-ending streams. He visited the troops in France, and would have liked to do much more. He wrote them a message: "I cannot share your hardships, but my heart is with you every hour of the day." On one visit, he was seriously injured when his horse was startled by a sudden noise and threw him to the ground. In spite of the private grief for dead loved-ones and fears for the living who were in danger, the whole nation was alarmed at the accident.

Once, when Field Marshal Earl Kitchener, the Secretary for War and the creator of the volunteer armies of Britain for the war, was attacked in the press for a shortage of ammunition supply at the front, which was not his fault, the public protested violently, for they regarded that tall, moustached soldier as their saviour. Copies of the offending papers were burned in the street, and George, to show that he agreed with

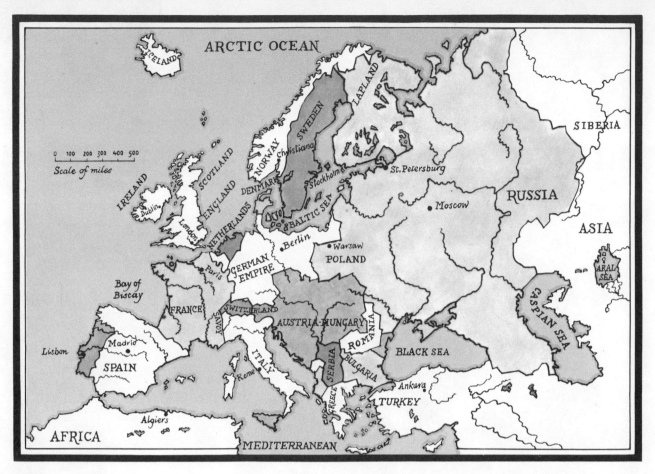

Europe in 1914

the people at once created Kitchener a Knight of the Garter. When Kitchener was drowned at sea on a voyage to Russia in 1916 to advise the Russian army chiefs on how best to stop the German advance into their territory, George led the nation in mourning for its great war leader.

After the war, Britain had time to turn to the many problems at home. The troops, coming back from the fronts, found that there were not enough jobs to go round, and many of them suffered terrible poverty. It was a poor reward for four years of fighting. Worse, the workers in the munitions factories were no longer wanted, and so the ranks of the unemployed swelled. The government paid out unemployment money, but it was not enough on which to live in many cases. So many countries had devoted their industries to production of war material that soon there was a shortage of ordinary goods. This pushed up the prices, but the wages of the workers did not

go up to meet them. Even those who were in jobs began to complain that they were not paid enough, and in 1926, there was a General Strike. This brought industrial production to a halt. But, the strike was broken when thousands of people from the professions rallied and kept the more urgent services, such as the delivery of food and milk, in motion.

One problem put off because of the interruption of the war was the campaign for women's voting rights. They had played so important a part in the war, by staffing military hospitals, by working in the fields and in the munitions factories, and by organising social services, that the government decided after all to give them the vote. In 1918, women over 30 were allowed to vote, and in that year the first woman member of Parliament, Lady Astor, was elected and took her seat. Later on, the vote was extended to all women over 21.

In 1931, the whole world was hit by a sudden falling off in trade, and its effects were felt deeply in Britain, as they were everywhere else. Prices rose again, unemployment grew, and for a time it looked as if there would be a general breakdown in industry. Then, gradually, as world markets improved, and as the government fought to prevent collapse by severe taxation, the position was put right.

The king was very disturbed by the plight of many of his people. There was little he could do, for it was the government's job to deal with the problems. What mattered most was the growth in confidence in Britain as a nation which would lead to better trading. So, he knew that this confidence would increase if the dignity and respect given to the monarchy continued, and he set out to achieve this aim. By his many appearances in public, his visits abroad, his sons' tours overseas, and his personal talks to the nation on Christmas Day every year over the new B.B.C. radio service, he provided the

country with an inspiration that earned the wonder of the world.

In 1935, George V and Mary celebrated their Silver Jubilee, and it was an event accompanied by rejoicing throughout the empire.

A little later that year he became seriously ill, and in January 1936, he died. The nation was plunged into grief, and many people thought that it was the end of an age of history. In Europe clouds of war were beginning to gather as Germany re-armed itself under a dictator, Adolf Hitler, and Italy, once the ally of Britain, now groaned under the heel of another dictator, Benito Mussolini. Both men aimed to expand the territories of their nations, and they threatened to use force to achieve it. How would Britain stand up to these men and their power? Did the death of the king mean that the empire would break up under this danger?

Edward VIII visits the coalminers in South Wales

EDWARD VIII [1936]

On December 11th, 1936, radio sets in Britain's homes, offices and factories were switched on. As they worked at their desks, turned their machines or rested in their armchairs, people from all over the country waited—to hear the voice of their king, Edward VIII, who had announced that he would speak to the nation. He had something of the greatest importance to tell them. Everyone knew what it would be, but they refused to believe it until they heard it from Edward himself.

And then, the recorded chimes of Big Ben were heard ringing out from the loudspeakers, an announcer introduced His Majesty the King, and with a clear, quiet voice he began his statement.

He told the nation that, after the most careful thought and with the greatest regret, he had decided to abdicate from the throne. He could not, he said, properly carry out his enormous responsibility without the woman he loved being at his side. As it was not possible to marry her and remain king, he must go.

It was the end of a short reign that had been full of promise for the future, and it was also the end of weeks of worry and unhappiness for him.

Why had the king to give up his throne to marry the woman he loved? His choice was an American lady who had divorced her first husband. Divorce was not so unusual, but this was different. The king was the Head of the Church of England, and divorce was not allowed by Church law. He could not marry a divorced lady without appearing to disregard one of the Church's basic teachings.

It was a cruel choice for him to make, and in it he had the sympathy and the understanding of the great part of the nation and the empire.

Edward was one of the most popular Princes of Wales in the history of the British monarchy. He was born in 1894, the eldest son of Prince George who became George V in 1910. He went to Osborne and then on to Dartmouth, two naval colleges, and afterwards studied at Oxford University.

When the first World War broke out, Edward longed to join the troops in the front line in France, but the king was loath to let him go. So he asked Lord Kitchener, a friend of the king's, to persuade him, but the great soldier would not. "What does it matter if I am killed?" protested the young prince, "I have four brothers." Kitchener looked down at him from his great height and answered: "If I were certain that you would be killed, I do not know if I should be right to restrain you. What I cannot allow is the chance of the enemy scoring you as a prisoner." All the same, he was eventually allowed to go, but he was kept away from the front lines.

After the war, Edward proved to be a most valuable help to his father, and he carried out many important duties. He travelled to most of the dominions on special tours and everywhere he was given most enthusiastic welcomes. The charm of his manner and the ease with which people found they could approach him won widespread affection, At home he took a keen interest in the plight of the unemployed ex-servicemen and grew to understand and sympathise with the grievances of the poorer people who suffered so much in the hard days of the 1920s. Many were the visits he paid to areas of unemployment, and unhappy as these poor people were, they always raised a thunderous cheer for the Prince of Wales.

Edward succeeded to the throne on January 26th, 1936, and at once he began to think of ways to bring the monarchy even closer to the people. It was then that he met Mrs Simpson and they fell in love. Unfortunately, when the government learnt of his desire to marry her, they brought all the pressure they could to prevent him. When it was clear that he would not change his mind, the prime minister, Stanley Baldwin, told Edward that he must make the choice. So he gave up the throne, and he was succeeded by his brother, the Duke of York, who became George VI.

Edward was created Duke of Windsor by the new king, but he left the country to live in Europe for a while. In June, 1937, he married Mrs Simpson, and they now live in retirement in France.

Prince Albert Frederick Arthur George, Duke of York, was the second son of King George V and Queen Mary. He went into the navy as a young man, for, like his father, he loved the sea and was immensely thrilled with the exciting new changes that were taking place in the building and equipping of warships. It was the age of the Dreadnought battleships, those great armour-plated vessels that carried turrets of heavy-calibre guns that could swivel through 180 degrees or more and discharge their batteries of shells either side of the ship. During the first World War he served in the Iron Duke, the flagship of Admiral Jellicoe, the Commander-in-Chief of the Grand Fleet.

Later on in the war, he transferred to the newly-created Royal Air Force and soon passed his test as an aeroplane pilot.

Like the Prince of Wales, he undertook many tours of the British dominions and colonies after the war, and on one occasion he went to Australia to open the new Parliament building at Canberra.

In 1923, he married Lady Elizabeth Bowes-Lyon, daughter of the Earl of Strathmore and Kinghorne, who was a descendent of the family of Lady Jane Grey, the Nine Days Queen. Their first daughter is now Her Majesty Queen Elizabeth II and their second is Princess Margaret, Countess of Snowdon.

Prince Albert was a quiet and thoughtful man, with the same charm of manner as his brother, Edward. He and his wife were immensely popular, and when in December 1936, Edward VIII abdicated, they were accepted with great enthusiasm as the new King and Queen. He was styled as George VI. They made a state visit to France in 1938, and the next year they went to Canada and the United States. George was the first British monarch to set foot on American soil. Both were given a wonderful welcome, and it was as well that they were for soon Britain and the whole empire was to be involved in a desperate war, and the mother country was going to need all the

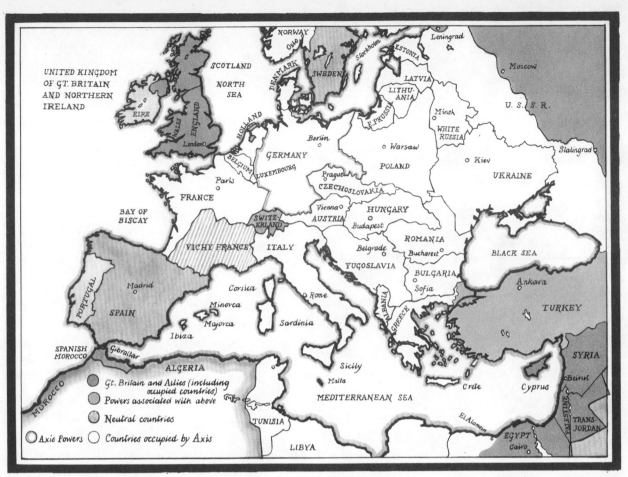

Map of Europe during the Second World War

help she could get from the dominions and the U.S.A.

Once more, Europe was threatened with war, and once again it was Germany that was the aggressor. The German dictator, Adolf Hitler, had begun to expand the territory of Germany. He bullied smaller nations, like Austria and Czechoslovakia, into surrendering their independence and becoming part of his empire by threatening them with aerial destruction of their cities.

Then, in 1939, Hitler went a step too far. Finding that he could not bully Poland with threats, he ordered his powerful armies to invade. At once Britain ordered Hitler to withdraw, or the country would go to war with him. He ignored the demand, and on September 3rd, 1939, war was declared. That evening, the king spoke to the nation over the wireless, and he asked the people to stand behind him and the government in the prosecution of the war to a victorious end.

By June 1940, France, Belgium, Holland, Denmark and Norway, all had fallen before the jack-booted German invaders, and Britain stood alone to face the seemingly unconquerable Hitler. It was then that the greatest man of our history came to the forefront as prime minister to direct the British war effort, and to defy the Germans. His name was Winston Churchill, a man who already had a long career of adventure, politics and soldiering behind him.

Churchill was one of the finest war leaders of all history. He inspired the nation to tremendous efforts by his stirring speeches. He organised the armed forces and the civilian population to resist German attacks by sea, by land and from the air. He encouraged the conquered nations of Europe to have hope that soon they would be liberated. When Hitler gave up the attempt to invade England, because his massive air fleets were crippled by a much smaller Royal Air Force in the Battle of Britain, in 1940, he turned his attention bombed areas, not only during air raids but also afterwards, when buildings beside him were in danger of collapsing about his feet. He visited ships of the Royal Navy at sea in the Atlantic, no matter that the waters were filled with German submarines, and later on he went to the army fronts in North Africa, Italy and France, to talk to the brave fighting men who were gradually driving the Germans back towards their own country.

The king and Churchill were very great friends. George took a deep interest in the direction of the war, and Churchill would frequently visit him and tell him of the latest government battle plans. When the British, American and Dominion forces crossed the channel to invade Normandy in June 1944, and so begin the liberation of the countries under German rule, both George and Churchill wanted to go with them. They had a long talk about it, but for every argument that Churchill put forward why the king should not risk his life, George answered with equally strong reasons that Churchill, too, ought not to go. So neither of them went, but later on, both the king and Churchill visited the troops in France and Germany.

At the end of April, 1945, Hitler, his dreams of world conquest having come to nothing, and he himself being besieged in an underground shelter in Berlin by advancing Soviet forces, took his own life. A few days later the Germans surrendered.

On the evening of Victory in Europe Day, May 8th, 1945, the king and the queen, with their daughters, came out on the balcony at Buckingham Palace to acknowledge the cheers of the colossal throng of happy people that filled the Mall and all the other roads leading to the Palace. With the royal family stood Churchill, the architect of victory.

The Japanese were finally brought to surrender when two of their cities, Hiroshima and Nagasaki, were obliterated by a most deadly weapon, the atomic bomb, in August 1945. The war was over, and now the world had to pick up the pieces and try

to U.S.S.R. On June 22nd, 1941, he launched a vast invasion of that huge country and within weeks he had overrun more than a million square miles of Soviet homeland. At once Churchill offered the fast retreating Soviet army the support of Britain in money and weapons. When, in December 1941, the Japanese treacherously attacked the United States naval base at Pearl Harbor in Hawaii, Churchill and the U.S. President, Roosevelt, joined hands and set out to destroy the forces of all three enemies, Germany, Italy and Japan.

The years 1940 and 1941 were hard for Britain. Convoys of supplies from abroad were attacked at sea by German U-boat submarines and many ships were sunk. German squadrons of heavy bombers poured thousands of tons of bombs on cities and towns. Even the king's own London home, Buckingham Palace, was heavily damaged by a stick of bombs.

During these days George showed great personal courage by visiting his people in to build a better place in which to live.

Soon after the victory in Europe, there was a General Election in Britain. The Labour Party, formed at the beginning of the century to fight for the interests of the working classes, had been growing steadily in strength, and now it won a sweeping victory over the Conservatives. Under its leader, Clement Attlee, later Earl Attlee, the new government began a number of reforms that were almost revolutionary. A national health service provided free medical treatment, no matter how prolonged or complicated, for the price of a few shillings a week. Certain industries which had been run by private companies were taken over by the government—a process which is called nationalisation—and these included the railways, the civil airlines and the coal mines. It was hoped that they would be run more efficiently, but if they were, it also cost more to buy their products or services.

The government also began the scheme of giving self-government to the regions of the vast British empire. India, of which the king was Emperor, was divided into two, the Republic of India and the Dominion of Pakistan, both new nations remaining within the British Commonwealth, a term to describe the association of all the former British colonies.

During these times of change, the king continued with his heavy and endless programme of visits, tours, official openings and meetings. It was very tiring and as his health had never been strong, it began to wear him down. In 1951, when he opened the Festival of Britain in London, to celebrate the centenary of the Great Exhibition of 1851, he looked very ill indeed. It was not long before newspapers wondered about him, and one of them asked, in large, black letters on its front page, "What is wrong with our King?" It demanded to know the state of his health and whether everything was being done to look after him.

In September that year he had a serious operation on the lungs. For days the nation waited in anxiety, until it was announced

George VI opens the Festival of Britain

that he was making good progress after the ordeal. But there were some who knew that it was only a respite. At Christmas, he spoke to the nation, as he had done every Christmas Day since his accession, but he did not sound at all well.

On February 5th, 1952, George was at his country home at Sandringham, in Norfolk. He was feeling quite well, and he had had a good day's shooting. After dinner he retired to bed and soon went to sleep. He never woke again, for during the night he had a heart attack and died.

143

Her Majesty the Queen was born on April 21st, 1926 in London, the elder daughter of the Duke and Duchess of York, who later became King George VI and Queen Elizabeth. During the war she served in Britain with the Auxiliary Territorial Service, a women's army corps attached to the British Army, and which later became the Women's Royal Army Corps.

On her twenty-first birthday, in 1947, when she was accompanying her father and mother on an official tour of South Africa, she made a speech to the peoples of the British Empire in which she pledged to devote her entire life to their service, and since that date she has carried out that promise in the greatest measure.

In the same year, she was married to her third cousin, Lieutenant Philip Mountbatten, who had the day before been made Duke of Edinburgh. The wedding was held in Westminster Abbey on November 20th, and it was the occasion for a splendid pageant. Huge crowds lined all the pavements along the route from Buckingham Palace to the Abbey, and the royal couple were given a wonderful reception.

It was while they were on a tour of the Commonwealth in February 1952 that the tragic news of the death of King George VI was announced. The Princess, now Queen Elizabeth II, returned to England at once. A year later she was crowned in Westminster Abbey, on June 2nd, and it was a coronation day that will always be specially remembered, for it was also the day on which the news came that the highest mountain in the world, Mount Everest, had at last been climbed to the top, by a New Zealander, Edmund Hillary, and a Sherpa, Tensing, in an expedition led by Sir John Hunt.

The Queen came to the throne soon after the Labour government of Mr Attlee had fallen and had been replaced by a Conservative government, led again by Winston Churchill. This great man, who had more experience of the world, of politics and of statecraft than anyone else in Britain, was to prove a great help to the young monarch. The world was beset with great problems—and indeed it is still troubled today.

Britain had her share of problems after the Second World War. Although the country, with its allies the United States and the Soviet Union, had won the war decisively, Britain came out of the struggle much worse off economically than she was at the beginning. To maintain enough armies, fleets of ships and squadrons of aeroplanes the country had had to borrow vast amounts of money from the generous United States government and from countries in the British Empire like Canada, Australia, New Zealand and South Africa. When it was over, something had to be paid towards the debts.

There were other problems. Britain's huge empire began to disintegrate. Canada, Australia, New Zealand and South Africa already had very wide powers of self-government. Now the other members quite rightly wanted independence, too, and the post-war Labour Government (1945–51) under Clement Attlee started the process of dismantling the empire by granting independence to India and creating the state of Pakistan. Independence for Burma soon followed. Winston Churchill's government (1951–55), Sir Anthony Eden's (1955–57), Harold Macmillan's (1957–63) and Harold Wilson's (1964–70) continued the process, and a host of new independent states took their seats in the United Nations Assembly, among them Ghana, Kenya, Uganda, Tanzania, Sierra Leone, Guyana, Malaysia, the Sudan, Malawi, Zambia and many others.

The word empire was dropped and the nations that had once formed it were bracketed under the term Commonwealth. Most—though not all—of the old colonies have remained inside the Commonwealth, and in this respect there is still a vital role for the Queen to play as its head.

In the chapters up to this one, the story of the development of the monarchy has been unfolded. Once, the kings were all-powerful and the people did much as they

were told. Gradually, the king's subjects obtained the right to make laws and carry out reforms, until in the present century all power lies with the elected representatives of the people in Parliament. This change has done more than reduce the power of the monarchy: it has made it much more popular, and while some of the kings of the past were loved and feared at the same time, now the monarchs are respected and admired without fear. It should also be understood that in many instances the monarchs stood as a brake against the aristocracy bullying the lower classes. John, for example, was well aware that Magna Carta was not going to do much for the ordinary man in the town or in the field.

The Queen has done as she promised in 1947—maintained the unity of the Commonwealth, and in this respect she must stand as one of the very few monarchs in world history to have kept her promise. To make it more effective she has travelled with her husband all over the Commonwealth, and she has visited many foreign lands as well. When she has not been able to go to a Commonwealth nation that has just been given self-government, she has

sent one of her relations to represent her.

It should not be overlooked that there have been more changes in society, in the ways in which we look at traditions and conventions, in the last twenty years than in any comparable period of history. As the monarchy has been kept constantly under the public eye through press and television, it has had to bring itself up to date. It is generally conceded that both Queen Elizabeth and Prince Philip have done this very well. All round the world kings have been toppled from their throne, some even murdered (like Feisal II of Iraq in 1958), and many monarchies have been abolished altogether. In some lands those that have remained have been reduced to equality with ordinary citizens. Throughout all this the British monarchy has remained intact and has been greatly strengthened. The royal family has come closer to the people of Britain and the Commonwealth. Much of the stiff formality and rigid protocol of the Court have been broken down or modified to fit in with the ideas of the times. Gallup polls consistently show, however, that Britain wants to retain its monarchy, and enjoys the pageantry and splendour of state occasions like the opening of Parliament and visits from heads of foreign states. Nor is there any serious opposition to the cost of the monarchy, namely, the price of a single packet of cigarettes in one year for every adult in the kingdom.

From Queen Elizabeth's accession in October 1964 the country was governed by the Conservative Party and in that time many changes took place. Britain provided, and still provides, a major contribution to the North Atlantic Treaty Organization, a union of countries in western Europe which is ready to stand up to any danger of war on the Continent. Millions of pounds are given every year to new and under-developed nations to help them stimulate their industries and agriculture and so take their place in the world.

At the end of January 1965, the Queen attended the state funeral of Sir Winston Churchill in St Paul's Cathedral. He had died, aged ninety, on 24th January, mourned by everyone in Britain, the Commonwealth, the United States and many other lands. It was the first time a sovereign had attended the funeral of a commoner—a unique tribute to the man who saved Britain, Europe—perhaps the world—in the dark days of the Second World War and who is rightly regarded as the greatest Englishman of all time.

In 1966 a general election took place and a Labour Government was returned to power with a majority of nearly 100 seats. This government set out to continue expanding British industry and improving the national economy. It passed a number of far-reaching acts of benefit to the community, dealing with such things as rents of houses and flats, profits made on property deals, and it tried as well to control wages and prices.

Map of the World in 1945

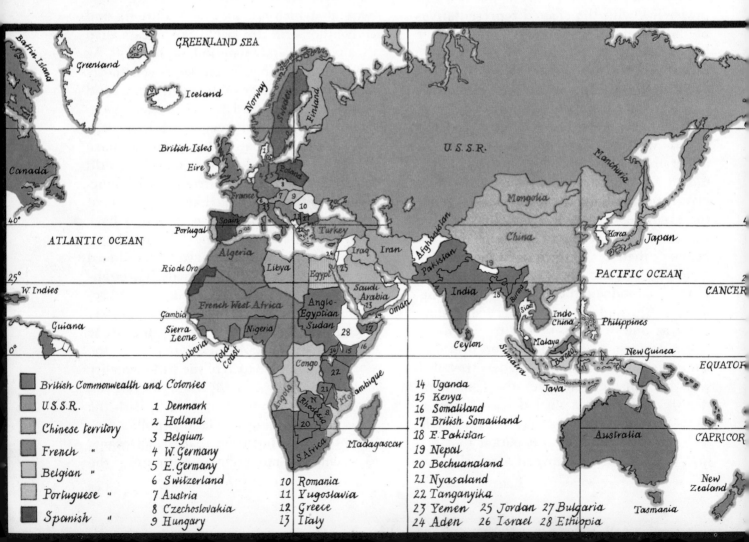

The State Funeral of Sir Winston Churchill

At a by-election at Carmarthen in Wales in June 1966 Mr Gwynfor Evans, a Welsh-speaking market gardener, won a seat in the House of Commons for the Welsh National Party, Plaid Cymru. It was the first time that a Welsh Nationalist has ever been sent to Westminster, and it was a sign of the nationalism that has for some time been growing strong in Wales. A year later, Mrs Winifred Ewing, won a seat for the Scottish Nationalists at Hamilton, evidence of an equally resurgent Scottish nationalism. Both countries were promised a greater measure of self-determination by the Conservative prime minister, Edward Heath, whose party won the general election in 1970.

Perhaps the most momentous event of Queen Elizabeth's reign so far has been the entry of the United Kingdom in 1972 into the Common Market, otherwise known as the European Economic Community. The nation has been sharply divided on this issue. Opponents say Britain will lose her independence and become part of some bigger United States of Europe. If this happens, it will threaten the position of the monarchy. Supporters deny this and say the union is an economic one, and that none of the member nations' existing forms of government should be affected. Time alone will tell, but whatever the Queen may have thought privately, she has welcomed the event publicly. If Britain cannot be a great power in the world there is nothing to stop it being a great power in Europe.

In a world which is at the present time largely a curious mixture of democratically run republics and one-party dictatorships, a monarchy may seem out of place. The Queen has disproved this by adapting her august position to the times.

147

Rulers of WALES

When the Britons invaded the Gael-inhabited isles and drove their kinsmen into South Wales, across the sea to Ireland, and up country to parts of Scotland, they settled in England and in North Wales. They did not mix very much with the Gaels, as we have seen in the Introduction to the Rulers of England section, and, if they did, often made their kinsmen their subjects and forced them to work as serfs.

The chief men among the Britons were the Druids, who were priests and scribes, men of learning; they wrote poetry and were able to devise a system of law. They worshipped their strange gods in oak groves, for they regarded the oak as a sacred tree. There, they would get involved in complicated rituals, which included sacrificing human beings to their gods. Such was the power of their religion that they could control the minds and the fears of the people.

When the Romans came to Britain, it was the Druids who put up the strongest resistance to them. The Romans considered the Druids barbarians, and wherever they went they tried to stamp Druidism out altogether. Though most of what is now England was conquered by them in the twenty years after the invasion of Aulus Plautius in A.D. 43, they had great difficulty in subduing the Britons in Wales. It took another twenty years to complete the conquest, and this was done when the Druids made a final but fruitless stand on the island of Anglesey, where they were said to have fought to the last man.

The Romans then built fortified towns, the two largest being at Deva (Chester) and at Isca (Caerleon-on-Usk), to keep the Britons under control. Then they constructed a network of roads through Wales, and placed smaller fortresses along them at regular intervals.

When the Romans had to abandon Britain to its fate at the beginning of the fifth century, the people had become Christians in England and Wales, and so far as Wales was concerned they were to remain so ever afterwards. The invasions of England by the Angles and Saxons uprooted the faith, for the invaders had gods of their own, like Woden, Thor and Balder. These invaders settled down in their newly-won lands, and so for many years the Britons in Wales were left alone.

Even in these times of relief from foreign invasion the Britons could not agree among themselves, and there was constant civil warfare between the tribal chiefs for the supreme power.

One chief who had a measure of success was Maelgwn, a tall and powerful warrior, who was capable of dreadful cruelty. He is said to have murdered some of his relations. At the same time, he was devoted to learning and he encouraged poets and historians.

Maelgwn, who was born towards the end of the fifth century, aimed at uniting all the people of Wales, but he seems only to have succeeded in doing so in Gwynedd, which was roughly the area of Merioneth, Caernarvon, Anglesey and part of Denbigh. He died in 547 and it is not known who was his successor. He was, however, the ancestor of Rhodri Mawr, the first prince of Wales about whom we are able to write a biographical piece.

The next three hundred years of Welsh history are very obscure. From time to time a strong man would appear and would assert some kind of dominion over his

Caedwalla, Prince of Gwynedd

neighbours, but it would vanish as soon as he died. Some of them fought against the English with success. Some even joined one English king in his war against another English king. One was Caedwalla, prince of Gwynedd at the beginning of the seventh century. He marched with Penda, King of Mercia, and together they defeated Edwin, King of Northumbria, near Doncaster in 633. A year later, Edwin's nephew, Oswald, fought Caedwalla at another battle and the Welsh prince was slain.

The civil warfare continued in Wales and it so weakened the country that it became an easy prey to border raiding parties of English warriors, who harried the countryside and slaughtered the people with great cruelty. Then, as had happened in England, Scotland and Ireland, Wales was struck by Viking raids. These warriors attacked monasteries and towns on the lengthy Welsh coastline, burned buildings and fields, and seized what riches they could find. Because the Welsh were not united they were unable to resist the attacks. The situation called for a strong leader, and in the ninth century such a man arose. He was Rhodri, called Mawr (which means "The Great").

Rhodri was a descendant of Maelgwn, and probably born on the island of Anglesey. In 844, he succeeded to the princedom of Gwynedd, and from the very beginning he determined to unite the different princedoms of Wales into a complete nation. It would have been a very hard task, for the Welsh were a proud race, but their pride was more local than national, and a man who had either succeeded as a prince or

churches and houses, burning farms and seizing goods, and then sailing off again, only to return later.

We know very little about Rhodri's career, but it is recorded that he succeeded in defeating the Vikings, almost as decisively as Ecgbert had done at Hingston Down. But Rhodri had another enemy, and that was the English, who wanted the lands of Wales.

By 855, Rhodri had become master of the northern half of Wales, and now he set

The Vikings crushed by Rhodri Mawr

fought and won such a position would not readily give it up to become an underling. Rhodri would have known about the aims of Ecgbert of Wessex, who by 828 had brought most of England under his rule, and he would have explained to other princes the value of joining together to present a united front against the Viking raids, which Wales, like England and Scotland, was undergoing at the time. The Vikings were behaving in much the same way on the Welsh coast, raiding, sacking

out to conquer the remainder. He marshalled an army and brought it down the mountainous tracks of central Wales and in Ceredigion (Cardigan) he defeated the local chiefs in a great battle and added their lands to his dominion. After this, the rest of the princes recognised him as their overlord.

We do not know what Rhodri looked like, nor what were his particular gifts. He must have been rather like Ecgbert or Alfred, or Kenneth MacAlpine, for he could only have reached his position by both courage and skill as a leader of men. He must, too, have had the same sense of national pride.

In 856, the Vikings raided Anglesey, at about the same time that their raids grew in strength against England. Rhodri assembled a force and there in a great battle he crushed them, killing their leader, Horm.

In the year when Alfred became king of England, that is, 871, Rhodri was again troubled with Viking attacks, as was Alfred, too. There is no record of the two men

ever having met, but we can imagine that had they done so, there would have been much in common for them to talk about.

In 878, Rhodri set out on another expedition against the Vikings, again in Anglesey, but, in the fighting, he was killed. At once his work of unity broke up. There was then no rule in Wales that an eldest son should inherit the main power or wealth of his father; these were divided between all the sons, and as Rhodri left several, it is easy to see why a civil war

followed, for none of them would allow the others to be richer than himself.

His supremacy over Wales was not passed on, though the princes of Gwynedd claimed to be overlords of all the other princedoms, and more often than not they managed to assert this claim.

With Rhodri the idea of a family of princes, however, was born, and all succeeding rulers, not only of Gwynedd, but of many of the other states, were in some way or other related to him.

Anarawd was Rhodri's eldest son, and he inherited the princedom of Gwynedd. His brothers received the other states, over which they had ruled as governors in their father's time. They began to war among each other, and this was a sad time for Wales, for it interrupted their progress of developing their agriculture, laws and way of life.

Anarawd had proved to be a courageous commander under his father in the fighting against the Vikings. When he succeeded, he joined with some of his brothers and drove the Vikings out of Caernarvonshire in a battle near Conway. Thus they avenged the death of their father, but no sooner was there peace than they fell out among each other.

Perhaps because he wanted to show the English king, Alfred, that Gwynedd was the leading princedom of Wales, Anarawd crossed the border into England and met Alfred for talks. The English king received him with great honour, and bestowed a number of gifts upon him. When Anarawd was baptised, Alfred stood as his godfather. Anarawd offered to recognise England as overlord kingdom, but of course this was not acceptable to his brothers.

We know no more about Anarawd, except that the rest of his reign was taken up with fighting with his brothers, and he died in 916.

HYWEL DDA [*Howel the Good: 916-950*]

Hywel was the grandson of Rhodri Mawr, by his second son, Cadel, who was under-prince of Ceredigion and Deheubarth. He is the only Welsh prince described as "The Good," and this was because of his achievement of setting down a new code of laws for the Welsh.

Hywel became prince of Ceredigion and Deheubarth, when Anarawd's son, Idwal, ruled Gwynedd. He was not a warlike man at all. He was, like Alfred, learned and specially interested in law. He believed that his grandfather's aim to unite the country would be easier to achieve if the people had one set of laws applicable to everybody, and that this unity ought not to be obtained by unnecessary fighting and slaughter.

In 918, he paid homage to Edward the Elder of England, and did so again to Edward's successor, Athelstan. For the first years of his rule he tried to bring order to his princedoms, by putting down local fighting between landowners. Then in 928, he made a pilgrimage to Rome.

For Hywel this was a most important step. We can assume that his domains were at peace for him to risk an absence from them of several months, which a journey to and from Rome would have entailed. He was greatly impressed by what he saw on his travels, and in particular he admired the systems of law which he observed. When he returned to Wales, he sent out letters to all the princes, summoning them and their chief advisers to an assembly at a large hunting lodge which he had on the river Teifi, near Whitland, in Carmarthenshire.

There was no reason why the princes, none of whom would recognise each other's superiority, should obey the summons, but they heard of his travels and they believed that he might offer some solution to the constant quarrelling that went on between them, fighting that must have been exhausting. So most of them came.

The conference lasted several weeks, and it was one of the most famous meetings in Welsh history. The laws and customs of all the princedoms were closely examined, and then, after much sorting out, in which confusions and peculiarities were removed, they were put down in writing in a code.

This code had two results. First, it gave the Welsh a law common to everyone, and secondly, it did a great deal to foster a spirit among the people of belonging to one nation. Though the wars went on between the princedoms for long afterwards, Hywel's code, more than anything, guaranteed the lasting of the Welsh feeling of nationalism, right down into the Middle Ages—perhaps even to this day.

Hywel's code had one unusual quality. It

Hywel Dda's assembly in Carmarthen

was very humane. Punishments for law breaking were generally in the form of fines. For example, if a local lord was detected fighting with another one, he would be made to pay to the prince a hundred or more cattle. This was a heavy penalty, for the main source of earning in those days was through cattle-farming.

This code made Hywel respected throughout Wales, and he was recognised as the leading prince. When he died in 950, the state of peace came to an end.

IAGO ap IDWAL [950-979]

When Hywel Dda died, his sons continued to rule Ceredigion and Deheubarth, but in Gwynedd the chiefs elected Iago, the son of Anarawd's son, Idwal. Iago had a brother Ieuaf whom he retained as his chief adviser. They believed that victory in battle was the best way to prove who was overlord, and they opened war on their neighbours. At Nant Carno they crushed the army of Powys, and then brought an even larger force down to Ceredigion, in 952. Two years later, Hywel's sons invaded

Gwynedd, but they were utterly routed at Llanrwst. It looked as if Iago's belief was justified, for he was now the most powerful prince in Wales.

Iago and Ieuaf then fell out, and the latter was captured and imprisoned. Iago continued to rule, and he was one of the princes who paid homage to Eadgar of England in 973, on the occasion when the English king was rowed across the river Dee by eight other princes.

In 979, Hywel, Ieuaf's son, rebelled against Iago and captured him. He seized Gwynedd for himself, and took as his chief adviser his brother Cadwallon.

HYWEL ap IEUAF [979-985] and
CADWALLON [985-986]

Hywel ruled for six years. We know nothing of his activities, but as he is described in Welsh histories as Hywel the Bad, presumably his rule was harsh and unpopular. When he died in 985, his brother Cadwallon succeeded him, but he was slain a year later by Maredudd ap Owain ap Hywel Dda.

MAREDUDD ap Owain ap Hywel Dda
[986–999]

Maredudd (Meredith) was the grandson of Hywel Dda, and he was prince of Ceredigion and Deheubarth. He was a courageous soldier and a skilful general. He determined to unite Wales, and to keep out the Viking raiders, and his whole reign was occupied with these two ambitions.

In 986, he invaded Gwynedd and slew Cadwallon in battle. He then declared himself prince of Gwynedd. He also brought Powys under his control and thus was ruler of the best part of Wales. He appears to have governed well, for in some later histories he is described as the most famous king of the Britons (the Welsh were called Britons by historians for many generations, because they were the descendants of the original Britons against whom the Roman conquerors had fought).

Like Aethelred II of England, Maredudd was vexed with Viking raids, but unlike that cowardly English monarch, Maredudd fought bravely against them and did not resort to paying heavy bribes to get them to go away. Indeed, there were occasions when Vikings paid him sums of money in exchange for captured warriors.

Maredudd died in 999, and he left no son. His daughter, Angharad, was married to Llywelyn ap Seisyll, a descendant of Rhodri Mawr, and this Llywelyn was later to be a powerful prince.

CYNAN ap HYWEL ap IEUAF [999–1008]

When Maredudd died, his dominions broke up because his son-in-law Llywelyn ap Seisyll was not strong enough to continue the rule. At once, all Wales divided again into separate and independent princedoms, recognising no overlord. Cynan, grandson of the Ieuaf who was captured and imprisoned in the time of Iago ap Idwal, seized power in Gwynedd, but the story of his reign—and indeed of all Wales—was the tale of endless fighting for supremacy. For twenty years no one prince emerged on top. Laws were broken, farming was neglected, families were divided against each other, and the whole country was in a state of anarchy. When Cynan died, probably in 1008, there was no clear successor, only a series of pretenders.

LLYWELYN ap SEISYLL [1018–1023]

Llywelyn ap Seisyll had been for years building up a small but tough band of followers, who, like him, were bent on ending the fighting and setting up one overlord prince. In 1018, he was ready to move, and he marched to Gwynedd, deposed one of the pretenders, Aedden, and made himself prince of the state. Then he turned on Ceredigion and Deheubarth and conquered them both. For a time, he was real overlord in Wales, for his army was superior to any of the hastily raised units that other chiefs could put into the field.

This overlordship was exceptionally prosperous for Wales, for the early historians have stressed the well being of the country. That is not to say that Wales was generally starving by any means, but this seems to have been a notable period. Tragically, however, it was short.

Llywelyn lived for some of the time in a mansion at Aberffraw, in Anglesey, and round him he gathered a court of chiefs and advisers who undertook the business of government at his direction. They were particularly concerned with seeing that the code of Hywel Dda was observed as far as possible, though because of the mountainous nature of the countryside in the north, communication between the regions was slow, and lawlessness was never completely controlled.

There are no accurate details of the kind of prosperity enjoyed by Wales at this time, but we do hear that cattle-farming, previously interrupted by the constant warfare, had a breathing space in which to develop. Possibly, some of the finer livestock were exported to England which had also suffered damage to its agriculture in the time of Aethelred II.

Llywelyn was occupied in dealing with Viking raids, and when, in 1023, he was racing across Ceredigion to Dyfed (Pembrokeshire) to come to the aid of the town of St David's he saw many houses in flames, as he came up to the walls. St David's was a centre of Christianity and of religious teaching, and the sight of the town being ravaged by the Vikings saddened him so much that he became ill and died. He left a son, Gruffydd ap Llywelyn ap Seisyll, who was only a child.

155

IAGO ap IDWAL ap MEURIG (1023-1039)

Iago was a descendant of Rhodri Mawr, and he became prince of Gwynedd on the death of Llywelyn. Some histories have said that he was overlord prince of Wales, but the whole of his reign was taken up with fighting between the princes, and the state of anarchy, which prevailed in the time of Cynan, was repeated. Iago seems to have held on to power in Gwynedd, possibly because the other princes were so busy fighting one another that they had no time nor resources to attack him. He was murdered in 1039, and the throne of Gwynedd was seized by Gruffydd ap Llywelyn ap Seisyll, who was now a fully grown man.

GRUFFYDD ap LLYWELYN ap SEISYLL
[1039-1063]

One New Year's Eve in the 1030s, a youngish man lay sprawled in a chair in a big house in North Wales, gazing into the crackling log fire. He had been sitting there for hours, interrupting his rest only by taking huge hunks of bread and cheese from a table, and washing them down with draughts of ale. He was Gruffydd, son of Llywelyn ap Seisyll, who had died at St Davids in 1023.

Suddenly, his sister burst into the room, shaking her fists at him.

"You have been skulking around here long enough," she cried. "I am tired of your idling. It's been going on for months. What would your father have said to you, a prince of the great house of Rhodri?"

Gruffydd looked at her, not stirring for a moment, not really taking in what she was saying.

She spoke again. "Now, take this," she shouted, throwing his coat at him, "and get out of this house. Don't come back again until you can prove that you are worthy of your father."

Slowly, the idle young man got up, put on his coat, and walked out of the front door. Outside, it was cold, and there was a bitter wind. He wandered along the road for a while, until he came upon a house

inside which was a crowd of people, talking, laughing and singing, enjoying the celebration of the New Year.

He went up to a window and he looked through. There he could see a gathering of people sitting round a huge cauldron on a fire, filled with boiling gravy in which were floating large lumps of beef. The men were digging at the beef with sharp sticks. He overheard one saying to another that he couldn't understand why, every time he pushed the lump to the bottom, it rose again to the surface as soon as he lifted off the stick. They tried again and again to make the meat stay at the bottom, but with the same result.

Suddenly, Gruffydd was struck with the obstinacy of the beef lumps rising to the surface as soon as the sticks were removed. He believed it was some sort of prophecy of his own future. He would try to make a kingdom out of Wales, he would be hampered and pushed down, but he would rise again.

From that moment, he became a changed

A Welsh raid into England

man, as the legend tells; there would be no more idling, for there was an important task to carry out.

Immediately, he set about raising an army of tough, brave and patriotic men, and after training it, he led it into Gwynedd, in 1039. Finding that Iago, the prince, had just been murdered, he seized the throne and challenged the chiefs to gainsay him. But none would come. Then he marched into Powys and conquered it, making himself lord of all north Wales.

Soon afterwards, now commander of a large and devoted army, he crossed the border into England and laid waste vast areas of land, capturing the livestock and defeating the local English levies that came came against him.

Then, near Welshpool, a large force of Mercian English gathered to fight him, but in a great battle he thoroughly defeated them. This victory spread his fame throughout Wales. Here was a real prince and conqueror.

A few years later, he crushed an army under a prince of Deheubarth and then added that princedom to his domains. The remaining chiefs recognised him as their overlord, and Rhodri's dream of a united Wales seemed to have come true. In the *Anglo-Saxon Chronicle* he is described as King of Wales, and on the Hereford and Shropshire borders his name was held in great dread.

To ensure that his domains would not be troubled by the English in the future, he married a daughter of Aelfgar, a son of the Mercian earl Leofric, thus cementing an alliance with central England. He took his bride to Rhuddlan where he had a mansion.

In 1063, Harold, Earl of Wessex, and chief adviser to Edward the Confessor led an expedition against Gruffydd at Rhuddlan. During the siege of his camp, Gruffydd was betrayed by one of his men and murdered. His head was cut off and sent to Harold as a peace offering.

The Welsh were soon to regret the sad end to their great prince, for the chiefs whom Gruffydd had conquered now began to fight among each other for the various parts of his dominion.

157

When Gruffydd was treacherously murdered, Bleddyn, his half-brother, became prince of Gwynedd, and lord of Powys.

Bleddyn was a gentle and courteous prince, and he had the same qualities of leadership and bravery of his half-brother. But, though he set out to keep the control over all Wales that Gruffydd had managed to assert, he could not command the allegiance of the south. He had rebellions in Gwynedd and Powys to deal with, and the southern chiefs took advantage of his preoccupation by re-affirming the old sway they had held before Gruffydd took it from them.

There was a new danger to Wales at this time, and this was the arrival of the Normans. When William of Normandy had defeated and killed Harold II in 1066, he set out to subdue the rest of England, and crush the pockets of resistance that held out for a few years. Bleddyn assisted the English in Shropshire, Herefordshire and Worcestershire, and in 1067, he carried out a raid on the Normans in Hereford. It was a temporary check, however, to the conquerors, and soon Bleddyn had to retire to Gwynedd.

Bleddyn was a man of great humanity and kindness. He earned a reputation for mercy over defeated enemies, and lives were spared wherever possible after a battle. He also had great interest in law, and in his time he made many amendments to the code of Hywel Dda, bringing it up to date to meet the changes of the past century and a half.

Once the Normans had established themselves as rulers of England, they turned their attentions to Wales. There were three main routes along which they planned to carry out an invasion, through the valleys of the Dee, the Severn and the Wye. They built castles along the English-Welsh border, at Chester, Shrewsbury, Montgomery, Hereford, Abergavenny and Chepstow, and so formed an impregnable line of fortification. Each castle was manned with hundreds of mail-clad troops, tough

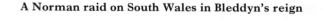

A Norman raid on South Wales in Bleddyn's reign

soldiers who had fought with the Conqueror at Senlac and in Normandy.

One of the Conqueror's barons, Hugh of Avranches, occupied Chester, and with his army he moved up the Dee Valley, along the north coast of Flintshire and Denbighshire. He reached Rhuddlan, built a castle and seized the old palace of Gruffydd ap Llywelyn. The people of Gwynedd were driven back into the Snowdon mountains.

From Shrewsbury, another baron, Roger of Montgomery, took a strong force up the Severn valley towards Montgomery (from which he took his name), and there set up a base for future attacks into the heart of Wales.

The third baron, William FitzOsbern, marched from Hereford down the Wye valley towards Brecon, where a fortress was erected.

Within a few years, then, the Normans had planted a firm foothold in Wales.

In the meanwhile, Bleddyn tried to keep his Gwynedd people together and urged them to resist the Normans, but after a fierce struggle with the governor of Rhuddlan, he was killed, in 1075.

TRAHAERN [1075-1081]

When Bleddyn was killed, his nephews and cousins began to fight for his throne. Gwynedd was by then the only kingdom that was not largely overrun by Normans. It was sad for the Welsh, that their chiefs should have preferred to fight each other rather than combine to throw out the invader. There was one of Bleddyn's cousins, however, who did try to inspire a feeling of unity, and that was Trahaern, a soldier of energy and ability, who marched into Gwynedd and seized the throne.

His reign was short, and the only event of importance was a revolt by Gruffydd ap Cynan, the grandson of Iago ap Idwal ap Meurig, who also claimed the throne of Gwynedd. Trahaern put this revolt down and drove Gruffydd into exile in Ireland.

Trahaern died in 1081, fighting against Gruffydd who had returned and defeated him at a battle at Mynydd Carn.

One day in 1094, the city of Chester was bustling with activity. Normally a busy town, as it was a centre of trade, on this day business was exceptionally brisk, for a number of merchants from Wales had come in with their wares. The taverns were filled with happy buyers and sellers, celebrating the results of a good day's work.

One of the merchants from Gwynedd, Cynwric, was walking near the newly-built Norman castle, when he espied, sitting outside the castle gate, a tall, powerfully-built, flaxen-haired man, who was loaded with chains round his wrists and his ankles. He was the object of derision among a crowd of onlookers, who were jeering him and throwing him bits of bread.

Cynwric approached the unfortunate prisoner, and at once recognised him as Gruffydd, prince of Gwynedd, who had been captured several years earlier by the Normans, after being betrayed to them by one of his own men.

Cynwric said nothing to the prince, but strolled around, waiting for the sun to set, when he knew that the onlookers would go home for their suppers. Then he got into conversation with the castle guards at the gate, and before long had persuaded them to join him in drinking some ale. He plied them with liquor, while he only pretended to drink, and when they had sunk to the ground in a stupor, he walked over to the prisoner.

Immediately, he undid the shackles and put a cloak over Gruffydd's head, and escorted him to his cart, where he bade him lie down so that he could be covered with the provisions that Cynwric had obtained that day.

Cynwric left the city and carried the prince many miles across the border, to his house in Denbighshire. There, the prince rested awhile, and then moved on to Anglesey, where a great gathering of friends, informed by Cynwric's messenger, were waiting to welcome their prince.

Gruffydd had arrived in Anglesey at a time when most of the Welsh people had

risen against the Norman invaders, and without waiting for a moment more than he could help, he put himself at their head. Well he might do so, for he was a bold and skilful general, who had already proved his worth in battle.

This great prince was the grandson of Iago, the Prince of Gwynedd who ruled from 1039, and he had defeated Trahaern in 1081, thus winning the princedom of Gwynedd, which he claimed was his by right of descent. The first years of his reign were filled with fighting, not only the Normans but also other Welsh chiefs. More than once he had been defeated, and after his last failure, he had been captured and sent to Chester by Robert, the governor of Rhuddlan. The Normans had then built fortresses along the Gwynedd coast line at Bangor, and at Caernarvon, and had crossed the Menai straits and erected a castle near Beaumaris.

By 1094, most of Wales had been overrun by the Normans, and only Gwynedd had any kind of independence. Even this was doubtful, for though the people kept the invader out of Snowdonia, they could not stop the Normans in their coastal towns. Down in the south, castles had been built by the Normans along the coast all the way from Chepstow to Pembroke, at such places as Neath, Kidwelly and Newport.

Many castles were built in Wales by the Normans, and this was because they acted as strongholds from which to control wide areas of countryside. When they invaded territories, they found houses and fortresses of timber and earth; they replaced them with buildings of stone, and, as the Welsh did not yet know about siege warfare, these buildings were all but impregnable. Inside them were battalions of soldiers, with living quarters. There they could carry out weapon drill, and when necessary, they could sally out, deal with raids, and then return to safety. As a result, one castle could dominate a large area.

The Norman barons who led the invasion forces settled down in parts of Wales and made for themselves small "kingdoms," where the ideas of the feudal system, already working in England, were copied. These areas were called marches, and the barons were called the Lords Marcher. They were very powerful, and from time to time they would support baronial risings against the kings of England. In time, they intermarried with native Welsh women, usually daughters or nieces of chiefs, and gradually they introduced English ideas and ways of life into their marches.

Gwynedd was the only large district unaffected by this merging, and this meant that the prince of Gwynedd was a practical ruler, although his territory was only part, and not all, of Wales.

In 1098, the Normans attacked Gwynedd again, and Gruffydd was driven into Anglesey, from which he fled and took refuge in Ireland. When he came back a year later, he was allowed to rule Anglesey, but that was all. A story of his life, written not long after his time, says that for the next few years "he spent his life in poverty and misery, hoping for the future providence of God."

These years were indeed painful, and it was some time before he was able to start to regain what he had lost. In 1114, Henry I of England invaded Gwynedd, probably because he heard reports that Gruffydd was building up a party of resistance to the English. The war was not decisive either way, and at the end of it, Gruffydd agreed to recognise Henry as overlord; in return he was given Gwynedd to rule, and from then on his reign was one of peace and order. More than once he visited the English court, and was received with all the honour given to visiting monarchs.

Gruffydd organised the building of many churches and abbeys. Forests that had been devastated in the fighting were re-planted, and, as his biographer says, "the inhabitants began to make orchards and gardens, and surround them with walls and ditches, and to construct walled buildings, and to support themselves from the fruit of the earth."

After the death of Henry I in 1135, the Welsh seized the opportunity provided by the civil war between Matilda and Stephen to rise and attack the Norman overlords. Gruffydd was by this time an old man, and he took no part in the fighting, but the Welsh were successful in many places, as they were led by two of his sons, Cadwaladr and Owain Gwynedd, both of them fine generals.

In 1137, blind and crippled, Gruffydd died, and was buried at Bangor. He left bequests of money to many churches and religious houses, including a sum to the Church of Christ in Dublin. He had not forgotten the hospitality the Irish had given him when he fled there nearly forty years before.

Owain was the son of Gruffydd ap Cynan, and with his brother Cadwaladr, he had managed the government of Gwynedd during the last years of the ageing prince. Owain was a handsome and majestic-looking man, skilled as a general and humane as a governor. At heart he was gentle and peace-loving, with high ideals, and he was learned and religious.

When the Welsh declared war on their Norman overlords after the death of Henry I of England, Owain and Cadwaladr were their leaders. The main centre of fighting was in Ceredigion, and Owain and Cadwaladr headed the troops who attacked the Marcher lord Walter de Bek's castle at Llanfihangel, and burned it to the ground. Then they went on to Aberystwyth and destroyed the stronghold of another Marcher, de Clare. Soon, the whole countryside was alive with tramping feet, as more and more Welshmen flocked to the national army.

Towards the end of 1136, the troops, now numbering more than 6,000 well-trained infantry, and nearly 2,000 cavalry, drew up outside the town of Cardigan, near the mouth of the river Teifi. There, a great battle was fought and the Welsh won a glorious victory. More than a thousand Normans were drowned as they tried to escape across the river, across a bridge that collapsed under their weight. The victors pursued the survivors right into Cardigan, one of the main centres of Norman power, and set the buildings on fire, capturing enormous amounts of treasure.

The next year, Carmarthen fell into their hands, and by this they won all south-west Wales. The old prince, Gruffydd, died, soon after he heard the great news, and his throne passed to Owain.

Owain, like many of his predecessors, set out to unite as much of Wales as he could under his leadership. He already had Gwynedd, and he had just won Ceredigion and Deheubarth. His reputation as a field commander earned him the respect of all Welshmen, even the smaller chiefs who never seemed to stop fighting with one another. This new power meant that he had to give up actual command, and turn to the business of government. The army was put in the hands of his brother, almost as great a soldier as Owain, and for some years, the war against the Normans continued, with increasing success for the Welsh.

Owain and Cadwaladr were devoted to each other, and the arrangement worked well. Then, suddenly, in 1143, Cadwaladr quarrelled with a young cousin, Anarawd, and killed him. This made Owain very angry, for Anarawd was engaged to be married to Owain's daughter. Moreover, his father was a local prince, and the success of the Welsh against the Normans depended very greatly upon the princes being united in action. This union was now threatened, for Anarawd's father demanded vengeance. Owain punished his brother severely; he drove him out of Ceredigion, and burned his mansion at Aberystwyth to the ground. Cadwaladr fled to Ireland for safety, but he did not learn his lesson, for within months he was plotting to return and to attack his brother. Eventually, the two were reconciled, but the close love and friendship between them had gone forever.

By 1152, Owain was master of all Wales that was not still in the hands of a few stubborn Marcher lords. It began to look as if the country would be free of English domination for good, for the English king was in no position to help the beleaguered Marchers.

It was a great time for Wales. The rise in national feeling produced a generation of poets, Gwalchmai and Cynndelw being the two best known. Owain himself promoted the building of abbeys and monasteries, and remains of these foundations can still be seen today at Valle Crucis, Strata Florida and Tintern. Learning spread throughout rapidly growing monastic communities. The Welsh developed their talent for music; competitions for special crowns to be awarded to the winners were organised for poetry and music, and these were called eisteddfods.

Owain Gwynedd and the great Welsh bard Gwalchmai

The Welsh had something to teach the English, too. It was among them that the spirit of chivalrous behaviour, so wonderfully displayed by the English in the time of Edward III, first appeared in the British Isles. Welsh law was already far more humane than any other in Europe, and this humanity and chivalry was best shown when a great many Welshmen accompanied the European Crusaders on the Second Crusade in 1147. This gentleness of nature affected the Norman Marchers and their followers. They had behaved badly in Wales; Hugh of Chester had used an Anglesey church as a kennel for his pack of dogs, and in a raid on Bangor, other Normans had burned the cathedral to the ground. The Welsh showed the invader that a respect for God and for the houses that were devoted to His worship was an essential thing for people who dared to call themselves civilised.

In 1157, when Henry II of England had succeeded in putting down all the revolts of the barons who had treated the population so harshly under Stephen, he set out on a great expedition to re-conquer the huge districts that the Welsh had wrested from the Marchers. The campaign was short, and it was not attended by any great success on either side. Although Henry was defeated by Owain here and there, Owain knew he could not forever resist the superior might of the English, led by a man who had the resources of more than half of France at his back. So they came to terms. Owain was to continue as prince of Gwynedd, but he had to acknowledge Henry as overlord.

In 1170, the great prince died, and was buried at Bangor. He had been, as a Welsh chronicler wrote "a man of great celebrity, and of the most extraordinary sagacity, nobleness and fortitude".

DAFYDD ap OWAIN GWYNEDD [1170–1194]

Dafydd was Owain Gwynedd's son, and when he became prince he also tried to keep the state together and control the remaining independent princedoms. But he believed in making even stronger ties with

164

England, and at a meeting in 1173 with Henry II, he begged the hand of the king's half-sister in marriage. At first, Henry was reluctant to agree. He did not understand the Welsh, and he had not yet grown to respect them. So long as they were quiet in their domains, he felt, he could regard them as a subject race, and their lands as just a few more territories in his already enormous empire. Then, a year later, he changed his mind, and Dafydd married the princess, who was called Emma, in great splendour and pomp.

The marriage was not at all popular among patriotic Welshmen. They were ready to accept Henry as overlord—indeed, from his very strength they could do little else—but, to become tied to the English king by family connection was too much like surrendering their independence of spirit altogether.

We do not know much about Dafydd's reign, except that most of it was taken up with fighting, struggles between the proud though often unruly Welsh princes against their immediate overlord, in an attempt to drive him off the throne of Gwynedd. His most serious danger was from his nephew, Llywelyn, who, by 1194, had captured most of his uncle's lands apart from a few isolated castles and their surrounding acres of pasture field. Three years later, Dafydd, who had been forced to abdicate in 1194, lost the remainder of his property, and he retired to England with his English wife and died there at the beginning of the next century.

LLYWELYN FAWR [*Llywelyn the Great : 1194–1240*]

Of all the princes to rule in Wales, whether as overlord or in one or other of the prince-doms, Llywelyn, grandson of Owain Gwynedd, was the greatest, and there is no disagreement about this opinion among Welsh historians. He has left an imperish-able name on the pages of the story of Wales; generations that followed him remembered the good that he did, and today people in Wales are given the

Christian name Llywelyn, in memory of his greatness.

We have no accurate description of his appearance, but we can imagine that the looks he had went with the character about which so many historians have written in terms of praise and wonder. He was a skilful general, specialising in the art of making rapid and unsuspected movements against his enemies. He knew how to besiege a thick, stone-walled castle and he had the endless patience to keep up the attack until he was successful. He had his own secret service system whereby if a rebel prince, or for that matter a Marcher lord, was planning to attack him, he would know about their plans before they had a chance to put them into action. By this system, he forestalled many a revolt, and struck terror into the hearts of would-be disturbers of the peace.

As a statesman, he modelled himself on Henry II; he ruled with justice, and, like Edward I of England, once he gave his word, he never broke it. Apart from his military skills, he was learned and de-voted to religious matters. He encouraged the Welsh poets, and held a number of eisteddfods in his time. He gave new buildings to monks, and urged them to develop and spread their knowledge of Latin, of history and of religious teaching.

At the same time, like his uncle, Dafydd, he believed in the policy of courting the friendship of England, and of using that nation's ideas whensoever they were found to be both practicable and good for Wales. He had come to understand that Wales could never be an entirely independent country, when it had the superior might of England at its doorstep. And yet, under this condition, he believed that Wales could develop into a united kingdom and could advance its national character, and exist as a separate nation at peace with its neighbour.

Not long after he became prince, he summoned a council of all the underling princes and put forward a plan for union. At first, they were not ready to agree, and the quarrelling, one of the features of Welsh history for centuries, began again.

Llywelyn was not to be deterred in his aim, although it is easy to see why so many Welshmen were unwilling to allow themselves to become what in effect were subjects of England. So he sought the alliance of John of England, and in 1204, he married that king's daughter, Joan.

Surprisingly, this match did not irritate the Welsh as much as Dafydd's marriage with Emma. Perhaps they had begun to learn that co-operation with England was a price worth paying for peace and for good government. For some years, the alliance lasted, and this gave Llywelyn time to re-model the government of Wales.

He created a council of chiefs, like the English Great Council, and its duties were to look after justice, finances, and local government matters. The members had to provide an army for Wales for dealing with rebel chiefs. The courts were to try to settle disputes over land ownership. And the Council was to approve the decisions taken by Llywelyn, so long as they were seen to be in the best interests of Wales.

In 1211, Llywelyn quarrelled with John, and the English king led an expedition into Gwynedd. Starting from Chester, John marched across the Dee and pushed as far as Deganwy. There, he found that Llywelyn had withdrawn his men into the mountains, and had taken most of the farm livestock with him. The countryside was bare of provisions for the English. The shortage was so acute that eggs cost 1½d. each, several shillings each in today's money, and animal flesh for roasting was a very rare treat.

John withdrew his army to Chester, but returned again at harvest time, and now he drove on to Bangor, where he burned the cathedral, a new one which had risen on the ashes of the one destroyed a hundred years before. But the Welsh would not give in, and peace was made.

When the barons of England combined to force John to sign Magna Carta in 1215, Llywelyn used this quarrel as an opportunity to strike out and recapture his losses of the previous years. In a swift campaign, he mastered all Gwynedd, and then turned south and took possession of Montgomery, Carmarthen and Cardigan. He met little resistance, for the marcher lords were involved in the civil war between John and his barons, who were supporting Prince Louis of France. (See page 52.) When John died at Newark in

Llywelyn Fawr nominates his son Dafydd as his successor

1216, Llywelyn summoned an assembly of all Welsh chiefs to discuss the distribution of the newly won territories.

From that moment, his position as overlord of Wales was never again seriously threatened.

Llywelyn now introduced a new idea into Wales. This was a new form of succession to the princes. We have seen that when a prince died, his lands and riches were divided between all his sons equally, and we have also seen the results of this custom, civil war, interruption of agriculture, general misery for the people. Llywelyn now announced that he would appoint a successor and he expected his council to agree to the choice. At a meeting held at Strata Florida, in 1238, Llywelyn, who was ageing and paralysed as the result of a stroke, compelled the council to recognise his second son, Dafydd, as his heir. His elder son, Griffin, was excluded because he did not like the alliance with England, and Llywelyn knew that if Griffin were to succeed him, it would only mean continued warfare with the English, a struggle that could not in the end prove advantageous for the Welsh.

Llywelyn died in 1240, and he was buried at Aberconway, a monastery which he had built and endowed. Such were the achievements of his reign and the respect that was felt for him among the English, that it was they who first called him Llywelyn the Great. It is hard to imagine a finer tribute to a ruler than that he should be so called by a more powerful neighbour.

DAFYDD ap LLYWELYN FAWR [1240-1246]

Dafydd succeeded to Gwynedd and its surrounding domains, according to the agreement reached at Strata Florida in 1238. He had married Isabella de Braouse, a daughter of one of the Marcher lords, and he was, like his father, a staunch believer in the alliance with England.

As soon as he came to the throne, he paid homage to Henry III, but soon afterwards a quarrel arose over the lands left by his father. Henry III invaded North Wales to recover these lands and he over-ran the princedom with little difficulty. The two rulers made peace at St Asaph, in 1241. Meanwhile, the Marcher lords further south took steps to recover many of the lands taken from them in the time of Llywelyn Fawr, and by 1243, Dafydd was really no more than a provisional chief, with sway over Gwynedd.

One of the terms of the St Asaph peace was that Dafydd's brother, Griffin, who was bitterly anti-English, should be sent to London as a prisoner. He was put in the Tower of London. In 1244, tired of his captivity, Griffin made an attempt to escape. One night, when all seemed quiet in the White Tower, he got out of bed, dressed, and then took off all the clothes from his bed. Tearing them into strips to make a rope, he tied one end to a parapet just above his window, some ninety feet from the ground.

Gently he began to lower himself when, suddenly, the coil snapped, and he went hurtling to his death below. The force of his fall, according to one report, was so great that his head was pushed between his shoulders.

Dafydd was very angry about his brother's death, although in Griffin's life-time, they had not got on at all well. He prepared to break his agreement with Henry and marshalled an army in the north and moved eastwards towards Chester. Henry brought an army against him and succeeded in checking this advance. Then he returned to England and left garrisons in the English castles and outposts. To make the Welsh feel the extent of his power, he put a ban on all trade in corn, salt, iron, steel and cloth with Wales.

The next year, Dafydd died, leaving no son to succeed him, which meant that a number of claimants came forward for the throne. The two with the best claim were Owain and Llywelyn, grandsons of Llywelyn Fawr. They agreed to divide the inheritance, and this was supported by many of the chief nobles and advisers.

LLYWELYN YR AIL [*Llywelyn the Last: 1246-1282*]

Llywelyn was the son of the prince Griffin who fell to his death in an attempt to escape from the Tower of London. Like his father, he was opposed to the alliance with England, but for the first years of his rule, when he was sharing the princedom with his brother Owain, he kept so closely to the terms of the alliance that for nearly nine years there are no details at all of his activities.

Then, in 1255, he quarrelled with Owain, captured him and put him in prison. Now he was sole ruler, and because of the difficulties which the English king was having with his own barons in England at this time, he began to lay plans for a great rising of the Welsh against their overlords.

One of the conditions of the alliance with England was that certain improvements would be made in Wales with English help. Another was that the Marcher lords would be stopped from carrying out raids on their Welsh subjects in their domains. Neither of these things were properly attended to, and when Edward, Henry III's son, visited Wales on an inspection tour of the English castles in 1256 and refused to do anything about the Welsh complaints, the chiefs decided on rebellion. They came to Llywelyn and asked for his help. This was his opportunity, and he seized it.

Together the princes, led by Llywelyn, organised a general rising of the people and set out to recover the dominions in Wales that belonged to the English Marcher lords. Within a year they had won Powys, most of Ceredigion and Deheubarth, and had ravaged vast areas in the south, reaching the borders of England. An attempt by the English king to stop them failed, and by 1258, Llywelyn had become almost as powerful as his grandfather.

In that year, the chiefs swore an oath of

Llywelyn Yr Ail cheered by his army after his victory over the English

loyalty to Llywelyn and he was now the real master of Wales. He made a treaty with the Scots, and a little while afterwards a truce was agreed with the English.

For the next few years, Llywelyn spent his time ordering the government of the Welsh. He had got most, though not all, of what he wanted in Wales, and he hesitated to get involved with further warfare with England until his own power was firmly rooted. There were of course the usual border raids and the skirmishes with Marcher lords, but for several years there was no full-scale war. During this time, the English barons, led by Simon de Montfort, rebelled against Henry III and defeated him at Lewes, compelling him to rule with the aid of a council of nobles, instead of acting on his whims. Then, too, de Montfort summoned the first real parliament of England in 1265. In that year he was defeated by Edward, the king's son, and killed at Evesham. There is evidence that the Welsh

were in some kind of alliance with de Montfort and his party, and they assisted the great earl by attacking those Marcher lords in South Wales who preferred to support Henry III.

If de Montfort had been the victor at Evesham, it is possible that Llywelyn would have been recognised as an independent prince and that Wales would have been given its complete freedom from English overlordship. So de Montfort's death dashed the hopes of the Welsh leader, but, fortunately for Wales, there were still many followers of de Montfort who were a danger to Henry and the English had no time to take any revenge on their Welsh subjects.

For the next ten years, Wales was at peace, and the nation was able to advance in agriculture and industry and in learning.

What was this great prince like? He was tallish, dark and majestic to look at. He had unbounded energy, tremendous personal courage, and he knew how to get men to follow him. Above all, he was a patriot, a quality which, however admirable, in the end led to his downfall. Like his predecessors, he was merciful, though when chiefs under him rebelled he dealt with them severely, preferring long terms of imprisonment to the more cruel punishment of execution. He must have been an outstanding person to be able to unite the bulk of the Welsh people and keep them in union for so many years.

In 1274, Edward I, having just returned from the seventh Crusade in the Holy Land, was crowned King of England. To the ceremony both the King of Scotland, Alexander III, and Llywelyn were summoned. The former answered and came, but Llywelyn would not. He had not forgotten the way Edward had behaved in Wales nearly twenty years before.

This refusal angered the English king, who, as we have seen in the tale of his life, was a brilliant soldier and statesman, and a man who believed that it was in the best interests of the peoples of the British Isles that they should be united. Several times

Llywelyn pays homage to Edward I

Edward summoned Llywelyn to pay him homage, and each time the Welsh leader refused. He said, on one occasion, that he would do so if he was given the English king's brother, Edmund of Lancaster, as a hostage, though he knew very well that Edward would not agree to that.

Then he sought the hand of Eleanor, daughter of Simon de Montfort, in marriage. This would have given Llywelyn a number of powerful supporters, not only in England but also in France, and Edward was determined to stop it. When Eleanor set out for Wales in a ship, it was chased along the English channel and captured, and the future bride was kept in confinement at the English court.

War then broke out, and the English were victorious. They drove the Welsh into the mountains of Snowdonia and were able to cut off their supplies to such an extent that Llywelyn surrendered in 1277. The peace treaty was more generous to Llywelyn than, in the circumstances, he deserved. He was allowed to keep the princedom of Gwynedd, without Denbighshire, and he was permitted to marry Eleanor. Edward, realising that by this time many Welsh people had grown to accept the presence of Englishmen in the marches and that therefore any spirit of nationalism in Wales would be much more confined to districts over which Llywelyn had power, took the risk of granting easy terms. Then he introduced English law into districts held by the marchers, and followed this up by sending English officials to enforce it.

For five years, there was no disturbance. Then, in 1282, Llywelyn rebelled again.

He marched along the coast of North Wales, sweeping the country with fire and sword. This provoked the English king, and he brought an enormous army into Flintshire, drove Llywelyn's forces back along the coast and into the mountains of Snowdonia. Once again, Llywelyn was compelled to surrender, but this time the terms offered were much more harsh. Gwynedd was to become an English province; Llywelyn was to be given an English earldom only and a yearly payment enough to maintain a court of some standing.

Llywelyn, ever a nationalist, refused these terms, and swiftly left the Snowdonia fortresses. He raced downwards towards Brecon, hoping to stir up revolt there.

One day in December, he went out with a small patrol party not far from Builth. Suddenly, it was attacked by an English patrol, and a Shropshire soldier, Stephen Frankton, charged against the prince and killed him, not knowing at the time who his victim was.

Frankton bent down over the body and began to search his pockets. Papers were found which showed that it was the Prince of Wales. Immediately, he cut off his victim's head, and had it sent to Edward,

who dispatched it to London where it was exhibited on a spike on London Bridge, near the Tower. A Welsh prophet had once said that a Welshman would one day be king of England; Edward, to make a mockery of this prophecy, ordered that the head should be adorned with ivy. He could not have guessed that, two hundred years later, this prophecy would come true, when Henry Tudor became Henry VII.

The revolt against England collapsed almost as soon as the news arrived in Gwynedd that Llywelyn had been slain. One of his brothers, Dafydd, continued the fight, but he was betrayed by his own men and handed to the English at Shrewsbury. There, he was tried and convicted, and then executed.

It was the end of Wales as an independent kingdom. Its superior neighbour had triumphed and had brought the nation into the kingdom of England. Thereafter, Edward, as we have seen in his life story, brought English government into Wales, and began the process by which the Welsh people have become an essential part of the nation of Britain. There were revolts, later on, as we have described in the time of Henry IV, but never again was Wales to assert its independence.

Rulers of SCOTLAND

In the last centuries before the Roman invasion of Britain, that part of Scotland north of the river Forth and now known as the Highlands was occupied by the Gaelic Celts, who had been driven there by their British Celt kinsmen. These Gaels mixed with the more savage inhabitants who had been living there for hundreds of years, and this resulted in a race of people who were less developed than those in the rest of Britain. Indeed, the habit of painting themselves with woad before going into battle, which had been given up elsewhere in Britain, stayed with them long after the arrival of the Roman legions. The first Romans to see these Gaels called them the Picti, that is, the painted men.

These Picts knew little about farming, and they relied on hunting and fishing. They were, however, a tough, brave and warlike race, and they were to give the Romans a great deal of trouble during the occupation of Britain.

By about A.D. 84, the Roman governor, Julius Agricola, had completed the conquest of Britain as far north as the river Forth. Then, in that year, he fought a great battle with the Picts, under their leader Galcagus, at a place in Perthshire near the Grampian mountains. The Picts were utterly defeated and more than ten thousand of them are said to have died.

Agricola planned to conquer the rest of Scotland, and also to turn his attention to Ireland, but he was called back by the emperor Domitian, who had become jealous of his governor's great military fame.

Thereafter, the Picts began to raid the Lowlands and caused much damage to new settlements there. In 119, the emperor Hadrian came to Britain and decided to build a great wall right across the country from the Solway Firth to the mouth of the Tyne. It was made of stone and it was provided with forts at one-mile intervals. From its forts, and with extra troops supplied from the main Roman city in north England, York, the Romans hoped to keep the Picts out of England and also to frighten them away from the Lowlands. But the raids went on, and twenty years later, another emperor, Antoninus Pius, ordered a further wall to be constructed from the Forth to the Clyde.

Even this wall was not entirely effective, and for the next seventy or more years the raids continued. In the years 208-10, the emperor Septimius Severus brought a vast army into Scotland, went beyond the Antonine Wall and began to make inroads into the heart of the Pictish countryside, building roads and setting up forts on the hills. Severus might have conquered their land, but he died at York in 211, and his successors did not pursue the adventure.

The raids grew worse, and just when the Saxons began their attacks on the East Coast of Britain in the third century, the Picts took advantage of the disorder and came down into Britain in great strength. They never attempted to settle, for they were interested only in plunder and killing. Whenever Britain had a strong governor, the Picts were kept at bay, but as soon as his firm hand was removed, they started to come southwards again. Finally, when Britain was abandoned by the Romans at the beginning of the fifth century, the Picts were bringing their savage bands right down as far as the south coast of England. It was for help to drive off one of these bands that Vortigern, King of Kent (see page 12), appealed to Hengist and Horsa of Denmark.

The story of Scotland from the departure of the Romans is almost unknown for nearly two centuries. During that time, the Picts continued with their raids and they also fought bitterly among each other. Then, Gaels from Ireland crossed the sea from Ulster in large numbers and began to settle in the west of Scotland, in the district of Argyll and the islands. This new colony became known as Dalriada, which was said to be the name of the region in Ireland from which the settlers came. They were Christians, and it was from among them that the first real king of Scotland came, Kenneth MacAlpine.

Scotland was by now divided into four kingdoms; Dalriada, the Pictish kingdom, Strathclyde, which was peopled with Britons, and Bernicia, which was part of Northumbria and which later became known as Lothian. (See page 175.) But it was not by any means a nation. Part Christian, part savage, containing a variety of races, it was to wait nearly two hundred years before anyone was strong enough to weld even some of the peoples into one kingdom.

In the middle of the sixth century, an Irish missionary called Columba sailed to the Island of Iona, with a band of devoted followers, and there he set up a monastery. Then he and his workers went to the mainland and began to preach Christianity to the pagan Picts. Their king, Brude, allowed him to go through the land without interference, and before very long many Picts gave up their heathen gods and were baptised into the Christian faith. This was followed by the conversion of Lothian by Cuthbert, another missionary, while both Dalriada and Strathclyde were already Christian kingdoms.

For some time, the Lothians were most powerful in Scotland, but when their king, Ecgfrith, was defeated by the Picts and slain at the battle of Nechtansmere in 685, their power decreased. Had he won, it is possible that all Scotland would have fallen to the English and the kingdom of England would have stretched from the Orkneys to the Isle of Wight.

In the next century, Scotland, like the other countries of Britain, was subjected to Viking raids, and as the different kingdoms were always quarrelling they were not able to drive the raiders out. Then in the middle of the ninth century there rose a man who dealt the Vikings a crushing blow, and also made the first practical move towards building a Scottish nation. That was Kenneth MacAlpine.

The Picts burn a Roman settlement in the 4th century A.D.

Kenneth MacAlpine became king of the Scots in Dalriada, that is, the district of Argyll and its surrounding islands, in 834. Although there are very few details known about his life, he has become one of the most famous names in Scottish history. It was he who not only dreamed of building one nation out of the various kingdoms but also went some way towards achieving it.

Like most regional princes throughout the British Isles in the ninth century, Kenneth was harassed by incessant Viking raids. We have seen how Ecgbert of Wessex and Rhodri Mawr of Gwynedd dealt with these invaders, and how only a tough, determined and skilful leader was able to stave them off. Kenneth proved to be as resolute, and by 841, he had defeated the Vikings so decisively that they were cleared out of Dalriada altogether.

Then he turned on the Picts in the Highlands. There, the district was equally vexed with Viking invasions, and for years no leader had come forth to deliver the people from them. So Kenneth invaded their kingdom, and by 843 he had conquered it and put the Vikings to flight. It was the first time that so large a part of Scotland had been under the sway of one ruler.

Kenneth was not only a great war leader; he was also an able governor. The royal headquarters were moved from Argyll to Scone, in Perthshire, which, in about 850 became the capital of the newly built kingdom. He also brought some relics of St Columba from the island of Iona and put them in a church which he built at Dunkeld, not far north of Scone. His aim was to establish the government in the centre of the kingdom, so that he could the more easily control affairs. Apart from anything else, this discouraged the Vikings, and Scottish historians have said that for the rest of his reign the new nation was free from attack.

Having made himself King of the Scots, Kenneth now decided to enlarge his empire, and he invaded Lothian several times. Settlements of Angles at Dunbar and Melrose were burned, but he was never able to conquer the district completely.

In 860, Kenneth died, undisputed master of northern Scotland, above the river Forth. He was the founder of a new dynasty of kings, and every succeeding ruler was descended in some way or other from him.

DONALD I [860-864], CONSTANTINE I [864-877], AEDH [877-8], EOCHA [878-889], and DONALD II [889-900].

The historians who have told us a little about Kenneth MacAlpine have said hardly anything about his immediate successors, apart from the fact that they had to deal with Viking raids, and that some of them tried to conquer Lothian.

The kings were elected by the royal advisers, as in England, and they were chosen from Kenneth's family. But, a brother often followed a ruler, and was then succeeded by his nephew, son of the ruler before.

Donald I succeeded his brother Kenneth, and reigned for four years. He is said to have given Scotland some good laws.

Assembly of chiefs and clergy at Scone

When he died in 864, Kenneth's son became Constantine I. He ruled for thirteen years, during which time the Scots were plagued by Viking raids. He was killed in battle in 877, fighting, it is said, some allies of Guthrum, the chief who was so soundly defeated at Ethandune by Alfred the Great the following year. He was succeeded by his brother Aedh, who was murdered within a few months. The next king was Eocha, a grandson of Kenneth, and we know nothing of him, except that he died in 889.

The throne then passed to Donald II, son of Constantine I, and it was in his reign that the Vikings began to settle in parts of Scotland, just as they had started to do in the time of Aethelwulf in England. Donald died in 900, and he was followed by Aedh's son, Constantine II.

CONSTANTINE II [900–942]

Constantine II ruled for forty-two years. Although there is little known about his career, it seems that his reign was an important one. He was successful against the Vikings in the early years. Then, he arranged a great assembly of chiefs and clergy at Scone, over which he and the Bishop of St Andrews, Kellach, presided. This meeting was an attempt to organise the church on a national basis, to encourage the development of the monasteries and to spread learning among the clergy. We do not know much about Kellach, but perhaps he was like Dunstan, the able and scholarly adviser of Eadred and Eadgar of England.

During this reign, the king of Strathclyde (see map) died, and before the local chiefs could elect another one, Constantine chose a successor and compelled him to recognise Scotland as the overlord kingdom. By this, the Scots added to their growing empire.

In 918, the Vikings were defeated by Constantine at a great battle fought at Corbridge, on the river Tyne.

Constantine was then defeated, along with Anlaf, the Viking chief, at the battle of Brunanburgh, in 937, described in the chapter on Athelstan of England. In 942, weary of fighting the Vikings, he decided to give up the throne, and retired to a monastery at St Andrews, where he died ten years later.

176

MALCOLM I [942-954]

When Constantine II retired in 942, he was succeeded by Malcolm, the son of Donald II. It was in his reign that Edmund I of England invaded Scotland and ravaged Strathclyde, the Celtic kingdom which recognised the Scots as overlords. Edmund gave the kingdom to Malcolm, "on condition that he would be his faithful fellow-worker by land and sea." After Edmund died in 946, Malcolm renewed the agreement with Edmund's successor, Eadred.

Although Scotland and England were separate nations, and from time to time fought each other for the territories which lay between them, that is between the Forth and the Tyne, they abandoned their rivalry when it became necessary to fight off heavy Viking raids. Both countries were Christian, and both were being built into compact units of government, and both wanted no interference from the Vikings.

Malcolm was killed in 954, fighting against the Vikings, and he was succeeded by his cousin Indulphus, the son of Constantine II.

INDULPHUS [954-962], DUFF [962-967], COLIN [967-971], KENNETH II [971-995], CONSTANTINE III [995-997], and KENNETH III [997-1005]

Details of these kings are scarce. Indulphus defeated the Vikings, and also managed to extend the boundary of Scotland a little way below the Forth, but he, too, retired to a monastery in 962, and was succeeded by Malcolm I's son, Duff. Duff was a weak ruler, unable to stop the Vikings, and before long he was driven off the throne by Indulphus' son, Colin, in 967. Colin reigned for four years, and when he died in 971, he was followed by Kenneth II, another son of Malcolm I. Kenneth reigned for twenty-four years but all we know of him is that he was probably one of those kings who rowed Eadgar of England across the river Dee at Chester in 973.

After Kenneth II came Constantine III, the son of Colin. He was murdered after two years on the throne, and was followed by Duff's son, Kenneth, who became Kenneth III. This Kenneth was killed in a civil war in 1005, and he was succeeded by his cousin, who became Malcolm II.

Malcolm II was a skilful general and leader of men; he was also wise and learned. Although he was a patriotic Scotsman, he knew that the nation would gain by government as practised in England.

Malcolm defeated his cousin Kenneth III in a civil war, and then began to rule a nation that was to see great changes. Unfortunately there are large gaps in our knowledge of him, but two events stand out as milestones in the history of Scotland.

In 1018, after years of preparation, during which he had instilled into his people a sense of national pride, he assembled an army and made ready to march southwards to conquer the district of Lothian. It is said that his force was so large that its numbers could not be counted. They crossed the Forth, poured down the roads of Lothian, and reached the banks of the river Tweed. There, at Carham, a battle was fought, and the Scots were triumphant. Viking settlers, Guthrum's Danelaw people and English alike, who made up the elements of the opposing army, were cut to pieces on the field. An English bishop wrote "Wretched me! Who have served as a bishop in these times. The land will never again be what it was." And indeed it never was, for all Lothian became part of Scotland as a result of the victory.

It must have been a tremendous moment for the Scots. For centuries they had been split up into different tribes, constantly warring with each other, knowing no peace, an easy prey to Viking raids, a temptation to English kings. Now they could see the beginnings of nationhood. But this was not the only achievement of that famous year. In Strathclyde, where princes ruled as subject lords of Scotland, Malcolm brought the people under his direct control. Now Scotland was a nation occupying very much the same territory that it does today.

Although he had defeated the English, Malcolm realised that the new nation could not progress without the use of the more highly developed arts of government understood in England. So he encouraged the spread of English ideas and language.

There is little to tell of the next twelve years of his rule. He is reported, in the Anglo-Saxon Chronicle, to have acknowledged Canute as overlord, but this does not appear to have affected the power he wielded. What really mattered was whether the new nation would survive after his death, as it was a country of people who could not always agree with one another.

Malcolm II acknowledges Canute as overlord

Death of Duncan I at Bothgouanan

DUNCAN I [1034–1040]

When Malcolm I died in 1034, he had no sons to follow him, but he had three daughters. One was the mother of his successor, Duncan I, and another was the mother of Macbeth, a very great Scottish king.

Almost as soon as Duncan succeeded, Scotland was racked with civil war. A nation put together by a strong, determined ruler will only survive if that rule is carried on. But Duncan was a weak man and he had no ability to maintain the new domains of his grandfather. Worse, he surrounded himself with favourites who cared little for the new Scotland, and before long a revolt against him broke out.

To divert the attention of the nation from its own disorders, Duncan embarked upon an invasion of Northumbria. This was unnecessary, for Malcolm had established a workable agreement between his people and the Northumbrian English. Duncan led an army down to Durham where he laid siege to the city. The attack failed, and the result was a murderous defeat for the Scots. It is said that the castle at Durham was covered on its battlements with the heads of leading Scotsmen who died in the siege.

Duncan retired northwards, only to find that most of the nation was against him. The leader of the rebels was his cousin, Macbeth, who was lord of the Highland counties, and at a battle at Bothgouanan the king was killed, in 1040.

Macbeth is received by the Pope

MACBETH [1040–1057]

Macbeth is the subject of one of Shakespeare's most famous plays. In it, Duncan, an ageing king of Scotland, is murdered with daggers by Macbeth and his wife when he visits them. Macbeth, a weak man, ruled by his wife, finally meets his end at Dunsinane when a chief, Macduff, leads an army against him and destroys him in battle. It is a wonderful story but it has no relation to the truth about Macbeth.

When Duncan was killed in the civil war, Macbeth was elected to succeed him. Apart from winning the civil war, Macbeth had proved himself a great general against other enemies. He was also very popular among the peoples in the north of Scotland.

As soon as he became king, he set out to

180

put down all discontent in the land, and the historians have said that for the next fourteen years there was peace. This gave the new nation time to expand its agriculture and industry. It allowed farmers an uninterrupted period in which to improve their livings, and it gave the people, in general, time to settle down after the civil war. One of the early chronicles says that "his administration was conducted with great ability, to the satisfaction of his people."

Macbeth was devoted to the Church, as were many kings of those days, and he gave lands for the building of monasteries and churches.

In about 1050, Macbeth made a pilgrimage to Rome where, it is recorded, he distributed silver pieces to the poor in the surrounding villages. To make a pilgrimage to Rome in those days, which was more than a thousand miles from Scotland, would have meant being away for several months, and a king could only have managed to do this if his kingdom was in good order. There was, in fact, no serious trouble in his absence.

In the Highlands, there were bands of highway robbers, not unlike those of whom we have read in the time of Edward I of England, and they would take advantage of the civil disturbances to increase their raiding activities. Macbeth organised a police force to deal with these people, and, after a vigorous campaign, finally succeeded in putting them down.

One of the great barons of England, Siward, Earl of Northumbria, was sent by Edward the Confessor to Scotland to compel Macbeth to acknowledge England as overlord kingdom, something that Macbeth had hitherto refused to do by request. Siward marched into Scotland, crossed the Forth and at Dunsinane, near Perth, in 1054, he defeated Macbeth in a great battle. Such were Siward's losses in the field, however, that he had to retire to England.

Macbeth, though defeated, was not altogether beaten. He continued to rule, spending his time in the Highlands. In 1057, Duncan's son, Malcolm, who had

fled from Scotland in 1040 and lived for a while in England, led another army into Scotland. At Lumphanan, in Aberdeenshire, after a fierce struggle, Macbeth was slain, and the kingdom fell to the victor, who became Malcolm III.

MALCOLM III [Ceanmor : 1057-1093]

Malcolm III was a short, stocky man, with a very large head. His nickname "Ceanmor," which means "Big-head," was a description of his appearance, just as Edward I was known as "Longshanks" because of his very long legs.

When he fled to England after the death of his father, Duncan I, in 1040, he was received with great hospitality. There, he learned all about England, its laws, its language and its ways of life, and so when he returned to Scotland and defeated Macbeth, he was as much an Englishman as he was a Scot. From the start, then, he determined to introduce English ideas, just as Malcolm II had done.

This may have been acceptable in the southern half of the country, but it was resisted strongly by the Highlanders, who were proud of their history and preferred to speak in the Gaelic tongue. So Malcolm's reign was continually vexed with division between the two halves.

Like Macbeth, Malcolm was a great general, and he crushed the Highlanders with little difficulty. Then he invaded Northumbria, but though he did this on several occasions, he never succeeded in conquering it.

In 1066, William of Normandy won the battle of Senlac, in which the English king, Harold, was slain. He then crushed all resistance to his rule, and by 1072 was ready to invade Scotland. He marched northwards, ravaged Lothian and crossed the Forth. At Abernethy, near Perth, the two kings met, and instead of fighting, they came to an agreement. Malcolm was allowed to keep the kingdom of Scotland, but he had to recognise England as overlord.

It was in the time of the Conqueror's son, William Rufus, however, that war

Jugglers entertain Malcolm III at Scone

broke out again, and Rufus succeeded in capturing Cumberland, where he rebuilt the castle at Carlisle.

In 1069, Malcolm had married Margaret, the sister of the Eadgar who had been suggested as an alternative king of England by some of the old Anglo-Saxon Witan after William's victory. This meant, among other things, that their descendants would be half-English, and in the southern half of Scotland, where English ideas had already begun to take root, the union was accepted. On the other hand, the more nationalist Scots of the Highlands did not like the arrangement at all.

Margaret's influence on her husband and on Scotland was very great. She insisted that Malcolm should be served not by common people but by noble and gentle families. She introduced into the Scottish court fine clothes and jewellery, so that the court would be brought more into line with those of other European countries. She also persuaded him to reform the church, which had been growing slack in its duties. It was perhaps due to her that the church of Scotland became properly united, under the Church of Rome, for up to then the Highlanders had preferred their own kind of Christianity.

In 1093, against the urgent advice of his wife, Malcolm invaded England again, but in Northumberland, at Alnwick, he was defeated and killed. This news broke the queen's heart, for she loved him dearly, and within a week she also died.

DONALD III [1093-4], DUNCAN II [1094], DONALD III [1094-7], EDGAR [1097-1107] and ALEXANDER I [1107-1124]

Almost as soon as Malcolm III and his queen, Margaret, had died in 1093, Scotland was plunged into civil war. Donald Bane, Malcolm's brother, drove Malcolm's sons, Duncan, Edgar, Alexander and David, out of Scotland, and began to rule as Donald III. Within six months, however, he was defeated in battle by Duncan, who became Duncan II.

This Duncan lasted only a few months, too, and he was killed in a skirmish at Mondynes, in Kincardineshire, by Donald Bane who was determined to regain the throne.

In England, William Rufus regarded the situation in Scotland with some concern. He wanted to see on the Scottish throne a king who would not only be his friend, but also his underling. He therefore encouraged Edgar, Malcolm's second son, to rebel against Donald Bane, and provided him with forces. In 1097, Edgar defeated his uncle and captured him, putting him in prison for the rest of his life.

Edgar then reigned for nine years, but all we know of him is that he surrendered some of the north-western islands of Scotland to a Viking chief called Magnus, something that his warlike and courageous father would never have done without a fight.

Edgar died in 1107, and was succeeded by his next brother, Alexander. Alexander I divided the kingdom between himself and his young brother, David. This was a dangerous thing to have done, for it weakened the Scottish nation. The partition seems to have survived without difficulty, and when Alexander died, David became king of all Scotland.

DAVID I [1124-1153]

It was a warm day in August, 1138, and outside the town of Northallerton in Yorkshire, two armies were drawn up opposite each other, ready for battle. One was a host of Scots, under their king, David I, and

their numbers were enormous. They had crossed the Tweed, swept down through Northumberland and Durham, laying waste the countryside, and meeting little resistance from the terrified English. Now they were face to face with a hastily assembled force of Yorkshiremen, under Thurstan, Archbishop of York, and Raoul, Bishop of Durham, two brave men who had rallied the English and determined to make a stand.

In the centre of the English army was an extraordinary sight. A huge wagon stood on the field. On it was the mast of a ship, and on top of this was a cross, surrounded by banners, belonging to St Cuthbert, St Peter of York, St John of Beverley, and St Wilfred, all of them famous Northumbrian saints. Round the wagon stood the men of Yorkshire, armed with a variety of weapons, waiting for the signal for the struggle to begin. Thurstan moved towards the wagon, and held up his hands to the sky. At this the throng became quiet, and he blessed the army, urging it to fight for God and for country.

The signal was given, and the front ranks of the Scots, the men from Galloway, charged towards the English lines. They wore no armour, and were no match for the mail-clad knights of Yorkshire who cut them down in great numbers. For two hours the armies were locked in the fight, and each time the Scots were driven back they were pursued by volleys of arrows. Then, just as Eadric Streona had done at the battle of Sherston in 1016 against Edmund Ironside, a Yorkshire knight held aloft a Scottish head, crying out that king David had been slain. At this the Scots lost heart, turned and fled from the field. It was a crushing defeat for David, but we shall see that he derived an unexpected piece of good fortune from it.

David was born in 1084, the youngest son of Malcolm III and queen Margaret. He had spent much of his youth in England, when his uncle Donald Bane was ruling Scotland and in the time of his brother Edgar, and he had grown to admire the

Wagon with standards, at the Battle of the Standard, Northallerton, 1138

ways of the Normans and the English. In 1124, he succeeded to the throne.

While in England, he married Matilda, daughter of Waltheof, Earl of Huntingdon, who had owned lands in Northumberland and Durham. On his accession, he wanted to have these lands to add to the Scottish kingdom, but his first task was to deal with revolts in the Highlands, and this took several years. Then, soon after the death of Henry I of England, he had an opportunity to fight for the two English counties.

When Henry I died, his heir was his daughter Matilda, but we have seen that the English council preferred her cousin, Stephen. As a result civil war broke out, and for some time the issue was undecided. David, whose sister was the wife of Henry I, and so their daughter was David's niece, now had good reason to invade England, on Matilda's behalf.

After his defeat at Northallerton, a battle better known as the battle of the Standard (after the banners displayed on the wagon

in the English lines), he retired to Carlisle. There, he was approached by Stephen, for whom things had not been going well, and offered money and lands to leave England alone and give up the support of Matilda. This was an unexpected piece of good fortune, for by the arrangement he obtained Northumberland, except for the castles of Bamborough and Newcastle, and Cumberland, both counties being given to his son, Henry, to rule in his name. For the rest of his reign, these two counties remained in Scottish hands. Scotland was larger in area than it had ever been before or than it has ever been since. Now he turned to the business of governing it.

One of the things he admired in England was the new feudal system of the Conqueror. His father had begun to introduce it into Scotland, but it was David who converted the nation into a proper feudal kingdom. But, as in England, the system could only work so long as the king was a strong man, able to keep the feudal lords under control. To ensure this, David gave many lands to his Norman friends. Annandale went to an ancestor of Robert I, and Renfrew was given to an ancestor of the Stewarts, to mention only two of the allotments.

He also appointed Normans to the highest positions of state; the Constable, who commanded the royal army when the king was not present, the Chamberlain, who managed the royal exchequer, and the Chancellor, who was the chief adviser and the keeper of the royal seal with which all official documents and acts were stamped.

David was a great lawgiver, and like Alfred of England and Hywel Dda of Wales, he reformed the existing laws which had got into confusion. He was also a benefactor of the Church. He founded many monasteries, some of them with huge abbey buildings, the remains of which can still be seen today, Kelso, Melrose, Holyrood, Jedburgh and Dryburgh. He gave the Church great sums of money, increased the number of bishops, and instituted a programme of education in the monasteries that was far-reaching.

David's last years were sad, for his son Henry died before him, and this meant that the throne would pass to a grandson, Malcolm, who was then only ten years old. You can imagine how David dreaded leaving the kingdom, with its new feudal system and its spirit of unity, to one so young, knowing that the barons would take advantage of the minority to try to upset the kingdom's stability. He died in 1153. An historian of the time said: "He was the comforter of the sorrowing, the father of the fatherless, and the best of all his kind."

Kelso Abbey

Malcolm came to the throne when he was eleven years old. He was a tall, slim, graceful youth, so young-looking that though he lived to the age of twenty-four he was known as Malcolm the Maiden, for his childlike looks. As soon as he succeeded, rebellion broke out in the Highlands, and it was with great difficulty that his Norman followers were able to put it down. Then the people of Galloway rose, and it took three separate armies to crush them. Already it was clear that David I's system was breaking down.

Malcolm's worst danger, however, was from England where, in 1154, young Henry Plantagenet had come to the throne as Henry II and had set out on his campaign to reorganise the country and crush the warlike barons after the awful period of Stephen's reign. Henry, once he had established himself as undisputed master of England, and had got Owain Gwynedd of Wales to accept him as overlord, now set out to recover the counties of Northumberland and Cumberland from the Scots. Then he aimed to get Scotland to accept him as overlord, as well.

Malcolm was advised by his Norman lords to return the counties to Henry without fighting, for, if he were to make an issue of it, he would probably lose far more than just two districts that did not really belong to Scotland. The border was readjusted to the Tweed-Solway Firth line.

We know little else about the young king, except that, like David, he was generous to the Church. He died at Jedburgh in December 1165, and was succeeded by his brother, William.

WILLIAM [*The Lion: 1165-1214*]

The reign of William the Lion was the longest in Scottish history, and yet there are few details about his career. He was called "The Lion" from the drawing of a lion that he carried on his shield and on his banner. Born in 1143, he succeeded his brother Malcolm IV in 1165.

He was a brave and warlike man, proud

William the Lion surprised by English troops

of his nation and anxious to do good for his people. But he was rash, and often acted without forethought, and so he would get into difficulties that could easily have been avoided.

William wanted to recover the counties returned to the English king by his brother, and at first he believed that he might get them by making friends with Henry II and asking for them at the right moment. It seems that the English king led him to believe that the counties would be returned, but after some years when nothing had been done about it, William took advantage of a revolt by one of Henry's sons.

When Henry returned from subduing Ireland in 1173, he found that his sons, Henry, Richard and Geoffrey, had risen against him in various dominions of the Plantagenet empire. The eldest son, Prince Henry, knowing that William the Lion wanted Northumberland and Cumberland, offered him the former if he would assist him in his revolt against Henry II by leading an army into England. William could not resist this opportunity, and at once marshalled a great army.

In 1174, he set out across the border and reached the town of Alnwick, where he laid siege to the great fortress. In the meanwhile, some of his troops were harrying the surrounding districts, setting fire to towns and fields, driving the English people before them. When Henry heard of this, he sent a Yorkshire baron, Ralf de Glanvil, with a force, against the Scottish king.

The 12th July was a foggy day, and Glanvil's men managed to reach Alnwick

unnoticed by William who, with several of his knights, was amusing himself jousting under the castle walls. Suddenly, the fog lifted, and to his horror William espied the English detachment, which outnumbered his men several times. With reckless courage, he spurred his horse forward, shouting to his knights: "Now it will be seen who are true knights," and charged into the English. Within minutes he was unhorsed, and fell to the ground. As he tried to get up, he saw, standing around him, many men with their swords drawn, points directed at his throat. Thus he was captured, along with his followers.

The Scottish king was a prisoner of the king of England! At once Glanvil had him conveyed to Richmond Castle, in Yorkshire, and sent the joyous news to Henry, who ordered William to be brought over to France. There, at Falaise, he was imprisoned, manacled with chains about his wrists and his ankles.

It was a bad day for Scotland, and we can imagine how the people felt, and what they feared. After a few weeks, William was allowed to return to his kingdom, but he had to acknowledge Henry as his overlord, and he had to give up the castles of Edinburgh, Stirling, Berwick and Roxburgh to the English. He was not allowed to make war, treaties or any other arrangements without the permission of the English king. It was a most humiliating set of conditions.

This situation lasted for fifteen years, during which we know very little of what happened in Scotland. Then, when Richard I became king of England in 1189, there was a change.

Richard was anxious to raise all the money he could to finance his army for the Third Crusade. He sold all sorts of offices and privileges, and he offered William the release from these conditions for the sum of £7000, and William gladly agreed. Scotland was independent again.

The rest of his reign was taken up with putting down revolts, and in 1214, tired out by his exertions, he died at Stirling, aged seventy-two.

Alexander II was the son of William the Lion and he succeeded to the throne in 1214 when he was sixteen years old. Though young, he decided to rule by himself, and before many weeks he had been approached by the barons of England, who were fighting against John, and asked to invade England on their behalf. At the beginning of the next year, he led an army across the border and began to harry the supporters of the English king in those districts. He took no part in the proceedings of Magna Carta at Runnymede, but we find that after John's death, Alexander was assisting Prince Louis of France in his struggle in England with the supporters of the young Henry III. After Louis had to give up and return to France, Alexander and Henry came to terms, and for many years they were great friends. In 1221, Alexander married Henry's sister, Joan.

One of the only events of his reign of which we know anything is his successful expedition against the rebels in Argyllshire and the islands. This region, though part of Scotland ever since the time of Kenneth MacAlpine, had nevertheless been unwilling to obey the kings of Scotland, and its people would often be found supporting rebellions elsewhere in the country. It was in the islands that the chief centres of rebellion lay, and in 1222, using a large fleet of ships, Alexander took an army to the islands and forced the people to submit.

Alexander was also vexed by the king of Norway, who ruled through some chiefs in the Hebrides. These chiefs were continually crossing over to the mainland of Ross and Inverness and raiding the inhabitants, stirring them into revolt against the Scottish kings. Alexander prepared an invasion fleet and set out on an expedition of conquest. On the way up the Argyll coast, however, he died, on the island of Kakerry, in July, 1249. He was succeeded by his son, Alexander III, one of the greatest of all the Scottish kings.

Alexander II sets out on his last expedition

On the 19th March, 1286, the forty-five-year-old king of Scotland, Alexander III, sat at the head of a table in the council room in Edinburgh Castle. Round him were his chief nobles and bishops, and they were discussing the succession to the throne, for the king had no living children. Outside, the weather was stormy, and heavy seas lashed at the shores just north of the city. Suddenly, the king pushed back his chair, and stood up.

"My lords, I think we have discussed this matter long enough. I must leave now and go to see my wife. As you know, we have been married only a few months, and I have seen so little of her lately. Forgive me."

He walked out of the room, down the stairs and into the courtyard, where some attendants were waiting. Mounting his hourse, he set off with them along the road to Queensferry and there crossed the Forth by ferry-boat. When the party reached the other side, it was dark, and the rain was still pouring down, blown about by great gusts of wind. The party continued down the road towards Burntisfield, where the queen was staying, but in the storm, the riders lost their way. Each man followed wherever his horse led him. Then, when some of the attendants had reached the outskirts of Kinghorn, they heard a great crash, followed by a piercing cry.

At once they rushed to the scene, at the top of a cliff. As they looked over it, down into the swirling waters of the Forth, they could hear the neighing of an injured horse, splashing about on the sand. Swiftly, they dismounted and climbed down the cliff. There, at its foot, lay the body of the king, covered with blood, and lifeless.

Thus ended Alexander III, of whose reign an historian said: "there was peace and love in the land, abundance of ale and bread, of wine and wassail cake, and of sports and mirth." And his tragic death led to untold miseries for the Scottish nation, miseries that were not to be ended for a quarter of a century.

When he came to the throne in 1249, Alexander was eight years old. He was crowned at Scone in great splendour, in the company of a host of nobles and bishops. The throne on which he sat contained the famous Stone of Destiny. This stone was believed to have been the very one on which Jacob, according to the Old Testament story, laid his head when he had his dream about the ladder, and it was supposed to have been brought to Scotland by a daughter of an Egyptian Pharaoh.

At first, the nation was ruled by a council of regency, but the members were unable to agree with each other and they soon fell to fighting. When Alexander was of age, he took over the government himself, and in a short time put down all the quarrelsome barons. As his reign is described as "most peaceable" by some historians, we must assume that he managed to control these barons effectively.

He maintained good relations with Henry III of England, having as a boy been betrothed, and later married to the king's daughter, Margaret. They had two sons, both of whom died before the king, and one daughter, Margaret, who was married to the king of Norway. Her daughter, Margaret, became the heir to the Scottish throne.

Alexander was a great warrior, and he had all the chivalry and gentleness that we find so admirable in the person of Edward III of England in the next century. He was powerfully built, handsome and fearless, and he knew how to make men obey him.

In 1263, Haakon, King of Norway, disturbed by news that the Hebrides were in danger of being attacked by Alexander, planned an expedition to deal with the Scottish king. He set sail from Norway in July with a fleet of more than one hundred ships, containing thousands of warriors.

Within a few days, he reached the Orkney Islands and then moved westwards and down past the Hebrides, pushing towards Argyll.

Alexander, informed of the expedition, assembled his fleet off the coast of Ayrshire, gathered an army and brought it to the district around Glasgow. In the meanwhile, he arranged for the fortresses along the west coast to be strengthened.

At the end of September, Haakon was drawn up at sea off the town of Largs, waiting to meet Alexander's ships, and ready to land his invasion force. Suddenly, a terrible storm arose, and many of the Norwegian king's ships foundered or were smashed to pieces on the rocky coast. With some difficulty, he brought the remainder of his men to land near Largs where, the next morning, the Scottish army was waiting for them. The battle began soon after dawn broke, and it was fought with all the strength and the courage of both sides. It went on all day, but by the evening, the Scots had triumphed. Haakon had been driven back to his ships with but a remnant

Battle of Largs

of the splendid fighting force he had brought with him. He set sail for Norway, but died on the way back, somewhere in the Orkneys.

It was one of the greatest victories in Scottish history. Alexander took advantage of it, invaded the Hebrides and in a short but tough campaign conquered them, adding them to the Scottish kingdom.

There is little more to tell of his reign, but from the descriptions of his rule, it is clear that he brought a measure of peace and prosperity that the Scots had not often before enjoyed. The tragic nature of his death brought a splendid reign to a very sad end. His heir was a little girl of three, his granddaughter, and this was to be the cause of a long period of suffering for the nation.

MARGARET [*The Maid of Norway : 1286–1290*]

The little girl, granddaughter of Alexander III, was born in Norway, as her mother was the wife of Norway's king, Eric. On her grandfather's death, Scotland was again ruled by a council of regency, and once more its members spent most of their time fighting among each other. This was an opportunity for the English king, Edward I, flush with his recent victory over Wales, to add Scotland to his dominions. He suggested to the Scottish regents that the young queen should be betrothed to his young son, Edward, who was then about the same age. The regents agreed, on condition that Scotland did not lose its independence and merely become an English province.

Then in 1290, when young Margaret was being brought by ship from Norway to her kingdom, she died. This was a tragedy. Who was now to be the next king of Scotland? Immediately, a dozen different nobles, all of them asserting some descent or relationship with the royal family, put forward their claims. It could mean only one thing—civil war. For two years, the position was undecided, and these years are called the First Interregnum, as there was, in effect, no monarch.

Because of the many claimants, and as no one in Scotland seemed to be able to say who was the best one, the regents invited Edward I to decide. Edward was delighted. He answered the invitation by saying that he would make a choice, but that before doing so, certain conditions must be observed by the Scots. His choice was to acknowledge him as overlord of Scotland, and the principal castles of Scotland were to be handed over to English barons. These terms must be agreed, not only by his choice, but by the successor of that chosen person.

The Scottish nobles were in a quandary. Faced with a desperate civil war between the many claimants, such war which could only result in the devastation of the country, and yet knowing that if they accepted Edward's terms they would be surrendering the nation's independence, they put off a decision.

Then, under pressure from Edward, they at last agreed to accept his choice and his terms, though it is likely that many of them thought to do so because they believed that the day would come when they could break the arrangement.

Edward and his advisers carefully examined all the claims, and after much deliberation, picked John Balliol, a great-great-grandson of David I. The only other claimant worth considering at the time was Robert Bruce, Lord of Annandale, who was a great-great-grandson of David I, but through a junior branch of the family.

JOHN BALLIOL [1292-1296]

The choice of John Balliol as their new king did not please the Scots at all. He was a weak and ineffective man, intimidated both by his nobles and by the English. Although he was a Scot, he seemed to have none of the fiery patriotism of the earlier kings.

He ruled for four years, but they were sad ones for the nation. One moment, he would do as the English king demanded, the next he would give in to his Scottish advisers, and so nobody could trust him. When he agreed to make a treaty of alliance with France, England's enemy, in 1295, and followed this up with an invasion of Northumberland, he brought the wrath of the English king down upon the whole nation. Edward marched northwards, and at the battle of Dunbar in 1296 utterly defeated John Balliol, compelling him to resign his crown. Edward had had enough of the Scots, he said, and now they would have no king of their own any more. He would be king of Scotland, and would rule through an English Governor. For ten years he ruled, and this is called the Second Interregnum.

SECOND INTERREGNUM [1296-1306)

Though Edward kept control of Scotland during this period, it was a most difficult task. In the story of his life, we have seen something of the resistance put up by Sir William Wallace. When Wallace died, the spirit of Scottish nationalism did not die with him.

Edward decided to make the Scots obey the laws of England, and William Ormsby was made Chief Justice. Another Englishman, Hugh Cressingham, was put in charge of the country's finances. The English decided what taxes the Scots should pay and used their officers to collect them. English judges sat in the courts, and English soldiers garrisoned the major castles and military camps.

The Scots were—and still are—an intensely patriotic race of people. They were not going to tolerate foreign domination without a struggle, and the whole of the Second Interregnum was racked with revolt. It cost England huge sums to try to keep the Scots down, and whenever they were successful in one district, in another the people rose again. After Wallace was executed, another national hero rose to fight for his nation's freedom—Robert Bruce, one of the best known of all Scottish leaders.

ROBERT I [*Bruce : 1306-1329*]

One day in 1306, Robert Bruce, who had decided to assert his claim to the Scottish throne (it was his grandfather's claim that had been considered by Edward I in 1292), went to a church in Dumfries to meet Sir John Comyn, another claimant. They had earlier come to an agreement whereby Comyn offered to forgo his claim and support Robert Bruce if he would give him certain lands. Then they had quarrelled, and Comyn is said to have reported the bargain to Edward I.

Inside the church, the two men soon fell into bitter argument, and loud voices were heard by their friends outside. Then, a shrill cry rent the air, and immediately Bruce ran out of the door, calling for his friends, telling them he had killed Comyn. They rushed into the church, and found the man, lying on the ground, seriously injured. They drew their swords and despatched him.

A thrill of horror spread throughout Scotland when it heard the story. A claimant to the throne had murdered another claimant—and in the sanctuary of a church, too! When Edward I heard of the crime, he was furious, and determined at once to punish Bruce. This was the main reason for his invasion of 1307, on which he died at Burgh-on-Sands. The Pope, also, was angry, and he excommunicated Bruce immediately. Nothing like this had happened since the murder of Becket, over a hundred years before.

Bruce, meanwhile, was not to be frightened by the protests of other people outside Scotland, and within a month of the deed he had himself crowned king at Scone, notwithstanding that Edward I was, in name, already King of Scotland.

The attendance at the ceremony was very small, for few of the nobles, remembering the fate of Wallace, were ready to risk their lives for a man who would

The murder of Sir John Comyn

share exactly the same fate if he were caught—and they as well. The Stone of Destiny had been removed by Edward I, and placed in a coronation chair at Westminster, where it can still be seen today. So it was not the kind of coronation that usually attended the succession of the kings of Scotland.

To make something of the position he had seized for himself, Bruce had to be a man of strength and courage, able to command followers, capable of enduring all kinds of hardship, prepared to risk everything for what he believed to be right for Scotland. Such were his qualities, and soon he won a reputation for daring leadership, and the admiration of all Scottish people who longed for their independence.

Bruce was a broad-shouldered, middle-sized man, with a fine head and deep-set eyes. He was possessed of considerable inventive powers. In armour, he looked what he was, a magnificent leader of men, an inspirer of courage. And yet there were defects in his nature. He was selfish, quick-tempered and at times dishonest, and nothing could forgive the rashness that led him to murder Comyn. He could be cruel when he had to be, without regret, but he also had a strict sense of justice.

This great leader, who had entered the stage of history with a wicked crime to his name, began a reign in which he was king in name only, for as soon as he was crowned, he was hunted across the countryside by the English, with a reward set on his capture, and eventually he was driven out of Scotland altogether.

A year later he returned and succeeded in defeating an English army under de Valence, Edward's Governor of Scotland. When Edward set out to punish Bruce, and died at Burgh-on-Sands, the continuation of the war was entrusted to his heir, who became Edward II.

Edward II disbanded the army and returned to London, leaving the English barons in Scotland to fend for themselves. For the next seven years, Bruce harried them either in open warfare or by guerilla

Robert Bruce

194

tactics, capturing their castles one by one, until in 1314, he completely destroyed a vast English army at Bannockburn (see Edward II of England).

The results of this battle were glorious for the Scots. Huge stores of treasure fell into their hands, not only from Edward's camp and the tents of his commanders, but also from the rest of the castles which surrendered to him after the victory. This money, urgently needed by Scotland, for the people had had to pay heavily for the "privilege" of being ruled by the English through all kinds of taxes, was more than doubled when Bruce released nobles captured at Bannockburn in exchange for large payments. Now he had the resources to rebuild the Scottish nation, and the people had the will to help him.

The victory of Bannockburn was not the end of the war, for Edward II refused to recognise Scotland's independence. This meant that fighting must go on, but now the position was different. No longer was Bruce a hunted man, with a price on his head; he was a conqueror, and he could lead armies with confidence into England to fight them on their own territory.

This he did, several times, often with great success. Strongholds fell, prisoners were captured, and more booty was taken. In 1318, he captured Berwick, a vital town that the English had used to guard the river Tweed and to supply her forces spread about Scotland.

Still Edward would not recognise Scotland's independence. So Bruce and the nobles decided to appeal to the Pope. At a meeting held at Arbroath, in 1320, they drafted a letter to Rome, begging for recognition as a separate nation. "We have been delivered by the strong arm of our Prince, our Lord Robert," the nobles wrote, "who, like a second Joshua, endured cheerfully toil, weariness, fasting and peril. We are never minded to bow beneath the yoke of the English. It is not for glory, riches or honour that we have fought; it is for liberty."

This letter, known as the Declaration of Arbroath, was one of the important documents of Scottish history. It was regarded in much the same way as Englishmen looked upon Magna Carta, for it was a statement that all Scotland believed it had the right to be free.

The Pope refused to grant the recognition, and so the fighting continued. At last, when Edward III became king in 1327, things changed, for the time being. A year later, Scotland was recognised by Edward, at the Treaty of Northampton, as an independent kingdom, and to cement the agreement, Bruce's son, David, was married to Edward's sister, Joanna.

In 1329, the great patriot died at Cardross, in Dumbartonshire.

Although most of his time had been taken up with fighting, Bruce had undertaken some improvements in the land. He was particularly anxious to put the nation's forces into good order. He built a navy with which to deal the pirates crushing blows, for these rovers were making the seas unsafe for English and Scottish mariners and merchantmen alike. He reorganised the army, so that it should be able to to win.

Every year, everybody over sixteen and under sixty had to come to an appointed place in their neighbourhood and show to officers what weapons they had and to prove that they knew how to use them. This was called the "wapinschaw," or weapon-showing. Every man who had lands worth more than ten pounds had to own his own suit of armour. Every man who was able to own a cow had also to possess a bow, a quiver and a bundle of twenty-four arrows. Though these regulations were sometimes broken, they did enable the Scots to be prepared for war and to acquit themselves well against any attack from abroad.

Bruce had given back to the Scots not only their nation but also their national pride, and for this he was remembered ever afterwards, especially in the many periods of distress that were to follow once he had gone.

David Bruce was Robert I's son, and he was five years old when he became David I in 1329. Eighteen months later, he was crowned at Scone by the Bishop of St Andrews who anointed him with holy oil, bought from the Pope for a great price. It was the first time that a Scottish king had been sprinkled with oil at his coronation, a ceremony practised in England for some generations.

Robert had left the country in the capable hands of his best friend and most trusted adviser, Randolph, Earl of Moray, who became Regent. Moray had commanded a wing at the battle of Bannockburn, and in many other battles he had shown the highest courage and skill as a field commander. He was respected by everyone in the land. He governed wisely for the first two years.

Then, in 1332, Edward Balliol, King John Balliol's son, who had been living in England, planned an invasion of Scotland to capture the throne. He spoke to Edward III about it, and that king offered to support him, provided that if he won, Scotland was once more to become a subject kingdom of England.

Balliol, accompanied by some Scottish nobles who had been banished by Robert I for taking sides with the English, set sail from Yorkshire and landed in Fifeshire. At once, Moray prepared an army, but, to the misfortune of the nation, he died before he could lead his troops out of camp. His successor, the Earl of Mar, was a very different kind of man, headstrong, unwilling to take advice, and within days of his appointment he met Balliol in battle near Perth and was completely defeated. Balliol then had himself crowned at Scone. There were now two kings of Scotland!

Balliol was driven out of the kingdom by followers of David a few months later, and at this Edward III decided to come out in the open and invade Scotland himself. Together, they marched towards Berwick, and at Halidon Hill a battle was fought.

The English army was arranged on one hill, facing the Scots who were on another. Between them there was a treacherous marsh. When the signal was given, the Scots charged down their slope, right into the wet, boggy valley where, floundering helplessly about, they were a splendid target for the English archers. The slaughter was frightful, and it was said that the Scots died in their hundreds where they stood. Not one of them reached the English close enough for hand-to-hand fighting. Among the Scottish dead were Lord Douglas, Mar's successor as Regent, four earls and many knights.

Edward and Balliol divided Scotland between them, Edward taking the southern half. David and his wife, Joanna, fled to France for safety.

The Scottish people had not forgotten their triumphs under Robert Bruce, and they resisted the rule of Edward and of Balliol. After many skirmishes, they drove Balliol out, and as Edward was occupied with the war in France, he was unable to help his brother king. David was invited to return from France and arrived home amid great rejoicing. As he was now seventeen, he decided to take over the government himself.

The Scots soon found that he was an unworthy successor to his great father. He was weak, extravagant and hot-headed. He spent huge sums on his own pleasures and had little interest in the details of government. When Edward was in France in 1346, the year of the battle of Crécy, David took advantage of his absence to invade England, but he misjudged the strength of the English army of the north, and at Neville's Cross, near Durham, he was defeated and captured. Taken to London, he spent the next eleven years as a prisoner of the English king.

Scotland was then ruled by David's nephew, Robert Stewart. This Robert was in fact several years older than his uncle, because David was born in the later years of his father's reign, whereas Robert Stewart's mother Marjorie had been Robert

Bruce's daughter by his first wife. Stewart governed well, although it was a hard time for the nation; it was the period when all Europe suffered so grievously from the Black Death.

When this plague reached England and began to spread, the Scots were not at first affected. Indeed, they regarded it as "the foul death of the English" and some thought of it as God's punishment for English aggression in Scotland. All the same, it eventually extended to the country and before it had gone about a third of the population had died of it. We can imagine that the same kind of distress came with it as did in England and in Europe.

Not long after the English victory at Poitiers, in 1356, Edward III decided to allow David to return to his kingdom. But the terms of his return were hard. Scotland had to pay 90,000 marks, in yearly instalments for ten years. Everybody had to contribute a sum to this ransom money, nobles, clergy, merchants and common people alike. It was a vast sum, and it was all the more painful to pay because the king was not really worth the money. When he came home in 1357 he went on with his expensive living, to the disgust of everybody. In 1371, he died, mourned only by those few associates who had enjoyed helping him to spend his money.

197

David II had no children, and so the throne passed to his nephew, Robert Stewart, who had governed the nation when the king was a prisoner in England.

Robert was a tall and good-looking man, with kind features. He had a strange defect of his eyes, for they were always red and watery, and this earned him the name "King Blearie." He was gentle and easygoing, and though he was devoted to the idea of keeping law and order in his kingdom, he did not have that tough and fearless nature necessary for controlling the warring barons who continued to struggle for power after David's death.

During his reign a treaty was signed with France. For a long time, the two countries had been on friendly terms, as they had one thing in common, above all others. Both had been subjected to invasion and conquest by the English. Now, by this treaty, they agreed that if one nation was attacked by England the other would come to its aid. So, when the fighting on the border began again in the time of Richard II of England, the French sent an army to help its ally.

Surprisingly, the Scottish people were not at all grateful for this aid. They did not

understand the French, their language or their ways of life, which were more luxurious. Frenchmen had grand houses, lavishly furnished, and the barons and knights lived like little kings, with their own courts. This was one of the reasons why the English were so successful in France in Edward III's time, for these little "kings" often refused to help the King of France when he was attacked, and so the nation, divided, was easier to overcome. The Scots, on their part, lived a much harder life. Their houses were generally built of wood and plaster. They did not have comfortable beds or decorative furnishings, and, as the climate was much colder for most of the year, they were a vigorous race, used to rough conditions.

The two peoples did not get on at all well when they met on common ground. Moreover, their methods of fighting were very different. The French loved a grand battle, in which the nobles and knights would be decked in all the fineries of armour and drapery that we associate with the legends of King Arthur. The Scots did not like major engagements, and preferred to attack their enemies by swift raids under cover of darkness, or by hiding behind trees and then springing out upon smaller

detachments of troops on the road. After a while, the French troops returned to their country.

In 1388, a famous battle was fought at Otterburn in Northumberland, between the English and the Scots. Two powerful Scottish nobles, the Earl of Moray and the Earl of Douglas, led a raid into the county, and at Otterburn they came upon a force, three times the size of theirs, under "Hotspur" Percy, who later rebelled against Henry IV of England. It was evening, and the sun was going down when the two armies clashed. The Scots pressed so hard into the English ranks that the latter's archers dared not let loose their arrows for fear of killing their own men. The fight went on for an hour, until Douglas, right in the thick of the fray, fell to the ground, pierced with many lance-wounds. His followers took up the cry—"A Douglas! A Douglas!" and with incredible bravery they overcame Hotspur's force, which abandoned the field, leaving nearly two thousand dead behind. It was a great victory, and it deterred the English for some time to come.

By this time, Robert was a very old man. He had been ill for many months and in 1390, he died.

ROBERT III [1390–1406]

Robert II was succeeded by his son, John Stewart, Earl of Carrick. There is a legend that this John changed his name and became Robert III, because it was thought that John was an unlucky name for a king. Certainly, there had been some unfortunate Johns in history, John of England, John of France who was captured by the Black Prince after Poitiers in 1356, and John Balliol who was forced to resign the crown of Scotland in 1296.

He was born in about 1339, and in his youth he had suffered an accident which affected both his body and his mind. When he came to the throne, the effective government of the nation was therefore entrusted to his brother, the Earl of Fife, who had also managed the kingdom in the last years of Robert II.

Scotland was safe from attack by England for the time being, but the internal fighting between the great feudal lords went on, and the story of this reign is really the tale of how Fife managed to deal with it.

Fife was a remarkable man, in many ways fit to be a king. He was perhaps the boldest Scot alive at the time, fearing absolutely nobody. He was a fine soldier, a sound governor and he was devoted to keeping order within the kingdom. He was a match for any of the rebel barons, and he was particularly loved by the merchant class and the common folk, chiefly, it is said, because he raised as few taxes as he possibly could. He was immensely rich himself, but was ready to spend his own money, rather than other people's, to further his aims.

During this reign, we hear about the difficulties which the king and Fife had with the peoples in the Highlands, those mountainous and wooded stretches of land, separated by rivers and lakes which today provide perhaps the most beautiful scenery in the British Isles. Here, the people lived a semi-barbarous existence, and because of the nature of their countryside they were most difficult to keep in order. They were divided into clans, just like the old tribes of Britain which the Romans found when they came in the time of Julius Caesar and again in the days of the Emperor Claudius. They did not grow crops, but lived by hunting and fishing. If they were short of food, they raided their more civilised neighbours further south, generally at harvest time, and carried off the crops. The most that the kings were able to do was to confine them within their region, but it was an impossible task to get these Highlanders to observe the laws of the nation. If a clan had a difference with another clan, it would not think of discussing the matter at a conference. The sword was the only answer.

Fife was able to keep them within their district, but he could do no more.

In 1399, the feudal lords, tired of being kept under strict control by Fife, begged the sickly king to dismiss him and appoint a new governor of the realm. The king agreed and gave the position to his eldest son, David. To compensate Fife, Robert III promoted him to be Duke of Albany, a title which brought with it considerable tracts of land.

It is not surprising that the new Duke was angry. He had more than proved his worth as a manager of the kingdom, and he knew that his successor would not do as well as he. And so it was, for David surrounded himself with worthless favourites, who were both greedy and arrogant, and raised taxes to pay for the extravagances of these people. Not long afterwards, David was found dead at Falkland Castle, and he was believed to have been murdered on the orders of Albany, who was not tried for the offence.

In 1406, the king's heir, James, a boy of eleven, was on his way to France when the ship in which he was travelling was captured off Flamborough by English seamen. He was sent to London when Henry IV put him in the Tower. He was to remain in England for the next eighteen years.

When the news of his son's capture was brought to the feeble Robert, he was stricken with grief and died at once.

Robert II's son, James, is captured on his way to France

JAMES I [*1406-1437*]

James was the first in a row of five Scottish kings of that name. They were all children when they succeeded, they were all gifted in some way, and they all met tragic ends.

Though he was a prisoner in England, James was declared king by the Scottish council as soon as Robert III died. The government of the nation was placed, once again, in the hands of Albany, an appointment which pleased the people but was not to the liking of the nobility. At once he set out to keep the lords under control, confiscating their lands if they rebelled, forcing them to observe the laws of the country.

During his Regency, James Resby, who was a Lollard (a follower of John Wycliffe, the religious reformer of Edward III's and Richard II's time) came to Scotland and preached the Lollard doctrines up and down the country. The Scottish Church viewed this with alarm, and it begged Albany to put an end to the Lollard teachings. Before long, Resby was caught, tried for heresy, and burnt at the stake. He was the first man to be put to death in Scotland for his religious beliefs.

At this time, although there were many schools attached to the abbeys and cathedrals of Scotland, and elsewhere in the countryside, there was no place where boys could continue their education after they left school. They would have to go abroad to foreign universities, and this was an expensive undertaking. It was decided, therefore, to found Scotland's first university, and it was established at St Andrews, by Wardlaw, the Bishop of St Andrews. It was a great moment for the Scots when the new college was opened, in 1411. Soon afterwards, it was blessed by the Pope, who sent a special messenger to convey his greetings. St Andrews is now one of the most famous universities in the world, and the scholars, writers, scientists and engineers who have studied in its lecture rooms and laboratories are too numerous to mention.

In 1420, the great Regent Albany died, aged eighty. To the very end he had kept a tight grip on the nation's government. He was succeeded by his son, Murdoch, who was utterly unworthy of the position. Immediately, the barons refused to accept him, and they agitated for the return to Scotland of the king. Talks were opened with the English, and in 1424 James was allowed to come home.

When he came back many people in Scotland were agog with interest. He had

James I returns to his kingdom

not been seen for eighteen years, and in 1406 he had been a boy. Now they wondered what he was like.

James was a big man, muscular and agile. He loved outdoor activities, and he was said to be one of the best athletes and riders in Scotland. During his confinement in England, he spent some years at Windsor where he was well-treated and where he got to know Prince Henry, who became Henry V in 1413. We may not be wrong in supposing that Henry, who was also a great athlete, encouraged him in these outdoor sports. James was also learned and artistic. He could write poetry, he could play musical instruments, and he loved painting and sketching.

When he returned to Scotland, with his wife, Joan, the granddaughter of John of Gaunt, he was crowned at Scone. At once he set out to make the nation obey him. He started by dismissing Murdoch, great Albany's son, and then he turned on the Highland chiefs. Some of them were

punished for their refusal to conform to the nation's laws, as a warning to the remainder.

James was a stern ruler, but this was necessary because for too long the nobles had been having things their own way. It was time that they had a king whom they feared. And yet, he had a strict regard for justice. When, for example, he found out that some of the clergy had not been carrying out their duties properly, such as helping the poor, he told them that they could hardly be surprised if the people took matters into their own hands and rose against them. If they wanted the respect of the populace, they must earn it. If they would mend their ways, then, he would protect them.

These tough measures made him enemies. For generations, the Scottish feudal lords co-operated with the kings if it suited them to do so, but they also seized every opportunity for advancing their own power, and they did not like to be disciplined by a king who had spent so many years in a foreign country. In 1437, a rich knight, Sir Robert Graham, who had been imprisoned earlier in the reign for unruliness, murdered the king when he was at Perth. It was a shocking crime, and James's widow, Joan, vowed to avenge his death. Graham and his associates were hunted up and down the country, and when they were caught, they were put to death after suffering the most frightful tortures. As a popular rhyme went:

> Sir Robert Graham, *that slew our king,*
> *God give him shame.*

JAMES II [1437–1460]

James was six years old when his father was murdered at Perth. Unfortunately for Scotland, there was no strong and wise man like Albany to rule as Regent, and though the boy's mother, Joan, tried to govern in his name, she could not get the support she needed. For several years the country was racked with warfare between the rich lords who fought among each other for the supreme position of power. When a brave and popular young noble, William, Earl of Douglas, whom the boy-king admired, was made lieutenant to the royal household, he was soon seized by other nobles and put to death.

One would have expected that England would take advantage of this civil warfare in Scotland to lead an invasion, since it was still the dream of English kings that they should become rulers of Scotland. At this

Death of James II

time, however, Henry VI had his own troubles, not only in France, where the empire of Henry V was fast disappearing, but also at home where the Lancastrians were not managing the country very well. And so, for a while, Scotland was safe from English aggression.

When James was sixteen, he took over the government himself, and at once continued his father's policy of suppressing the lords. He was not as learned as James I, but he was more popular. His soldiers adored him because he would share their hard, outdoor life in camp on military expeditions, and he would mix with them, talking to them as equals.

He was to reign for another thirteen years, but he was so occupied with dealing with baronial wars that he had little time for any other activity. His main danger was from the Douglas family, relatives of the young man who had been put to death earlier on. They were a tough, fighting family, but they were popular, as for years they had been the leaders of the armies that had harried the English on the border. One of them was killed at Otterburn, as will be remembered. The present earl, William, was for some time one of James's chief advisers, but secretly he was increasing his own power by making arrangements with other lords to build up a party that would be strong enough to bend the king to their will. It was the story of who should rule Scotland, a king through the nobles and the parliament, or the nobles on their own, with no regard for the wishes of the country.

At that time, Scotland, too, had its Great Council of nobles and bishops, and also its parliament of knights, prominent citizens and country landowners. Parliament would be summoned from time to time to discuss affairs of government or to grant the king money for military campaigns. But there were differences from the English model.

In Scotland, all the members would meet in one place. If every member appeared, however, there was no room large enough to hold them. So, each county selected two representatives to speak for its inhabitants. As there were fewer bishops and fewer nobles in Scotland than there were in England, it was possible to hold these meetings in one large room, and it often happened that some of the members never bothered to attend at all.

In time, James discovered Douglas's secret plans, and at a meeting in Stirling Castle, he suddenly asked Douglas to give them up. Douglas refused, whereupon James took a dagger from his belt and stabbed him in the neck. His attendants finished the assault by plunging their knives into his heart.

It was a wicked crime, for Douglas was popular. All the same, it helped James to break the Douglas power, and he managed to get Parliament to pass an act whereby the extensive Douglas lands were to be confiscated.

For the rest of his reign, James managed to keep the lords under his control and even got them to work with him. In 1460, he determined to win back the castles of Roxburgh and Berwick, which were in English hands. One morning, as he stood beside the cannons which were discharging their explosive missiles against the great thick walls of Roxburgh Castle, one of them burst. A large splinter of iron struck him, and he fell dead on the spot.

JAMES III [1460–1488]

One day in 1482, James III was encamped outside the town of Lauder with his army. He had declared war on England because his brother, the new Duke of Albany, had fled to the court of Edward IV and begged his help to get James deposed from the throne. Approaching the other side of the town was another army, led by the Earl of Angus and Lord Gray which, he hoped, was about to join him for the march into England.

Angus's army stopped outside the town, and the two lords went into Lauder church for a discussion. They were tired of the king's favourites, and were bent on removing them.

Meanwhile, in the royal camp, James was amusing himself in the company of these favourites, who included an architect, Cochrane, recently made Earl of Mar, Homyle, the king's tailor, a musician called Roger and Leonard, a blacksmith. When Angus's army did not appear to be coming any nearer, Cochrane set off for the town

and reached the church. Dressed in a fine suit of black velvet, with a gold chain about his neck, he knocked on the church door. The door opened and he rushed in, up the aisle, to where the two lords were standing in discussion. Immediately, Angus seized hold of the gold chain and pulled it away, breaking the jewelled clasp.

"Is this a joke?" asked Cochrane, nervously.

"No, it is not, as you will soon find out," answered Angus. Then he turned to Lord Gray. "Go and get the others. I'll keep this one here," and he held the point of his sword at Cochrane's throat.

Gray departed, and collecting a guard outside, set off for the king's camp. When he got there, he lifted up the flap and cried out to the startled James: "My Lord, the people of Scotland are tired of your favourites, and they are disgusted with the company you keep. You are under arrest." Waving to his soldiers, Gray pointed towards the favourites. "Take them out," he ordered.

The soldiers dragged the frightened men out of the tent, and took them along the field to a bridge, where Angus was now waiting with Cochrane. Over the parapet were a number of ropes, looped at the end. Without further ado, the soldiers put the halters round the victims' necks and lowered them over the parapet, so that their feet dangled above the water underneath.

Then Angus and Gray took the king to Edinburgh Castle and held him in custody. The march against England was abandoned, but this was to have a permanent result, for the English advanced against Berwick, captured it, and it has remained part of England ever since.

James had come to the throne in 1460, when he was only eight. The nation was governed by the council of nobles, at the head of whom was a pious and learned man, James Kennedy, Bishop of St Andrews. Kennedy, a kind-hearted man, nonetheless knew how to handle the most unruly barons, and for the first five years of the reign there was little internal disorder. He

was a great benefactor to the Church, and he built a college which was added to the university of St Andrews.

Unfortunately, this wise rule ended when he died in 1465, and almost at once the warfare between the feudal lords began again. Four years later, James decided to rule for himself.

James was a strange man, gifted, fond of music and deeply religious, and yet he was weak-minded, and did not understand the problems that had to be solved in his kingdom. He disliked the nobles as a class, and he surrounded himself with people of humble birth, who were generally craftsmen and artists whose work he admired. This would have been understandable if he were not king, but they were not the sort of people who knew anything about government and so they could be of little help to him. He quarrelled with his brothers and imprisoned them. One, the Duke of Albany, escaped and fled to England where he was entertained by Edward IV.

James also quarrelled with all of his barons, and he angered the people, who might in different circumstances have supported him, by debasing the value of the coinage (as Henry VIII did in the last years of his reign). Most of the money thus raised was spent on his favourites.

Eventually, the nobles rose in revolt, and Angus and Gray captured him at Lauder. When they had imprisoned him in Edinburgh Castle, they allowed Albany to return from England and he was given back the lands which had been taken from him. James was released, on condition that he stopped filling up the court with what the nobles considered as useless advisers and friends.

No sooner had he obtained his release, however, when James went back on his word. He confiscated lands from those nobles who had resisted him, and gave some of them to a crop of new favourites. In 1488, the nobles rose again, and at the battle of Sauchieburn they defeated him. He fled from the field but was overtaken the same evening, and stabbed to death.

James IV was the son of James III, and he came to the throne when he was sixteen years old. Although he was still a boy, he made up his mind that he would give Scotland the kind of government it needed, that is, direction of all affairs from a strong central authority. It would be a difficult task, and most of his predecessors had failed in it, but James began with certain advantages. He had a splendid appearance, of medium height, well-built, with a fine brow and a long beard (in days when not many people wore them at all) and no sooner had a description of his looks been spread around the nation than he was recognised wherever he went. This was a most useful thing, and its value was increased by the fact that the possessor of these features was also learned in a vast number of subjects. He could speak seven languages, apart from English, and he was

James IV

interested in everything that was going on around him. He employed scientists and encouraged them to pursue their discoveries, he picked out the best lawyers and gave them high positions, instructing them to bring the laws of the nation up to date. He studied the lessons of warfare by reading about the famous generals of Europe of the time, and in many encounters he showed himself to be a skilful commander. A man with so many gifts, and with a presence that was immediately recognisable, was bound to be able to command the obedience and the loyalty of his subjects, high and low.

He came to the throne when great changes were taking place throughout Western Europe, in an age when nations were sending their ships and their men to the hitherto undiscovered corners of the world, like the Americas, the East Indies and the remote parts of Africa and Asia. Although Scotland was not able to join in this great new adventure across the seas, it could, and it did, benefit from the new ideas of learning that were spreading over Europe. Printing had reached England in the time of Edward IV, and James encouraged printers in his own land, so that learning could be advanced.

Like his predecessors, he was bothered by baronial warfare, though in his time it was not so violent or widespread. He had already decided to bring the nation into line with other countries in the advancement of new ideas of government, and as the nation in general was anxious to accept them, the barons found that they could only survive at all if they gave up the sort of aggression to which their fathers and grandfathers had been accustomed.

There was one area where James was more successful than his forebears. This was in the Hebrides and in north-western Scotland.

For a long time, these districts, though part of the Scottish kingdom, had nevertheless been pursuing a separate existence, paying little attention to the more orderly government of the south. The Hebrides were ruled by a Lord of the Isles, as he was called, and a succession of these lords had given much trouble to the kings. Sometimes, these lords had been allowed to keep their power, provided that they acknowledged the Scottish kings as overlords and agreed to observe the nation's laws. But James decided that this power must be brought to an end, and in a hard campaign he crushed the chiefs and their followers, and abolished the title altogether. He seems to have won great respect in the north, for among the troops who fought in his last battle, there were none so brave or so loyal as those that came from the Hebrides.

By the beginning of the sixteenth century, both Henry VII of England and James were anxious that their nations should be at peace with one another, and to cement an alliance James married Margaret Tudor, the English king's daughter, in 1503, at a ceremony that was to be the finest of its kind yet seen in Scotland.

So much of Scottish history seems to have been filled with warfare and unrest that it is indeed pleasant to read about the general growth in prosperity of the nation under James. In his time, a number of industries expanded swiftly, none more quickly than the fisheries. The wool trade developed, agriculture was improved, more houses were built and they were, for the most part, constructed of stone and brick. James also built a royal navy, and one vessel, called the Great Michael, became the largest ship in the world at the time.

James turned his attention to law, and he set up a Daily Council which met in Edinburgh, or wherever else he might be staying. At this court, anyone could bring a complaint before a panel of judges appointed by him to hear cases. He also regulated the travelling of judges to county courts, and would sometimes attend these hearings himself.

He encouraged trade with other countries on a far greater scale than ever before. He brought craftsmen and merchants from Europe and invited them to settle in Scotland to teach their skills to the people, providing them with worthwhile livings. In

Battle of Flodden

particular, the fisheries experts were able to show the Scottish fishermen how best to preserve and pack their catches. Wool, fish, cloth and pearls, among other goods, were exported in increasing quantities, and in return Scotland received fine silks, wines, jewellery and metals.

Nor was the field of education neglected. A law was passed which made the upper classes send their children to school, and then on to the universities. Two more had been founded since St Andrews was established one hundred years before, Glasgow in 1451, and Aberdeen in 1494, and so there was room for those scholars who wished to develop their learning.

James made Edinburgh the capital city of Scotland, which it still is, and he arranged that the great mansion at Holyrood should become the palace of the royal family. It was in Edinburgh that Parliament, on most occasions, met.

This great king, leader of his people into the new age of learning and government that was spreading throughout Europe,

died in battle. It happened in this way.

When Henry VIII of England decided to make war on France in 1513, James, anxious to help Scotland's oldest ally, invaded England. In August of that year, after harrying Northumberland and attacking some of its smaller fortresses, he met an English army at Flodden, on September 9th. A battle began, and to begin with the Scots easily crushed one of the English wings. But, as the sun went down, the Scots were hard-pressed in their centre. Then an English cavalry charge broke the centre up, and the slaughter began. Soon, James and his nobles were fighting for their very lives, and by eventide the king and his chief leaders had fallen. When the rest of the Scots heard of the death of their great king, they turned and ran from the field. And they did not stop until they had crossed the border into Scotland.

A splendid reign had come to a sudden end. The Scots were long to regret the passing of their king in battle, for his heir was a boy only eighteen months old.

JAMES V [1515-1542]

When James IV fell at Flodden, the Scots were alarmed lest the English should march into the country and try to overrun it. Every English king since Edward I, and many before him, had at some time or other been ambitious to bring Scotland under his rule, but now there seemed to be little to stop the Earl of Surrey, the English commander, doing what he liked. In Edinburgh the terror was so great that the citizens immediately built a large stone wall round the city, and throughout the rest of the country the people were urged to arm themselves and be ready to fight.

Surrey, however, had lost so many men himself at Flodden that he gave up the attempt to take advantage of the victory, and Scotland was spared.

The new king, James V, was a mere baby, and so a Regent had to be appointed to rule. Some of the nobles chose his mother, Queen Margaret, and as she was the sister of Henry VIII, the English king was anxious to give her any support he could. Other nobles, however, wanted John Stewart, Duke of Albany, son of the Albany who had fled to England in the reign of James III. The next few years of Scottish history are chiefly the sad story of continual internal fighting between the two parties. Sometimes the Queen ruled, and sometimes it was Albany who was Regent. And every time Albany was supreme, there was danger from England and border fighting took place.

Life for the young king, meanwhile, was hard. He was moved about from house to house, so that he would not fall into the hands of unscrupulous nobles who wanted to wield their power in his name. He never had a permanent home, and so his education was interrupted, although he had, for part of the time, the great poet and scholar, Sir David Lindsay, as his tutor.

In 1528, when he had been confined in Falkland Castle for a while by the Douglas family, he managed to escape to Stirling, and there he announced that he was going to govern Scotland himself.

In many ways, James was like his father, strong, brave and determined to keep the nobles under his control. He had a thin face, with a long nose and bright red hair. What he lacked in learning he made up with a spirit of patriotism and a sense of justice. He became known as "The Poor Man's King" because of his concern for the welfare of the ordinary people.

Once he began to rule he set out to crush the Douglases. They were banished from Scotland and their lands were confiscated. Then James turned on the Highland clan chiefs who had used the disturbed period of his minority to wage war on each other, and to ravage the Lowlands. They boasted of the fifty or more churches which they burned, of the houses which they ransacked, but when James captured many of their chiefs, he executed some and put the remainder in prison.

James introduced a number of good laws,

and he set up a Court of Session in Edinburgh which made it easier for people to obtain justice directly from him or from special judges appointed by him. He believed that ordinary folk should have protection from greedy and lawless nobles, and that their grievances were better put right in law courts than on the field of battle. This Court of Session is today the chief law court of Scotland.

James continued the policy of maintaining friendship with France. In 1537 he married a French princess, Madeleine, daughter of Francis I, and when she died a few months later, he married another Frenchwoman, Marie of Lorraine. This alliance with France angered Henry VIII and in 1542 full scale war between the Scots and the English broke out.

At Solway Moss, on the border between Cumberland and Dumfriesshire, the Scots were routed and many of the leaders were killed.

The news of this defeat broke the king's heart, and he was taken ill. While he lay at Falkland, he was told that his wife had given birth to a child. He asked whether it was a boy or a girl, and when told that it was a girl, he said, "It came with a lass, and it will go with a lass." By this he meant that the Stuart royal line had begun through a daughter of Robert Bruce marrying a Stuart, and that the same line would end through a woman—his daughter. He was not far wrong, for Mary ended her life upon an English execution block and her son James became James of England and Scotland together, in 1603. Even when the Stuarts became monarchs of both countries, the last of the direct line was a woman, Queen Anne, who died in 1714.

A week later, James V died, having lost the will to go on living. His advisers had resented his friendship with France, and the unruly nobles had hated his protection of the people from them. He felt a great sense of failure, and on his deathbed he must have dreaded for the future of the nation, now to be ruled in the name of a week-old baby girl.

On a cold February night in 1567, Mary, Queen of Scots, bade farewell to her husband, Henry Stewart, Lord Darnley, who was lying ill with smallpox in a little house on the outskirts of Edinburgh. As she prepared to mount her horse in the thick snow outside, a servant, nicknamed Paris, appeared, his face black with dirt.

"Jesu, Paris," exclaimed the Queen, "how begrimed you are!" Then, without waiting for an answer, she turned to her attendants and gave the signal to set off down the street towards the other end of the city where they were to attend a wedding feast.

Three hours later, the still of the night was shattered by a violent explosion. The little house, called Kirk O'Field, in which Mary had left her sick husband, had been blown to pieces by gunpowder. In the garden lay the bodies of Darnley and his servant, Taylor.

Quickly, a crowd gathered round the corpses, and at once something curious was noticed about them. Neither showed the slightest trace of gunpowder nor any injuries arising from its detonation. Both men had been suffocated.

This crime, for which Mary was blamed, took away the last trace of popularity that she had enjoyed with the Scottish people, and within a year she had been forced to abdicate and had become a prisoner of the Queen of England, Elizabeth.

Mary succeeded at the age of only seven days, and as had happened so often before, the succession of a mere child led to a breakdown of law and order. This time it was very bad for Scotland, for not only was the nation invaded several times by the English, but it was also bitterly divided over the Reformation, and many people suffered for their beliefs.

Mary's mother, the widow of James V, was a Frenchwoman and a Catholic, and her supporters wished to see the alliance with France continue. The Regent, the Earl of Arran, however, who was a cousin of the queen, was a Protestant, and his party looked to friendship with England and sought to break away from Rome. Arran agreed with Henry VIII that Mary, when she was eleven, should marry the king's son, Edward, who would then be about sixteen. Until that time, the two countries were to remain at peace.

The royal party of the queen's mother did not like the arrangement at all. One of its leaders, Cardinal Beaton, a rich, powerful and very learned man, who was Archbishop of St Andrews and Lord Chancellor, took the baby Mary to Stirling and there had her crowned, in 1543. He then packed a Parliament with his allies and managed to get them to cancel the agreement with Henry VIII. He also managed to win Arran over to his side.

Henry was furious. He sent his brother-in-law, Lord Hertford, at the head of a fleet of ships to the Firth of Forth, and when it arrived off Leith, hundreds of armed soldiers were landed ashore. They marched to Edinburgh, drove the defenders off and burnt the city. Unable to capture the castle, they set fire instead to Holyrood Palace. Then they returned to England, burning the villages and fields as they went.

The Scots still refused to accept the agreement, and a year later Hertford again invaded the country, burning the abbeys of Kelso, Melrose and Dryburgh.

In the meanwhile, Protestant followers of the new religion which was spreading throughout Europe, had been coming into Scotland and preaching against the Church of Rome. Beaton, a devout Catholic, dealt harshly with these heretics, and a number were caught and burned at the stake. One was George Wishart, a great thinker and a powerful speaker, who was burned before Beaton's own palace at St Andrews.

A few weeks after Wishart's death, Beaton himself was killed, in his palace, but it was not the end of the Catholics in Scotland. The Protestant persecutions went on, and now they were encouraged by Arran and Queen Mary's mother.

The warfare with England also went on. In 1547, when Edward VI was king and his

The Lords of the Congregation

uncle Lord Hertford, now Duke of Somerset, was Protector, a great battle was fought at Pinkie in which the Scots were defeated. They sent to their allies in France for help, and soon a large French army sailed across the sea and landed in Perthshire. Together, the Scots and the French drove out the English, but no sooner had they done so when they began to quarrel with each other, just as the Scots and French had done in the time of Robert II.

In 1554, Mary's mother seized the Regency from Arran, and at once she filled all the empty offices of state with Frenchmen. This angered both nobles and people in Scotland, and civil war followed. Mary's mother held on to the Regency, and in 1558 she arranged for Mary to marry Francis, the King of France's son and heir, a match that was not liked by the Scots at all.

Some of the Protestant nobles got together and drew up a covenant, that is, an agreement, whereby they promised to devote their energies to making Scotland Protestant. Calling themselves the Lords of the Congregation (the Congregation being the rapidly growing number of Protestants in the country), they vowed to use the sword, if it were necessary.

It was at this time that Scotland's most famous reformer began to preach. He was John Knox, one of Wishart's followers, and he had spent many months as a galley slave for his Protestant beliefs. Now he was free and he went up and down the country, thundering against Rome, just as Wycliffe had done in England in the times of Edward III and Richard II. Knox was a short, thin and slightly-built man, never in good health. But he had the courage of a lion, and he feared no one. His powers of speaking were superb, and it was said that he could by his voice put more spirit into his audiences than "five hundred trumpets continually blustering."

In May, 1559, when he was preaching a

John Knox

powerful attack on Rome at Perth, the congregation rose and destroyed the inside of the church, smashing all the pictures and statues. Then they charged out, and ran to two neighbouring monasteries which they also destroyed. Wherever he preached, this kind of violence was likely to follow. He did not wish for it at all, but he was powerless to stop it.

The Regent decided to punish the Perth mob, as an example to others, and she led an army against them. But the Protestants also raised a force and dreadful fighting began. It spread throughout Scotland, Catholic against Protestant, which sometimes meant brother against brother, or father against son. In 1560, a peace was made, and it was a victory for the Protestant cause. French soldiers were to leave the nation at once; a council of twelve nobles was to rule (for the Regent had died a few weeks earlier) and a Parliament was to be summoned to agree to a break with Rome. Thus, Scotland became Protestant, and remained so ever after, though there were many occasions when strong forces tried to disturb the new church.

In 1559, Mary's husband, Francis, succeeded to the French throne. This meant that Mary was queen of both Scotland and of France. It looked as though the Scots would soon become just another province of France, but the young king died soon afterwards, and Mary decided to come home to Scotland. When she arrived at

Holyrood, there was a huge crowd waiting to welcome her.

Mary was eighteen. Tall, slim, with delicate hands and lovely features, she was regarded as one of the most beautiful women in Europe. She was also gifted. She could speak several languages, she had read volumes of history, of religious books, of law and of politics, and she could play musical instruments. Living for years, as she had, in France, she had learned much about Europe, its buildings, its art and its ways of life. She was gentle-mannered, and she was kind to her servants. She also had great personal courage.

But Mary had many faults, too. She could not be trusted to keep her word, she was obstinate, she was two-faced, and she would not take good advice when it was offered to her. Her short period of rule was filled with troubles, and it was to end tragically, just as her own life was to do, many years after.

Mary picked two chief advisers, her half-brother, James Stewart, Earl of Moray, and William Maitland, one of the most brilliant men in Scotland. They were both Protestants, and so they were able to enforce the acts of the 1560 Parliament.

Before long, Mary quarrelled with Knox. Mass had been forbidden as a church service in Scotland, but the queen had been allowed to have private celebrations of it at Holyrood. Knox objected strongly; if the queen can continue to practise Roman Catholic rites, he said, it would not be long before all the other Scottish Catholics could do likewise. So he attacked her in sermons and in pamphlets, because he feared that she was really planning to restore the Roman faith in Scotland, just as Mary I had done in England.

When Elizabeth I became queen, Mary was the heir to the English throne. She tried to get Elizabeth to name her as such, but that wise woman would not do so, for she feared Catholic risings in England on Mary's behalf—and indeed this fear more than once came true.

In 1565, Mary married her cousin,

Henry Stewart, Lord Darnley, a tall, attractive man, who had many bad qualities. He was easily led, given to heavy drinking, cruel and arrogant, though at first these things were not obvious.

The marriage alarmed Elizabeth. Darnley, too, was in the line of succession to the English throne, as he and Mary were both grandchildren of Henry VIII's sister, Margaret, wife of James IV. It also frightened the Protestant Scottish nobles.

Mary and Darnley got on well enough for the first few months. She even promised to make him King-consort, but when she discovered what he was really like, she changed her mind. This only made him more unpleasant, and to get his revenge he murdered her private secretary, the Italian musician David Rizzio, of whom she had become very fond. Beforehand, Darnley had told Moray and the other Protestant nobles that he was going to do so, and they offered that if he was successful, they would get Mary to make him King-Consort. In return he was to ensure that the new Protestant Church should be safe in the country.

Mary was very upset, but knowing that her husband had the backing of Moray and his friends, she persuaded Darnley to give them up, and join her party, which was now led by the Earl of Bothwell.

In June, 1566, Mary gave birth to a prince, James, who later became James VI, and later still, James I of England, Scotland and Ireland. The Scottish people were delighted, and hundreds of bonfires were lit in Edinburgh alone to celebrate the event. But Mary was not happy. She now hated Darnley, and she sought comfort from Bothwell, a fierce, stout-limbed warrior, who had great courage, but very little intelligence, and who was ready to do anything the queen should ask of him.

When Darnley became ill with smallpox, Mary patched up her quarrels with him and nursed him. As he lay at Kirk O'Field recovering, the house was blown up and he was murdered. From that day to this people have argued whether or not Mary was involved in the murder. If she was innocent, who, then, was guilty?

One of the main things in Mary's favour was her remark to the servant, Paris, about his dirty face. The dirt was gunpowder, and he is supposed to have discovered the barrels of it in the cellars of Kirk O'Field. He rushed upstairs to warn his queen about them, but she was in too much of a hurry to listen. Now, if she knew about them already, and that they were to be used for murderous purposes, the very last thing

she would have done would be to draw attention to traces of gunpowder on Paris's face. Bothwell, on the other hand, was believed to have planned the crime, and he was even tried for it, but the judges could not bring a verdict against him, as the evidence was slight. The guilty parties may never be known for certain, but there are reasons for thinking that it was Moray's idea. He had no further use for Darnley and would have been glad of an opportunity to turn people against Mary, if he could show that she had killed her own husband. This would enable him to drive her off the throne and it would bring him to supreme power as Regent.

Mary did not help her own case at all when, three months after Darnley's death, she married Bothwell, and gave him enormous powers. Moray and his lords were outraged, and they rebelled. At Carberry Hill, near Musselburgh, his army came upon Bothwell's and prepared to fight. Bothwell's men deserted from the field, and the earl was driven out of Scotland, never to return.

Moray had won, and he forced Mary to abdicate and to hand the crown to her baby son, James. The boy was crowned at Stirling, as James VI, and John Knox preached the sermon at the coronation service. Moray then became Regent.

Mary was imprisoned in Loch Leven Castle, but within a year she managed to escape and raise an army among the Catholics. Moray, hearing of this, assembled his forces on a field at Langside, which is now part of the city of Glasgow. A battle was fought, but in less than an hour Mary's troops were scattered. She jumped on to her horse and rode hard without stopping for sixty miles, reaching Dundrennan where she hid for the night. The next morning, she continued to ride and crossed the border near Carlisle. There, she sent a messenger to Elizabeth I, and begged for protection. Elizabeth put her into confinement, where she remained for the next nineteen years.

After many plots against Elizabeth, in some if not all of which, Mary was actively involved, the English queen signed her death-warrant, and she was executed at Fotheringay Castle, in 1587. Her end was cruel and violent, but in all truth she had brought it on herself.

Mary's defeat at Langside and her flight to England removed the worst danger to the new Scottish Protestant Church, and it also strengthened the hand of the Regent, Moray, who had already showed himself a wise and popular ruler. The king was only two years old when Mary fled, and for many years his kingdom was to be governed by Regents. It is sad that none of his successors proved so able as Moray.

Moray was a striking and tough-looking man, with sharp eyes and a bold jaw. He was not handsome, but he appeared to be what he was—a strong man. He was a skilful general, and a sound governor. He had a strict regard for justice and he would not allow the rich to bully the poor. He had never cared for his half-sister, Mary, for he believed that her interests and ambitions were not those of Scotland, a country of which he was immensely proud. It was a tragedy that he was only an illegitimate son of James V, or else he would have become king—and made a very good one, too. As Regent, however, he had almost the same power, and in a short rule he used it well.

He put down revolts by Catholic nobles who longed for the return of their queen. He also dealt with other nobles who objected to his power. But, his great devotion to the interests of the lower classes, something that few Scottish rulers had bothered about, made him enemies among the rich, and in 1570 he was murdered while on horseback outside the house of someone whom he believed was a friend. It was a senseless crime, and it led to all kinds of trouble for Scotland.

His funeral in St Giles's Cathedral in Edinburgh was a splendid affair. John Knox preached a moving sermon, and, as an eyewitness has said, "he made three thousand persons shed tears for the loss of such a good and godly governor."

For the next few years, the nation was ruled by a succession of regents, each as hopeless as the next, none of them popular. The first, the Earl of Lennox, Darnley's father, was old, tired and weak, and he was quite unfit to rule. At once the Catholic nobles rose in favour of Mary, and were ready to go to war with England to rescue her from her imprisonment. Lennox was unable to deal with them, and before long he, too, was murdered, shot through the heart by a rebel soldier.

Lennox was followed by the Earl of Mar, a peace-loving man, but he also was not able to stop the rivalry between the Catholic and the Protestant parties. It was a very bad time for the nation, for soldiers on both sides behaved with great cruelty. Captives were never made prisoners; they were put to death on the spot. If the troops wanted fuel for their camp fires, they ripped off the timber roofs of the town houses and burned them. It was not unlike the miserable days of the reign of Stephen in England, four hundred years earlier. In the middle of the fighting, Mar died, and he was succeeded by the Earl of Morton.

Morton was a tough, courageous but cruel man, the kind of person who in better times might have made an able governor, for he feared no one and when he was not driven to cruelty, understood the meaning of fair play and justice. The bitterness between the Catholic party and the Protestants, however, was so great that kindness and chivalry, justice and mercy, were thrown aside for the sake of success by one party or the other.

In 1572, an event took place in France which had a deep effect upon the Scots. This was the massacre of St Bartholomew, in Paris, so named because it took place on that saint's day, August 24th. Nearly all the leading Protestants of France were in the capital for a meeting, when, suddenly, one evening, the Catholics, urged on by the King, Charles IX, descended upon the Protestants in their lodging houses, in restaurants and in their friends' homes, and slaughtered them, murdering several thousand. It was a frightful crime, and the horror of it rang throughout Europe. It made the Scottish Protestants even more determined to hang on to their new Church and to do everything they could to prevent the possibility of Mary ever returning and taking up her lost throne.

Morton's first task was to capture Edinburgh Castle, which had been occupied by supporters of Mary. He was not strong enough to achieve this on his own, so he begged for help from England. A detachment of soldiers was sent to his aid, and the castle was taken. Many of the defenders were put to death. So, Mary's cause collapsed, and the civil war was for the time being over.

Morton now began to govern. Stern and fearless, he put down all opposition. But he needed money, and he raised crippling

Mary, Queen of Scots, before her execution

taxes from all classes, and it was the poor who could least afford to pay. Soon, some of his followers turned against him, and they compelled him to resign.

His successor was a cousin of the king's, Lord Aubigny, a Scottish royal descendant who had spent his life in France. James made him Duke of Lennox, but he was hated because he was a supporter of the Catholic cause. He had Morton executed. Many Scotsmen had resented Morton's taxation, but at least he had been a true Scottish patriot, and his death only made Lennox even more unpopular. So, once again there was a rising against the government, and the Earl of Gowrie, the leader, managed to capture the young king and compel him to dismiss Lennox.

James was imprisoned at Falkland Castle, but he determined to escape so that he could be revenged on Gowrie. He succeeded, and at once took over the reins of government. He was eighteen, learned, obstinate and filled with a new idea of monarchy, namely, that kings ruled by right of God, and so were not answerable to other men on earth. He soon showed what kind of man he was, and, in the story of his life in the *Rulers of England*, his nature has been explained. He surrounded himself with favourites, most of whom only cared for him so long as he supplied them with money and titles, and who cared little for Scotland or its fortunes.

The next years were filled with plots against his life, and with risings of the Catholics. In 1587, his mother, Mary, was executed, but James, who had seen nothing of her for eighteen years, cared little for that. Her death made him heir to the English throne, as Elizabeth had not married. He wondered whether the English would accept him. He was a Protestant, but it was known that he would readily have given up the faith if it suited him. When Philip II of Spain sent his great Armada against England in 1588, James let it be known that he would become a Catholic if the invasion were successful.

When the Protestant nobles heard of

Robert Carey arriving at Holyrood Palace

this, they protested strongly, but James, with his clever tongue, persuaded them that he had only made this offer to ensure that Scotland would remain free from English interference. After the Armada ended in disaster for Spain, James began to make friends with the English. It was better to be on the winning side, he thought, but many of his councillors felt they could no longer trust him.

On Saturday evening, March 26th, 1603, an envoy, Sir Robert Carey arrived at Holyrood Palace with news that the great Elizabeth of England was dead, and that he, James, was now king of England. He set out for London, and in July he was crowned King of England, Scotland and Ireland. Thus, the Scottish throne was absorbed with the English, something that for centuries, apart from a few years in the time of Edward I, the Scottish people had successfully resisted.

Though it took some time for the Scots to get used to not having their own separate king, the union proved to be of immense value to both nations. Scotsmen still call themselves Scotsmen, and they are rightly proud of their heritage. Their scholars and scientists have made their names famous in every corner of the world; to name but a few, Lord Kelvin was one of the most gifted physicists of all time, Alexander Graham Bell invented the telephone, and there was Sir Alexander Fleming, the discoverer of penicillin, a wonder drug that has saved countless lives. There are other names, too; Field Marshal Earl Haig, the British commander in the First World War, Ramsay MacDonald, the first Labour Prime Minister, Robert Louis Stevenson, the author of *Treasure Island*, Sir Walter Scott, one of the world's most famous story-tellers, Lord Dalhousie, perhaps the greatest governor-general that Britain ever sent to India, and countless others.

Today, there is a strong nationalist movement that would like to see Scotland a separate nation again.

Rulers of
IRELAND

Ireland was settled by the Gaelic Celts several hundreds of years before the birth of Our Lord. It seems that the country was divided into a number of kingdoms, each with their own chiefs, in much the same way as Britain was regulated before the arrival of the legions of Rome. Stories of some of these chiefs, and even family trees showing unbroken lines of descent, have been written by very early Irish poets and historians, but they are so entangled with legend and fairy tale that it is almost impossible to separate fact from fiction.

We know definitely that when the Roman governor of Britain, Julius Agricola, began his attacks on the Picts in Scotland (see introduction to the Rulers of Scotland), he considered also the invasion of Ireland. His son-in-law, Tacitus, the famous Roman historian, says that Agricola believed he could achieve the invasion with a small force. He might well have made the attempt after his victory over Galcagus, but he was recalled to Rome.

All the same, Roman ideas and customs were brought to Ireland in those times, peacefully, by visitors, traders, and later on by Christian missionaries. This had an unusual result. The best talents of the native Gaels were so well mixed with the qualities of Roman civilisation that in the dark days which followed the fall of the Roman Empire, when much of Europe was plunged back into darkness, Ireland had a Golden Age of learning and art.

At the beginning of the fifth century, an

Irish raiding party from Ulster landed in Wales and captured a number of hostages. One of them was a youth called Patrick, the son of a Roman official, and he was imprisoned in Antrim. While he was there he is said to have had a dream in which an angel told him he would one day convert the Irish people to Christianity. He managed to escape from Ireland and he went to France to study theology. When he felt that he had learned enough, he went to the Pope, Celestine I, and asked for his blessing to embark upon a mission to Ireland. The Pope gave it to him and Patrick set sail at once. He landed at Wicklow and proceeded northwards to Strangford, near Belfast, to the court of Laoghaire O'Neill, then the chief king, who allowed him to preach throughout his territory.

By the time that Patrick died, in about 460, he had succeeded in making nearly all Ireland Christian.

The descendants of Laoghaire, like him and his ancestors, claimed to be chief kings of Ireland, but as a rule the claim was contested or ignored by the other kings, and the story of Ireland in those days is largely the tale of constant fighting between the kings for supremacy.

Despite this warfare, Ireland was to enjoy a glorious period of art and learning, and it was the Church rather than the kings that encouraged it. In metal-work Irish craftsmen became the most skilful in Europe. They developed the art of enamelling in many colours, and they made beautiful stained glass. They designed exquisite illuminations on manuscripts, they built lovely stone crosses and placed them in many parts of the countryside. They wrote heroic poetry and legend-packed histories.

Many monasteries were built in these days, and in them a standard of learning was reached that was among the highest in Europe. One historian who has produced a map of Ireland with the chief monasteries marked on it shows that there were over sixty of them by the sixth century. Of all the peoples of the British Isles, the Irish were the most devoted to religion. This

was to play a large part in their struggles against the English in later centuries. Indeed, when they resisted the governments of Elizabeth I and of Cromwell, it was as much because they objected to the new Protestant Faith as it was that they did not wish to be subjects of the English crown. Today, Ireland is a staunchly Roman Catholic nation, except in the North.

At the beginning of the ninth century, as was happening in England, Wales and Scotland, Ireland became the victim of Viking raids. These increased in number and strength over the years, and soon the raiders began to settle. They captured most of the ports and towns on the East coast, including Dublin.

The Irish kings did not help themselves or their people as much as they could because they continued to war with each other instead of combining to get rid of the invaders. It needed a strong man to do the two things at once—unite the kingdoms and rule them, and then defeat the Vikings. Such a man was Brian Boru, king of Munster, not by any means the first man to be called King of Ireland, but the first to make the title mean something.

St Patrick

It was evening on Good Friday, in 1014. Not far from the beach in Dublin Bay, a few miles north of Dublin, an army of Ireland had just inflicted the greatest defeat of its history against the Vikings, on the plain of Clontarf. Now the victorious men of St Patrick were chasing the northmen off the fields, helmeted and axe-bearing warriors who were running as fast as their legs would carry them.

In the corner of a field stood a large tent. It was the command post of the Irish army, and at its entrance stood an ageing and grey-haired man, who was watching with joy the headlong flight of his enemies. He was Brian Boru (Boru: the name meaning "Taker of Tributes") and he was King of Ireland. Though he was not far short of ninety years old, and so not able to take part in the actual fighting, he was still in full possession of his powers and had directed the operations throughout the day.

Suddenly, two or three of the fleeing Vikings came running towards the tent. In a moment they reached it, burst in, and before the old king could raise his great axe, they cut him down and killed him.

Thus died the most famous king of Irish history, about whom the poets wrote many songs. It was a sad day for the Irish, for it robbed the victory of its glory, in the same way as the death of Nelson at Trafalgar, in 1805, marred the enjoyment of that most splendid English naval victory.

Brian was born in about 926, in Munster, and his youth was spent in learning the arts of war to deal with the Viking raiders, who were ravaging his country as they had ravaged England and Scotland before. He was a descendant of the kings of Munster, and by 978, it was his turn to become king.

He was well aware that for centuries there had been a family which had supplied overlord Kings of Ireland, but he also knew that, grand though this title was, it did not often carry with it an effective control of the island. So, he set out to make himself King of Ireland, and once having done so, he would keep the position and hand it on

A poet sings ballads to Brian Boru at a banquet

to his family. Succession by birth was all very well, but he knew that such a position could only be kept by hard fighting and by being stronger than anyone else.

In 984, he invaded the kingdom of Leinster and in a swift campaign won it, forcing the Leinster king to pay him homage as overlord. Then he turned upon Connaught and Meath, with the same result.

By the end of the century, he was ready to deal with the Vikings, who had raided and settled in Dublin and its countryside, and in 1000 he defeated them in a great battle. This did not drive them out, but it kept them within the small territory they had occupied.

A year later, Brian assumed the title King of Ireland, although there was a descendant of the O'Neills who had the name, and he took rapid steps to have his claim supported. He went to Armagh and to the great St Patrick's Church there he gave generous gifts of gold. This church was regarded as the principal cathedral of Ireland. Then, in a charter, he recognised the archbishop of Armagh as head of the Irish Church, and in return was acknowledged as King. At once he set off on a tour of the whole country, and on his journey he compelled local kings and chiefs to pay him tribute, which is how he got his name Boru. This tribute was generally in the form of goods, such as copper cauldrons, linen clothes, silver chains, and even livestock like pigs and cows.

Brian then set up his own court, having heard about the splendid pageantry of the other royal courts in Europe. Though his palace was still a humble building with earthen floors and a thatched roof, he contrived to live the life of a real king. He surrounded himself with officials of state, with properly appointed duties, and he employed educated men to write the story of his time. Most of these men wrote their tales in verse, which allowed them to sing the praises of the king in exaggerated terms.

The rest of his reign was, until the end, fairly peaceful. There were revolts by kings of the states under him, but he kept them down. In this time he arranged the building of many churches and monasteries, and he showed great interest in the development of learning, for in many ways the Irish were much more cultured than their English, Scottish and Welsh neighbours.

In spite of his efforts to keep peace, Brian was at heart a warrior, as every leader in Ireland had to be at that time, and it was hard for him to resist the temptation to fight rather than meet over the council table with rebels. The first half of his life had been taken up completely with warfare, and so, to him, the sword spoke louder than the tongue.

In 1013, the Dublin Vikings declared war on him, and they managed to obtain the support of the men of Leinster. Brian marshalled a great army, chiefly of his own Munstermen, and at Clontarf, where his son Murchad commanded in the field, the Vikings suffered a crushing defeat. Sad it was that he should have been killed in the hour of victory. He was taken to Armagh and buried in St Patrick's Church.

Brian had made one kingdom out of the many states of Ireland, but no sooner had

223

he gone than his power broke up. It was not given to him to produce a family of great men to carry on his work, such as Alfred of England had done over a hundred years before.

INTERREGNUM [1014–1064]

When Brian Boru was killed after the victory at Clontarf, many of the Irish wanted to have as their overlord the descendant of the O'Neills that Brian had overruled, Maelsechlainn, known in shorter form as Malachy. He took over the title King of Ireland, but almost at once Brian's heirs resisted it. For the next fifty years there was no real King of Ireland; the story of the country, so far as the ancient chroniclers relate, was nothing more than the tale of fighting between the local kings for this title.

By 1064, Brian's grandson, Turlough O'Brien, assumed the overlordship.

TURLOUGH O'BRIEN [1064–1086]

Turlough O'Brien was King of Ireland for about the same period of time that William of Normandy ruled England as William I. He was born in 1009, and was educated at a monastery in Limerick. We know nothing of his early life, but by 1055 he became king of Munster, and set out at once to claim the overlordship, by virtue of his descent from Brian. His reign, however, was filled with wars with his neighbours, who regarded the O'Briens as usurpers, but there are reports in the chronicles that in the intervals of peace he ruled well. He kept his court at Kinkora, in what is now County Clare, and he tried to maintain the same government as that which his grandfather had begun.

In 1074, Lanfranc, Archbishop of Canterbury in William I's reign, wrote Turlough a letter in which he described him as King of Ireland. This must mean that at the time Turlough had managed to get the other kings to acknowledge him as overlord. Then he was taken ill, and he died in 1086.

224

MURTOGH O'BRIEN [1086–1119] and DOMHNALL O'LOCHLAINN [1094–1121]

Murtogh O'Brien succeeded to the kingdom of Munster in 1086, but he was soon to find that the other Irish kingdoms were not going to accept him as their overlord. Warfare broke out, and for some years it went on, with no decisive results on either side. He had some successes against Connaught and Leinster, but later on was defeated by the king of Connaught. He continued to harry these kingdoms, however, and also attacked Meath.

His main rival for the overlordship was Domhnall O'Lochlainn, king of Ulster. As he was a descendant of the O'Neills, he claimed the title King of Ireland. He was in a good position. The headquarters of the Irish Church was at Armagh, part of his kingdom. The archbishop, a man of peace and learning, did not like the continual fighting between the Irish kings, and more than once he persuaded them to give up their wars. According to one authority, Ireland was divided in 1094 between Murtogh and Domhnall, and this division gave both kings time to attend to their internal affairs. Murtogh was especially interested in the church and he reformed its organisation, appointing new bishops and setting down the dioceses over which they were to have control.

Murtogh, like his father, was recognised as King of Ireland by an English archbishop, this time Anselm, who wrote to him in 1096. But the division of the country was not a happy one, and for many years the two kings fought, supported on either side by other lesser kings. In 1103, Domhnall defeated Murtogh at Cobha in County Tyrone so decisively that Murtogh acknowledged his conqueror as overlord.

In 1114, Murtogh, tired of the business of government, and by now ill with consumption, entered a monastery, just as Constantine II of Scotland had done seventy years before. He remained there for five years, during which time his brother Diarmaid O'Brien managed the kingdom of Munster. Murtogh died in

1119, and Domhnall became undisputed King of Ireland.

We know very little about Domhnall, except that he was a thick-set and majestic-looking man, who won the love of the people of Ulster. He, too, was devoted to the church, and endowed many monasteries. He died in 1121, and the struggle for the overlordship began all over again.

TURLOUGH O'CONNOR [1121–1156]

When Domhnall O'Lochlainn died, Turlough O'Connor, who had become king of Connaught in 1106, had himself proclaimed king of all Ireland. It was an easy claim to make, but it was not so easy to enforce. Warfare broke out, and times were so bad that the historians have described the period as one of complete anarchy. Agriculture and learning were interrupted, and fine buildings were burned to the ground. It was much like the state of Wales after the death of Llywelyn ap Seisyll in 1023.

Turlough's claim was supported by the archbishop of Armagh, possibly in return

Part of an illuminated manuscript

ŀ̇ʒeneracio

for a generous gift of gold to the church of St Patrick. But the years were spent in fighting. Turlough is said to have been a great builder of bridges, and a number were constructed across the river Shannon, which then divided Connaught from Munster. These enabled him to bring his armies swiftly into Munster. In 1128, he made a tour of that kingdom and received tribute from its king and its local chiefs. Copying the example of the Normans in England, Turlough built castles at advantageous points to enforce his control of the peoples.

Turlough was a great benefactor to the Church. He endowed monasteries, for he believed that the Irish should not give up their opportunities of education merely because their chiefs seemed to want to spend their lives fighting. In his time, Irish art became famous throughout Europe. Her craftsmen were second to none in making fine metal-work, in sculpture and in illumination of manuscripts. The monasteries were staffed by great scholars, many of whom were widely respected on the Continent for their works. The art of handwriting, calligraphy, was a speciality in the monasteries of the day, and some of the best examples of medieval script were produced in Ireland.

So far as the ordinary people were concerned, their lives were those of hard-working peasants, farming under difficult conditions because their efforts were so often interrupted by war. They could barely produce enough goods for themselves, and export was practically unknown.

Turlough was said to have been a man of great mercy to enemies, and he was the first king of Ireland to show qualities of chivalry which we have seen in the time of Owain Gwynedd of Wales, and later on, in Edward III's reign. He loved poetry and encouraged poets to spend their hours at his court, to write the epic stories of the times, and to describe the former glories of Irish people.

Turlough died in 1156, and was succeeded by his son, Roderic, who failed to enforce a claim to be King of all Ireland.

Murtogh O'Lochlainn was the son of Domhnall O'Lochlainn. He had tried more than once to make himself King of Ireland, but Turlough O'Connor had been too strong for him. Once Turlough died, however, Murtogh claimed the title and because he knew that many people were tired of the endless wars, he tried to assert his claim in a peaceful manner. He called a meeting of the heads of the Church, and also local kings and chiefs, at Mellifont Abbey, in County Louth, and a large percentage of them arrived, including seventeen bishops, the archbishop of Armagh, and many lords. The purpose of the meeting was to discuss the future of the country, not only so far as the church was concerned, but also in matters of government. It was much like the meeting at the White Hunting Lodge held by the Welsh Prince, Hywel Dda.

We do not know exactly what happened at the meeting, except that while the Church business was attended to, no agreement was reached over government. Still, the very fact that he had called the assembly and that so many chiefs came must have meant that he was held in considerable respect.

By 1161, Murtogh managed to get all the undertakings to recognise him as King, and to pay him homage, though this was not achieved without some warfare.

Murtogh was a benefactor of the Church; he founded a great monastery at Newry and built an abbey there. He gave large presents to Armagh, and he rebuilt the cathedral at Derry (later Londonderry), which had been damaged in the fighting between him and Turlough O'Connor several years before.

In 1166, Murtogh's kingdom of Ulster was invaded by Roderic O'Connor, son of Turlough O'Connor of Connaught, and at the battle of Newton Hamilton he was slain, with many of his advisers and friends. Roderic then assumed the overlordship of Ireland.

Roderic was born in about 1116. Of his youth we know nothing, but not long after he came of age his father found it necessary to imprison him for treason, probably for plotting with one of the underkings. When Turlough died in 1156, Roderic inherited the kingdom of Connaught. The first years of his rule were taken up with fighting against his neighbours, and more than once he tried to unseat Murtogh O'Lochlainn.

When Murtogh died in 1166, Roderic announced that he was King of Ireland and took the unique step of having himself so proclaimed at a great ceremony in Dublin. There, a splendid pageant was put on, very much like the celebration of coronations in England. It showed that Dublin was to be the principal town of Ireland.

Before many months had passed, Dermot, king of Leinster, rebelled against Roderic, but he was swiftly defeated and driven out of Ireland altogether. He fled across the sea to Wales, and there rode to England to the court of Henry II, and begged that king for help to restore him to his throne. Henry II, busy as he was with troubles in his French domains, could not at once help. All the same, he had in mind the conquest of Ireland, and had even got the Pope, Adrian IV, to authorise him to lead a "crusade" against the Irish because they were running their church on separate lines from the rest of Christendom.

Henry told Dermot that he should try to get support from some of the marcher lords of south Wales. Dermot left and in Pembrokeshire he managed to persuade Richard de Clare, Earl of Pembroke, to agree to help him. This earl, nicknamed Strongbow, probably because he and his army had made a name for themselves with skilful use of archers in battle, set out with a force of cavalry and foot-soldiers across the sea to Ireland. With Dermot, they they drove Roderic out of Leinster, and

Assembly of nobles and clergy at Mellifont before King Murtogh O'Lochlainn

also overran the district around Dublin.

Strongbow then begged the hand of Dermot's daughter in marriage, with an agreement that if Dermot should die, he, Strongbow, should become King of Leinster. A year later, Dermot died, and Strongbow became King. His rule, however, was marked with cruelty and violence, and before long Henry II heard about it. So far as he was concerned, this was a danger to his empire; he could not afford to have barons ruling large districts and living like little kings on their own. The situation became more urgent when Strongbow defeated an attack of Roderic's.

In 1171, then, Henry embarked upon the invasion of Ireland. He knew that Strongbow was not at all popular, and that the Irish feared that other Welsh marcher lords might be tempted to cross the sea and build up small empires for themselves. He brought a great army to Waterford, marched up to Dublin, and in a short but victorious campaign compelled Strongbow to acknowledge him as overlord. Most of

Henry II in a skirmish with Strongbow

the other chiefs followed suit, but Roderic would not.

Henry called a meeting of the leaders of the Irish Church and showed them the authority he had from the Pope to make them bring their Church into line. They agreed, with unexpected willingness, possibly because they were tired of the constant warfare in the land and believed that a united Church, under the Pope, would inspire Irishmen to seek a similar kind of unity among themselves.

After supervising the government of Leinster and Meath, and after appointing a Justiciar to manage the kingdoms and to administer English law, Henry returned to England. In 1174, he came to terms with Roderic at a treaty in which Roderic was allowed to rule Connaught, and was also recognised as King of Ireland. He had, however, to accept Henry as overlord, and the English king had himself proclaimed as Lord of Ireland, a title passed on to his descendants.

Roderic ruled for some years at peace, but in 1186 he retired to a monastery, and died there twelve years later.

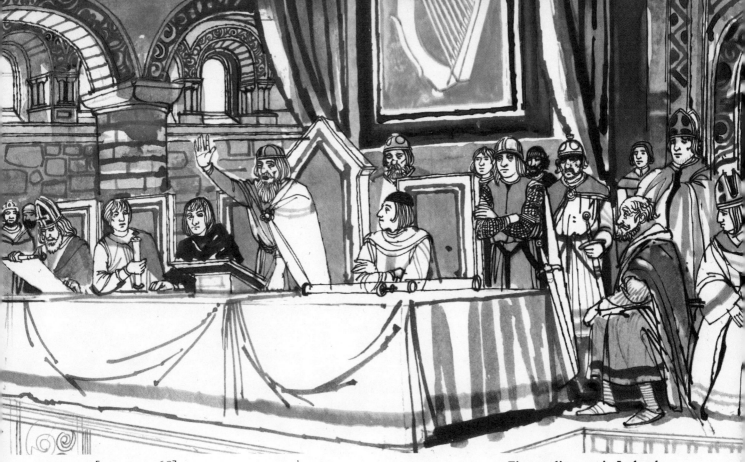

IRELAND [1172–1968]

First parliament in Ireland

Although the Irish people had never seemed to be able to accept one of their own kings as overlord for long without revolt, they objected most strongly to the invasion of their land by Henry II and his proclamation that he was Lord of Ireland. At that time, they were not powerful enough to drive the English out, nor indeed were they able to do so for centuries, though there were times when some or other brave and skilful soldier made a stout stand against the foreigner. The story of Ireland from that time is really the tale of continual fighting against the English. After hardships which no other nation of the civilised world has ever had to suffer, they finally won, when in 1922 the Irish Free State was established. Today, the Irish Republic is an independent State, it does not belong to the Commonwealth, and its language is still taught in its schools. Ulster, however, is not part of this republic, and it has become the dominion of Northern Ireland, joined to the kingdom of Great Britain. The fight for independence is a long and

complicated story, and it can only be summarised here.

When Henry II left the island, more English barons came over to Leinster and Meath and began to make settlements. These two provinces lie in the central plain of Ireland, flat, low-lying countryside that is very good for agriculture. They brought with them battalions of armed troops, built stone castles, and set up little feudal domains, in which the ideas of the manorial system were followed. English law was introduced, and in most ways the domains were like the marches set up in Wales by the Lords Marcher. The settlers expanded agriculture, and they founded towns, for up to then there were few communities in Ireland that were bigger than villages. Many Irish native people were forced into work as serfs.

Not long after the first parliament of Simon de Montfort in England in 1265, the English settlers created their own parliament, which consisted of nobles, clergy and knights. Gradually, as had happened

229

in Wales, the English began to mix with the Irish, and they married into the native kings' and chiefs' families. We shall call them Anglo-Irish people, to separate them from the pure Irish who refused to mix.

The hold on Ireland by the Anglo-Irish was never complete; sometimes the native people rose and drove whole communities of Anglo-Irish out of their towns, sometimes Anglo-Irish themselves rebelled against the government. From time to time the English kings had to send strong forces to deal with these risings, but when England was deeply involved with the Hundred Years War with France and then with the Wars of the Roses at home, it was a time when the native Irish could make trouble at will, with little fear of interference.

When England was in order again in the time of Henry VII, a new governor was sent to Ireland. He was Sir Henry Poynings, and he had a great act passed in the Irish parliament which compelled the Anglo-Irish government to remain under the control of England. Naturally, many Irishmen did not like this, and they fought against it, but their efforts were never completely successful, largely because even now the Irish people were not always able to agree among each other. Then, in the years following the break with Rome, Henry VIII turned his attention to Ireland and ordered that all positions of state in the country should be held by Englishmen. He also established a permanent English army of occupation in the country to keep order. In 1541, he had himself proclaimed King of Ireland, a title used by every succeeding ruler since then. After 1937, this title referred only to Northern Ireland, for then the Irish state had its first president.

When England became a Protestant country, the Irish wished to remain Catholics—as they are, for the most part, still Catholic today. Here was another reason for hatred against the English. Rebellions broke out time and again, and in Elizabeth's reign they were so dangerous that it

III. James came to Ireland, with money and troops supplied by Louis XIV of France, to try to drive the Protestants out, but he was soundly defeated at the battle of the Boyne in 1690. The Protestants were confirmed in their lands and given the exclusive rule of all Ireland. Catholics were not even allowed to stand for parliament.

Bitterness and hatred continued, for the next century, but it was not until 1798 that a general rising took place against the English government in Ireland. In 1800, the English government passed an act uniting the British and Irish parliaments. Irish lords and commoners were given seats in parliament at Westminster, and Ireland kept its own law courts.

After the defeat of Napoleon at Waterloo in 1815, when all Europe was in a state of confusion, the Irish Catholics, who were still a majority in the land, demanded that they should be allowed to stand for parliament at Westminster. In 1829, an act was passed which gave them this right.

Cromwell's troops in Ireland

was with great difficulty that in the end they were crushed.

In the early part of the seventeenth century, many English and Scots began to settle in northern Ireland, in what was the old kingdom of Ulster. They were mostly Protestants, and they acknowledged the overlordship of the British kings. It is not surprising that the Catholic Irish objected to these settlements, nor that civil war broke out. After the execution of Charles I, Cromwell had to come to Ireland to deal with the unrest, and this he did with considerable cruelty. It should be said that the main victims of his anger were not native Irishmen but Anglo-Irish who had refused to conform to the new English faith.

When James II was deposed from the British throne in 1688, the Irish took sides in the quarrel. The Catholic south and west supported James, and the Ulstermen remained firmly behind the new king, William

Starving peasants during the Famine

At this time, the population of Ireland was the largest per square mile in Europe, and yet because of strict trade laws enforced by the English, there was scarcely enough food grown on Irish soil to support it. In the 1840s a terrible disease struck at the potato crops and a great famine followed. Thousands of peasants died of starvation; about as many emigrated to the Americas, especially to the United States. Those that remained feared that their sufferings would go on so long as they were still subjects of the British crown. So they began to agitate for complete independence. English government officials and Protestant landlords, who were still treating the Catholic Irish as feudal subjects, were murdered; acts of violence took place all over the country. The Irish Members at Westminster called for a Home Rule Bill, which would grant them considerable independence, and they found much support from more democratic English Members, especially among the Liberal Party.

Home rule bills were introduced into Parliament by Gladstone, but they were all rejected. Then, in 1913, the Liberals brought in another bill. Ulster would have none of it, for it wanted to remain in the U.K. and tension was only relieved by the outbreak of the First World War.

Meanwhile, some of those who sought independence for Ireland were prepared to use force. In May 1916 about a thousand of them revolted in Dublin. They seized public buildings. On the steps of the General Post Office, one of their leaders, Padraic Pearse, read out their Declaration of Independence.

For a week this small band of patriots fought against overwhelming British forces before surrendering. Then the British committed the worst of a long catalogue of acts of violence in Ireland. They tried and executed all the rising's leaders, and many others as well.

The Irish (except Ulster) were now united in their determination to drive the British out. Members of the independence party, Sinn Fein, were elected to Parliament at by-elections.

In 1918, at the general election, Sinn Fein won a sweeping victory by gaining 73 out of 105 seats. Every member refused to take his seat at Westminster. Instead they formed a Parliament in Dublin, the Dail Eireann, and proceeded to take over the Irish government.

The British reacted to this with force. The army and police were strengthened by a division of ex-prisoners and out-of-work ex-army officers, known as the Black and Tans from the colour of their uniforms. This army behaved with appalling cruelty.

Against them the Irish pitched a band of tough and courageous volunteers, led by Michael Collins, regarded by most Irishmen as the greatest man of Irish history since Brian Boru. The Irish Republican Army conducted guerrilla warfare against the British for two years with such success that in the summer of 1921 the British government agreed to meet the leaders of Dail Eireann for independence talks.

After meetings in London, a treaty was signed, giving Ireland dominion status.

Ulster would have nothing to do with the Treaty (it had already been granted a measure of self-government), nor would Eamon de Valera, who wanted nothing short of a republic. Bitter civil war followed and the death-roll was high. Although the Treaty forces won, they lost their two leaders. Arthur Griffith, founder of Sinn Fein, died of heart failure, and ten days later, Michael Collins, to the grief of all Ireland, was assassinated on 22 August 1922.

The new Irish Free State had a governor-general representing King George V, but this office was abolished in 1936. A year later Ireland's first President was elected.

After the Second World War, a struggle in which many Irishmen fought with the greatest gallantry in the British Army, Ireland obtained complete independence, in 1949. Seven hundred and fifty years of fighting had at last achieved what the native ancestors of the Irish wanted— freedom. It was the end of the most tragic struggle for liberty in the history of Western Europe.

INDEX

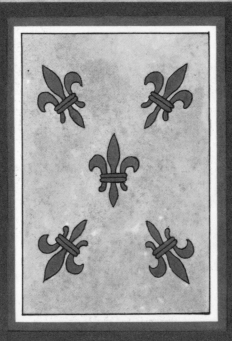